# Britain in the European Union

## Law, Policy and Parliament

Edited by

**Philip Giddings**
*Senior Lecturer in Politics*
*University of Reading*

and

**Gavin Drewry**
*Professor of Public Administration and*
*Director of the Centre for Political Studies,*
*Royal Holloway,*
*University of London*

First published 2004 by
PALGRAVE MACMILLAN
Houndmills, Basingstoke, Hampshire RG21 6XS and
175 Fifth Avenue, New York, N.Y. 10010
Companies and representatives throughout the world

PALGRAVE MACMILLAN is the global academic imprint of the Palgrave
Macmillan division of St. Martin's Press, LLC and of Palgrave Macmillan Ltd.
Macmillan® is a registered trademark in the United States, United Kingdom
and other countries. Palgrave is a registered trademark in the European
Union and other countries.

ISBN 1–4039–0451–0 hardback
ISBN 1–4039–0452–9 paperback

This book is printed on paper suitable for recycling and made from fully
managed and sustained forest sources.

A catalogue record for this book is available from the British Library.

Library of Congress Cataloging-in-Publication Data
Britain in the European Union : law, policy, and Parliament / edited by
    Philip Giddings and Gavin Drewry.
        p.   cm.
    Includes bibliographical references and index.
    ISBN 1–4039–0451–0 (cloth) — ISBN 1–4039–0452–9 (paper)
    1. European Union—Great Britain.   2. International and municipal
    law—Great Britain.   3. Constitutional law—Great Britain.   4. Great Britain.
    Parliament.   5. Great Britain—Politics and government—1997–
    I. Giddings, Philip James.   II. Drewry, Gavin.

KD4015.B75 2004
342.41—dc22
                                                                    2003067591


Printed and bound in Great Britain by
Antony Rowe Ltd, Chippenham and Eastbourne

# Contents

# Preface

This book has a long history, dating back to January 1990 when the Study of Parliament Group decided to establish a study group on Parliament and the European Community. The first product of that study group's work was *Westminster and Europe*, published by Macmillan Press in 1996, and the early history of the project can be found in the Preface to that volume, written by our colleague David Millar, who was one of the original convenors of the study group. The website of the Study of Parliament Group itself is http://www.spg.org.uk/.

But even before the ink on that first publication was dry, it was quite clear to the editors, and to all the other members of the team of academics and parliamentary officers who contributed to *Westminster and Europe*, that the continuing unfolding of events in Europe following the Maastricht Treaty on European Union (roughly, the cut-off point for the earlier book) meant that a successor volume would soon be needed. The urgency of this was compounded by parliamentary changes in the UK – in particular the Blair Government's decision to set up a Scottish Parliament and a Welsh Assembly, exercising devolved powers.

The study group was reconstituted and reconvened, with a substantial carry-over of membership from its predecessor – though with some new faces, several of them co-opted from outside the membership of the Study of Parliament Group, added to the team. This blend of continuity and change (to use that rather hackneyed but apposite phrase) enabled us to build upon the strengths of *Westminster and Europe* but also to take on board new themes and a lot of fresh material. We quickly abandoned early thoughts about producing a mere second edition of the previous volume when the extent to which the subject-matter and its context had changed made clear to us that a completely new book would be necessary. We also decided, in consultation with our publishers, to increase the book's appeal to lawyers, as well as to political scientists, by giving it a more explicitly legal and constitutional flavour.

The study group proceeded as before by holding two or three meetings a year to plan the structure and content of a new book and to benefit from the expert knowledge of specialist insiders (such as the clerks and advisers to relevant parliamentary committees) who came to address us. Our first acknowledgement of debt must be to such behind-the-scenes contributors who generously gave up their time to come and talk to the group and who often made themselves available in other contexts to give invaluable information and advice. Those who helped us in this way did so on a non-attributable basis, which is why this acknowledgement is in impersonal terms. And none of our advisers is in any way responsible for the contents of the book.

It was noted in the Preface to *Westminster and Europe* that the book had taken five years to come to fruition. The present book has been similarly slow in production, and for similar reasons. Apart from the familiar excuse of good intentions being thwarted by competing pressures of time, some authors underestimated the sheer volume and complexity of often highly technical subject-matter. And although the general cut-off point for new material was the 2001 general election, authors had in some contexts to update their material beyond that point – and, from the editors' point of view, the book would have looked strangely truncated had we not taken on board at least some aspects of the continuing debates surrounding M. Giscard-d'Estaing's Convention on Europe, or had we not noted Chancellor Gordon Brown's House of Commons statement on 9 June 2003 about the prospects of the UK signing up to the single currency. Even so, we were too late to take on board an important report by the European Scrutiny Committee, *The Convention on the Future of Europe and the Role of National Parliaments* (HC 63, 2002–03) which came out in June 2003, just as the book was being finalised.

In this context we take the opportunity to thank our publishers, Palgrave Macmillan, and particularly Alison Howson, for their patience and, more generally, for their support and encouragement for our project.

Finally, the editors must warmly thank all their fellow members and associates of the study group without whose hard work and expertise this book could not have been written. It would be invidious to single out individuals in this context, but we must make an exception in naming Priscilla Baines and Richard Ware who, as well as

contributing as authors, gave us an enormous amount of invaluable
editorial help and advice. We are also very greatful to Christine Fretten
for providing a comprehensive listing of Parliamentary reports relating
to the European Union. This list is published on the SPG's website.

The content of individual chapters and appendices is the responsibility of their authors. The co-editors are responsible for all matters
of editorial policy, including the structure of the book as a whole,
and for the material in the chapters that bear their names as authors.
Although the book is the product of a study group of the Study of
Parliament Group, it does not purport to represent any corporate
views of the SPG.

Philip Giddings
Gavin Drewry

Note: In the interests of space, the predecessor to this book, Philip
Giddings and Gavin Drewry (eds), *Westminster and Europe: The Impact
of the European Union on the Westminster Parliament* is cited hereafter
as *Westminster and Europe*.

# Notes on Contributors

**Carole Andrews** is Head of the International Affairs and Defence Section in the Research Service of the House of Commons Library. She joined the Library in 1972 as an International Affairs Researcher and was Head of Reference Services from 1985 to 1997.

**Priscilla Baines** has been House of Commons Librarian since 2000. Before that, she worked in the Library's research service from 1968 to 1991 and was Deputy Librarian and Director of Human Resources from 1993 to 1999.

**Gavin Drewry** is Professor of Public Administration and Director of the Centre for Political Studies at Royal Holloway, University of London. He is also an honorary professor in the Law Faculty at UCL.

**Christine Fretten** is Senior Librarian in the International Affairs and Defence Section of the House of Commons Library. She joined the Library in 1975, and since 1986 has been responsible for European documentation.

**Gabrielle Garton Grimwood** was until July 2003 a Senior Researcher in the House of Commons Library. She joined the Library on secondment from the Home Office, where she spent the early years of her career in the Immigration and Nationality Directorate.

**Philip Giddings** is Senior Lecturer in Politics at the University of Reading and has edited and contributed to a number of books on Parliament.

**Julia Lourie** has worked as a subject specialist in the Research Service of the House of Commons Library since 1969. Between 1989 and 2003, she was responsible for briefing MPs of all parties on employment law and policy.

**David Miers** is Professor of Law, Cardiff University. He has written extensively on the preparation and interpretation of legislation and on the role of Westminster in its making and scrutiny.

**Vaughne Miller** is Senior Research Clerk in the International Affairs and Defence Section of the House of Commons Library. She has specialised in the European Union since 1992.

**Alan Page** is Professor of Public Law at the University of Dundee. He is the author (with Terence Daintith) of *The Executive in the Constitution* and (with David Miers) of *Legislation.*

**Simon Patrick** is Deputy Principal Clerk in the Journal Office and Clerk of the Procedure Committee. Among other previous roles, he has been Clerk of the Treasury Committee. He runs the Study of Parliament Group's website.

**Richard Ware** was Director of Research Services, House of Commons Library 1997–2000 and is currently head of the Office of the Clerk. He was Joint Editor of *Parliament and International Relations.*

**Edward Wood** is Director of Information Services at the House of Commons Library.

**Alex Wright** is Lecturer at the Department of Politics, Dundee. He is currently an independent assessor of ministerial appointments to public bodies in Scotland. His published works include an edited volume entitled *Scotland: the Challenge of Devolution.*

**Joanne Wright** is Jean Monnet Professor of European Integration at Royal Holloway, University of London where she is also Dean of the Faculty of History and Social Science. Her main research interest is in the roles international organisations play in internal and external security problems.

# 1
# Introduction

*Gavin Drewry and Philip Giddings*

The European Community – now the main pillar of a more ambitiously conceived European Union – has permeated every aspect of public life. It has affected the culture and working of all government institutions, and the substantive policy agenda at every level and practically in every sector. The effects of this on the Westminster Parliament have been profound, and have become even more so in recent years with the widening of EU competencies, the enlargement of membership and the ongoing march of European integration.

## The four roles of national parliaments

In this emerging EU a national parliament has been able to play four roles. In the United Kingdom the first role has been a constitutional one – to give legislative effect both to the major changes in the treaties that define the role and structure of the Union and the functions of its institutions in Brussels and elsewhere. Second, the UK Parliament has had a legislative role – to deal with the unrelenting flow of European law in the form of the directives that require scrutiny in draft and then legislative ratification in their final form. Third, the UK Parliament has a representative role: it is to our elected parliament that we as citizens of a democratic and sovereign state look to represent our interests and make a significant impact on events and developments in Europe. Fourth, in the United Kingdom the Westminster Parliament has an accountability role, holding British ministers to account for their stewardship of the European agenda.

Notwithstanding those four roles for national parliaments, many citizens and parliamentarians complain about the remoteness of the EU and its 'democratic deficit'. And those of a 'Eurosceptic' persuasion add that the whole enterprise of European integration is a fundamental threat to national sovereignty and to healthy and effective parliamentary government. National parliaments have acquired an increasingly significant rival, the European Parliament, which has been given, during the period covered by this study, increased co-decision-making powers in the EU legislative process.

Whatever one's views about Europe, it was always clear that once Westminster had – after a bitter struggle – enacted the European Communities Act 1972, the UK Parliament was never going to be the same institution again. But what kind of institution has it become and how would it handle the political and policy issues which would arise on the European agenda? These are the central questions addressed in this book.

## Westminster politics

We began the concluding chapter of our previous book, *Westminster and Europe* by quoting Vernon Bogdanor's reminder that 'most community legislation does not fit into the binary conception of politics dominant at Westminster...'.[1] Much has happened in the decade since that was written. The Labour–Conservative duopoly has been dented by the Liberal Democrats at Westminster and replaced in the devolved parliaments/assemblies in Scotland, Wales and Northern Ireland (see Chapter 10). But the central truth of Bogdanor's comment still remains valid so far as Westminster is concerned. There, most parliamentary business continues to be set in the context of ministerial responsibility, exercised against the background of a winner-takes-all electoral system and an adversarial political culture. But when Parliament turns to European business, particularly legislative business, that context and background are of only marginal relevance. The complex dynamics of Westminster in Europe involve both structural and constitutional elements on the one hand, and political forces on the other – and both are reflected throughout this book.

But let us begin with the constitution, and that pivotal, if largely outmoded, convention of ministerial responsibility to Parliament. Here it is crucial to remember that ministers and their departments are not the authors of European Community instruments and proposals in the way that they are for 'domestic' primary and secondary legislation. Even in theory, therefore, they cannot be held directly accountable for them in the traditional way. This does not of course absolve them from responsibility for the individual and collective lines that they as Ministers take in respect of such matters. Indeed, this is the aspect with which British parliamentarians, and particularly MPs from the opposition parties, will be particularly concerned. This was the primary reason for introducing the mechanism of the 'scrutiny reserve' (see Chapter 4) whereby UK ministers have agreed to withhold their consent in the Council of Ministers until the process of parliamentary scrutiny at Westminster has been completed. This mechanism is designed to add teeth to the bark of the Westminster watchdog.

## Limited accountability

The effectiveness of that design has, however, always been open to challenge, even before the extensions of the EU's competence under the Treaties of Maastricht, Amsterdam and Nice. In the first place, some practical prerequisites of 'effective accountability' are manifestly lacking. In particular, the procedures of the Council of Ministers – the forum in which national governments make their final and definitive contribution to EU decision-making are – secret. They are not therefore open to public scrutiny and for that reason can hardly be conducive to ministerial accountability to national parliaments. As a recent report by the House of Commons European Scrutiny Committee observes:

> The Council of Ministers is by far the most important law-making body in the EU.... and yet it meets in private when doing so. That the Council legislates in private is not simply objectionable in principle but also has specific and harmful effects.

The detrimental effects identified by the Committee were that:

- It is impossible for national parliaments (and electorates) to hold Ministers to account if it is not clear how they acted in the Council. For example, a Home Office Minister was recently unable to tell us why an amendment he had promised would be made to the European Arrest Warrant proposal had not in fact been made. This is not primarily a matter of voting records, since votes are rare, but of how firmly governments argue particular points or pressed for particular concessions, The Minister for Europe told us that 'very often what you will find is that nobody will own up to having opposed a decision or having supported a decision. There is a lot of hiding behind other people';

- Secrecy makes it easy for governments to blame 'Brussels' for decisions they may themselves have agreed to;
- Private discussions in the Council result in deals which no government fully accountable to its own parliament would have agreed to; rather than balancing the interests of Member States, such deals may simply reflect the interests of governments;
- Private meetings make the Council, and thus a great part of the EU's activity, largely invisible to citizens.[2]

So even if a minister goes to Brussels armed with a strong message from Parliament's scrutiny procedures, it is difficult to ascertain how vigorously and how effectively that message has been carried into the Council's deliberations. In this and other contexts, transparency, a basic prerequisite of accountability, is not one of the EU's most conspicuous characteristics. The Commons Scrutiny Committee went on to welcome the fact that the UK Government is in favour of the Council meeting in public when legislating and has supported that proposal during the deliberation of the Convention on the Future of Europe. But at the time of writing that has yet to come to fruition.

The second major institutional challenge to the capacity of national parliaments to hold their governments to account in this context has been the growing provision for qualified majority voting (QMV) in the Council. To quote Desmond Dinan:

> As long as a government could veto EU legislation, its national parliament could hold it accountable for exercising (or not exercising) that veto. Once governments subscribed to qualified majority voting, however, national parliaments could not reasonably hold them accountable for being outvoted and abiding by a majority decision.[3]

As noted below, during the period covered by this book, there has been a considerable extension in the range of decisions covered by QMV and more were proposed in the Convention on the Future of Europe.

## The character of the parties

To turn from constitutional and institutional limitations upon effective accountability to the United Kingdom's political culture, we must first consider the character of our two major political parties. The normal stereotype is adversarial politics, characterised by cohesive and disciplined parties in confrontation across the floor of the House of Commons. But from the start the European Question has defied that stereotype. Periods of front-bench consensus have alternated with profound disagreement. It is certainly true that Conservative and Labour positions have for significant periods diverged in major respects on this issue. Back in the 1960s and 1970s, the Labour Party (and the trade union movement that constituted so much of its rank-and-file membership) was seen as hostile to the European Community; whereas the Conservatives, for both political and economic reasons (the EC being seen then as a beacon of free-trade) were generally in favour. On the other hand, the Conservative front-bench supported the Wilson Government's application in 1967 and eight years later campaigned with most of the then Labour Cabinet for a 'yes' vote in the referendum on continuing membership. In contrast again, by 1983 Labour, by then dominated by its left wing, was advocating withdrawal from the Common Market and Margaret Thatcher's Government was positively advocating an extension of European competence in the Single European Act. Since then the relative positions of the parties have radically shifted once more: whilst it would be mistaken to suggest that the Conservatives are now completely 'Eurosceptic' and Labour is 'pro-European', there has been a distinct shift towards those respective positions.

Part of the reason why that last view is mistaken is that Europe continues to divide the main parliamentary parties *internally* and has done so at least since the early 1960s when the United Kingdom first sought membership of what was then the European Common Market under Harold Macmillan. Divisions within both parties were apparent when Harold Wilson's Government made the United

Kingdom's second application in 1967. Edward Heath's European Communities Bill in 1972 only passed with the aid of pro-European Labour dissidents, which foreshadowed the breakaway of the Social Democrats a decade later. In the Conservative Party, neither Margaret Thatcher nor *a fortiori* John Major will need reminding that maintaining party unity – including the unity of ministers generally bound by the discipline of collective responsibility – has been an uphill and sometimes unavailing struggle. And, in Opposition after 1997, certainly until the renewed speculation in mid-2003 about a referendum on the single currency, the Conservatives were palpably fearful of articulating strong positions on big European issues for fear of reopening old wounds and presenting the electorally disastrous image of a divided party. Even 'New Labour' under Tony Blair, whilst generally more positive about many European issues (such as the Social Chapter, see Chapter 6), has experienced a subterranean rumble of disunity – most notably between the Prime Minister and his Chancellor, Gordon Brown, over the issue of joining the Euro (see Chapter 7).

## Parliamentary culture

When it comes to examining the nature and effectiveness of any aspect of parliamentary work, culture is every bit as important as constitutional conventions and procedural devices. And one relevant feature of parliamentary culture, by no means confined to the European agenda, is the limited range of things that MPs are actually willing to do. While they may often be willing to talk about the high profile issues that hit the headlines, persuading them to knuckle down to the important routines and detail of technical scrutiny may be quite another matter. Asked by the chairman of the Commons European Scrutiny Committee for his views 'on how the attention paid by the House to European matters could be increased and the House's handling of EU matters could be made more interesting to members, the media and the public?', the then Leader of the House, Robin Cook, replied:

> we both have a common problem which is that unfortunately, within the House, there is not the interest in European affairs that the matters really deserve. Broadly speaking, most vital departments

are now spending about a fifth or a quarter of their time relating to Europe coping with the consequence of initiatives taken in Europe, trying to influence the projects that may be passing through Europe. That reflects the reality and extent to which our trade, our law enforcement services, our environment requirements now have very much a continental, not just a domestic, dimension. ... I do not think in the House we have yet achieved that quantum leap, that gear shift, to recognise the extent to which what happens in Europe has such a big bearing on what happens in our domestic politics. When we debate Europe, we do tend to go for the grand theatre and the grand positions on the principles of whether we are in or out or on what structure the future architecture of Europe might have. We tend not to be so good at paying attention to the nitty gritty, the detailed issues, the way in which this affects a whole range of detailed policy considerations.[4]

Mr Cook confessed that he did not have an easy solution to this problem, which is a serious one. The cumulative extent and effectiveness of any national parliament's engagement with the voluminous but politically unsexy 'nitty gritty' of EU business is crucial to its claims to occupy an important part on the European stage.

## An expanding and deepening Europe

Our previous book ended with the great parliamentary struggle over ratification of the Maastricht Treaty. Since then much has happened in the 'grand theatre' of the EU both structurally and in terms of substantive policy development, that has impinged upon the Westminster agenda – and, hence, features prominently in the chapters that follow. In Chapter 2, David Miers gives a full account of how the EU has developed since Maastricht. Here we simply note the two major movements: first, the extensive implications of the Maastricht Treaty with its two new 'pillars', the 'Social Chapter' and economic and monetary union; and, second, the grand project of enlargement, occasioned to a large extent by the collapse of the Soviet Empire in Central and Eastern Europe.

In the early part of the period covered by this book the huge implications of the Maastricht Treaty came fully into play. Alongside the

European Community there were now two new 'pillars': a Second Pillar, the Common Foreign and Security Policy; and a Third Pillar, Co-operation on Justice and Home Affairs (subsequently renamed Police and Judicial Co-operation in Criminal Matters). Maastricht also set a timetable for economic and monetary union, and the introduction of a single currency; strengthened the legislative powers of the European Parliament; and brought in the so-called Social Chapter, in respect of which the Major Government initially opted out. The word 'subsidiarity', already part of the vocabulary of European discourse, was elevated to a key principle, albeit with limited consensus about its precise meaning.

As noted in the previous volume, the Maastricht Treaty foreshadowed the convening of another Intergovernmental Conference (IGC) in 1996 to review the operation of the Treaty. The main product of this was the Amsterdam Treaty of 1999. This considerably extended the legislative powers of the European Parliament, and it also extended the range of issues that could be decided in the Council by QMV (some of which had formerly to be decided on the basis of unanimity). The Social Chapter was incorporated into the Amsterdam Treaty, following its adoption by the United Kingdom, under the newly elected Blair Government, in 1997.

The next major landmark, following a further IGC, was the Nice Treaty of 2000, intended to pave the way for the grand project of enlargement of the EU by the addition of up to 13 new members states. The Nice Treaty further extended the range of matters subject to QMV and agreed, eventually, a new weighting of votes from 2005. The Treaty also set the membership of the enlarged European Parliament and provided that, from 2005, each member country of the enlarged Union was to have one member of the Commission, with a rotation if and when membership reaches 27. The Treaty also added to the powers of President of the Commission. The prolonged and complex negotiations about enlargement finally came to a conclusion at Copenhagen in December 2002 when ten states – Malta, Cyprus, Latvia, Lithuania, Estonia, Poland, Hungary, Czech Republic, Slovakia and Slovenia – were formally invited to join the EU in May 2004 (subject in most cases to confirmation by referendums in the countries concerned). Romania and Bulgaria hope to join in 2007, but at the time of writing, Turkey has suspended its membership negotiations.

These major changes to the Union – 'deepening and widening' – raised serious questions about governance – how decisions were to be made. In December 2001, the summit meeting in Laeken led to the establishment of a 'Convention on the Future of Europe' under former French President, Valéry Giscard D'Estaing, to consider the consolidation and simplification of the Treaties into a new EU (but will it still be called that?) constitution. This process continues at the time of writing.

## The shape of this study

In this book we cover the period from the ratification of the Maastricht Treaty to the UK General Election of 2001. We have, however, given latitude to our contributors to go beyond June 2001 where there have been significant developments between then and the submission of text for publication (April 2003 in most cases) which they wished to incorporate. And in Chapter 11 the editors have taken the opportunity to look at what may lie ahead in the light of continuing developments, such as enlargement and the products of the Convention on the Future of Europe.

Although this book develops a number of the themes of our previous book, *Westminster and Europe*, it is a completely different one. Readers may therefore find it helpful in some contexts to refer back to *Westminster and Europe*, to set themes in a longer historical perspective and to look at areas (like the Common Agricultural Policy) which have not been selected for coverage in the present work. Since the major focus of this book is on law and policy in particular areas, it is necessary to begin – as before – with setting the scene against which policy and law have been made. Thus in Chapter 2, David Miers takes the account of the development of European institutions from the ratification of the Maastricht Treaty to the Laeken Summit of December 2001 – the period in which the 'Community' became a 'Union', with new structures and more ambitious goals. In Chapter 3, Alan Page (like Miers, an academic lawyer) considers the impact of those developments in European Law on the United Kingdom's constitution and law; and in Chapter 4, Priscilla Baines reviews the complicated story of the evolution of post-Maastricht policy and legislative scrutiny machinery in both Houses of the UK Parliament.

With the context thus set, we then move on to examine the Westminster Parliament 'in action', illustrated by reference to some of the key European debates and issues of the last decade – many of them still live issues at the time of writing. There were several other policy issues (such as the BSE crisis and the Common Fisheries Policy) which might well have been included but which we reluctantly discarded, partly on space grounds. But we are confident that the themes that have been included are both important and interesting in their own right, and as a collection well-illustrate the wider issues of Parliament's handling of the European dimension of law and policy-making – that is, 'Westminster in Europe'.

Thus in Chapter 5, Vaughne Miller and Carole Andrews look at governance and institutional reform in the EU in the wake of the Amsterdam and Nice IGCs, and particularly how the continuing process of enlargement; has been handled. In Chapter 6, Julia Lourie discusses employment law, with special reference to the Maastricht Social Chapter which was the subject of an opt-out by the Major Government, subsequently reversed by its successor in 1997. Another so-called 'opt-out' is dealt with in Chapter 7, where Philip Giddings looks at the complicated saga of British ambivalence towards European Monetary Union and the single European currency. In Chapter 8, Richard Ware and Joanne Wright turn our attention to a different feature of governance, the second and third pillars of the EU, and the quest for a common foreign and security policy – a subject brought sharply into recent focus by events leading up to the invasion of Iraq in February 2003. Such international developments, and especially those following the terrorist attacks on the USA in September 2001, highlighted the difficult issues of policy relating to immigration and asylum which are reviewed in Chapter 9 by Gavin Drewry, with the assistance of two colleagues from the House of Commons Library. And a further, more domestic, aspect of governance is dealt with in Chapter 10, where Alex Wright shifts the focus from Westminster to examine the impact of the EU and its agendas on the devolved parliaments and executives of the United Kingdom. The book ends with a concluding chapter, written by the editors, bringing the story up to June 2003, and offering some reflections on the future, informed by the material in the preceding chapters – the basis perhaps (our publishers permitting) for a further sequel in a few years' time?

# Notes

1. *Westminster and Europe*, p. 299. The quotation is from V. Bogdanor, 'Britain and the European Community', in J. Jowell and D. Oliver (eds), *The Changing Constitution*, 3rd edn, Oxford: Clarendon Press, 1994, p. 8.
2. House of Commons European Scrutiny Committee, *Democracy and Accountability in the EU and the Role of National Parliaments*, 33rd Report, 2001–02, HC 152, para. 20.
3. Desmond Dinan, *Ever Closer Union*, 2nd edn, London: Macmillan, 1999, p. 296.
4. *European Scrutiny in the Commons*, evidence 5 November 2002, HC 1298-i, Q. 3.

# 2
# Britain in Europe: Community to Union, 1973–2001

*David Miers*

## Introduction

This chapter's purpose is to set the scene for the detailed accounts which follow of the relationship between Westminster and Europe. It does so in two interconnected ways. First, it reviews the main developments that took place following the United Kingdom's accession to the European Economic Community (EEC) on 1 January 1973. These are traced through key legislative events: the Single European Act 1986, the Treaty on European Union 1992 (TEU), the Treaty of Amsterdam 1997 and the Treaty of Nice 2001. Their cumulative and intended effect has been the progressive enlargement (widening) and integration (deepening) of the Community. The chapter comments, secondly, on the nature of the United Kingdom's ambivalent relationship with the Community, in particular concerning the question whether deeper integration would best serve its long-term interests. In terms of British politics, this was perhaps the most acrimonious question of the latter half of the twentieth century. Two of its most prominent casualties were Margaret Thatcher and John Major, both of whose terms as Prime Minister foundered on deep-rooted divisions within the Conservative Party over the question of European integration. Despite its pro-European rhetoric, New Labour has pursued a cautious policy, vividly demonstrated by the United Kingdom's non-participation in the launch of the Euro on 1 January 2002.[1]

Following this introduction, the chapter is divided into four sections. The section 'Aims, achievements, institutional arrangements and the awkward partner' summarises these features of the European Community, aims, and makes some preliminary comments about the United Kingdom's ambivalent attitude to the notion of 'closer union'. The section 'Enlargement' documents the expansion in Community membership which occurred between 1973 and the mid-1990s, and which is proposed for the first decade of this century. The discussion draws attention to some of the primary economic implications of enlargement for the Community. The section which follows reviews the steps that have been taken towards integration. It comments on the difficulties created for the United Kingdom by the drive towards political and economic union and on Member States' efforts to manage the institutional implications of enlargement. The section 'New Labour and the EU: a Europe of nations' makes some concluding remarks about the present state of the Union.

## Aims, achievements, institutional arrangements and the awkward partner

### Aims and achievements: the internal market and beyond

Upon its accession, the United Kingdom became subject to a political regime having unique aspirational, institutional and legal characteristics. These had been first established with the coming into force in July 1952, under the Treaty of Paris, of the European Coal and Steel Community (ECSC). Two further Communities were established under separate Treaties of Rome in 1957: the European Atomic Energy Community (Euratom) and the EEC. These three Communities had their origins in the wish of their founders to assist their countries' post-war economic regeneration and to create such a degree of integration as would prevent another European war. In the case of the Treaty of Rome, integration meant the promotion of 'a harmonious development of economic activities, a continuous and balanced expansion, an increase in stability, an accelerated raising of the standard of living and closer relations' between the States belonging to the Community.[2] This was to be achieved, first, by the creation of a common market. This would entail:

- the abolition of all internal tariffs and quantitative restrictions on trade;

- the creation of a common external tariff subjecting all imported goods to the same conditions irrespective of their place of entry into the Community;
- the prohibition of practices distorting competition within the Community; and
- the harmonisation of laws to the extent necessary to achieve a common market.

The Treaty was unambiguous in its contemplation of increasing Community involvement in Member States' economic affairs. In addition to the free movement of the four primary incidents of their economies – goods, persons (in particular, workers), services and capital – which would be brought about by the completion of the internal market, 'ever closer union among the peoples of Europe'[3] required other areas of integration, for example in agriculture and transport, as well as the progressive approximation of Member States' economic policies. The internal market was effectively completed in 1992 under the terms of the Single European Act 1986 (SEA). Closer union now extends well beyond a purely economic community, to include such matters as the environment, defence, criminal justice, immigration and animal welfare. In restructuring the Community, the primary achievements of the TEU were the creation of the EU and agreement on the stages to be completed for economic and monetary union (EMU). Further institutional changes were made by the Treaty of Amsterdam 1997 (TA). In addition to deepening, the Community has also widened its membership. From six in 1957 to fifteen by the mid-1990s, the commitment at the beginning of the 21st century is to incorporate another dozen Members, as the geopolitical notion of 'Europe' extends further eastwards.

### Institutional arrangements

The founders of the Treaties recognised that to achieve their aspirations it would be necessary to create an institutional framework which met two basic criteria. The first was to give the two groups principally responsible for formulating Community obligations and for securing compliance with them, that is, the central executive and the Member States, a balance of power at the expense of democratic accountability to their citizens. The second was to ensure that

Member States, upon whose political tractability success would inevitably depend, enjoyed sufficient representation in decision-making. These constraints were, in each of the three Communities, translated into essentially the same institutional configuration: one body to represent Community interests (the Commission, and in the case of the ECSC, the High Authority), one to represent national interests (the Council of Ministers) and one to provide a limited measure of democratic accountability (the European Assembly). A fourth body was established to provide authoritative rulings on the interpretation of Community Law (the Court of Justice of the European Communities – CJEC). From 1958 each European Assembly (known as the European Parliament (EP) from 1962) and the CJEC became common to all three;[4] in 1965, the 'Merger Treaty' established one European Commission and one Council of Ministers to serve the three Communities.[5]

The configuration and role of these institutions remain broadly as they were at the time of the United Kingdom's accession.[6] As the 'guardian' of the EU Treaties, the Commission's primary responsibilities are to initiate Community policy and to represent its general interests, both internally and externally. The President and the Members of the Commission are appointed by the Member States after they have been approved by the EP. The Commissioners are obliged to act in the collective interest, notwithstanding that it might operate to their own country's national disadvantage. The Commission exercises primarily both executive and legislative functions. The Council of Ministers is the 'embodiment' of the Member States. Comprising government representatives, it both takes decisions on a wide range of Community and EU issues, and co-ordinates Member States' broad economic policies.[7] Its Presidency rotates among the Member States on a six-year cycle, each holding office for six months. The Council exercises legislative functions and shares budgetary authority with EP. These overlapping functions between the Community's institutions are a product of the Treaty's conception, described above, of an institutional separation of *interests*, rather than, as in other legal systems, a separation of *powers*.

The stability and smooth functioning of these arrangements have inevitably been compromised by the inherent tension between the pursuit of collective at the expense of national interests. The informal 'summit' meetings between heads of government that became regular features of Community business during the 1970s reflected the necessity both of Member States' engagement in and consent to policy-making at the highest level. Formally recognised by SEA, the European Council is now established under TEU Article 4, and involves all three of the Treaty institutions. It comprises the Commission President and the heads of state or government, and is required to report to EP. The Council meets at least twice a year, chaired by the Member State holding the Presidency of the Council of Ministers. Its role is to provide 'the necessary impetus' for the development of the EU. In so doing, the European Council gives Member States the opportunity to influence the Community agenda during their Presidency. That influence will reflect their position on the questions, how fast and how far should closer union be pursued. The tension between collective and national interests finds expression also in the voting arrangements in the Council of Ministers. On most matters, decisions are subject to a system known as 'qualified majority voting' (QMV). Its purpose is to ensure that 'ever closer union' does not founder on the intransigence of one Member State. But on some matters, there must be unanimity. In these cases any Member State enjoys a veto over collective action. Inasmuch as this represents a retention of national sovereignty for each of them, its 'erosion', through the gradual transfer of matters to QMV, has been a matter of acute political sensitivity, and not only for the United Kingdom.

Voting in the EP, on the other hand, initially attracted less significance. It was a deliberate feature of the Treaty of Rome that its role would be advisory and not determinative. As a result of the incremental changes made by SEA, TEU and TA, it is the EP, of all the EU institutions, which has changed most significantly. Elected every five years by direct universal suffrage, EP, which sits in Strasbourg, has three main responsibilities: it shares with the Council budgetary authority and the power to legislate,[8] and it exercises democratic supervision over the Commission. The enhancement of EP's voice is an aspect of the EU's response to the widely shared view, acknowledged by the Commission's 2001 White Paper, *European Governance*,[9] that it is at once both remote (decisions taken by faceless and unaccountable bureaucrats in Brussels) and intrusive (decisions which require long-established local practices to be changed).[10] The introduction in TEU of the concept of 'subsidiarity' likewise was an attempt to bring decisions closer to those affected by them. But there continues to be concern about the transparency of the EU's decision-making, evidenced in 1999 by the Lords' Report on 'comitology', Euro-speak for a complex form of Commission law-making.[11] The objective of the European constitutional convention, agreed by the European Council at Laeken in December 2001, is to achieve greater openness, participation, accountability, effectiveness and coherence in the governance of the EU.[12]

### The awkward partner

Its declining industrial base, political history and geographically peripheral island position meant that upon accession in 1973, the United Kingdom joined the Community under different economic conditions and with a different political outlook than that shared by the six founding states. Subsequent differences over its budgetary contribution, together with its (declining) role within the Commonwealth and successive governments' desire to maintain the 'special relationship' with the United States, have cast the United Kingdom as an awkward, half-hearted, semi-detached or reluctant member of the Community.[13] If this implies that other Member States have always been *communitaire*, Young argues that the implication is misconceived.[14] Like all EEC members, the United Kingdom has pursued its national interest; unlike its founders, it has not equated that interest with integration. Margaret Thatcher's antipathy to what she perceived to be the erosion of sovereignty implied by political union was, during the late 1980s, tempered by her pragmatic support for the completion of the internal market. Economic and monetary union were, however, very far removed from the vision of a Europe of sovereign states economically liberal, deregulated and interdependent, and based on political co-operation but not integration which she described in her Bruges speech in September 1988. Likewise John Major, her successor as Prime Minister, found it virtually impossible to maintain a stance which was pro-European but which did not involve the 'F' (federalism) word.

Associated with the non-alignment of interests is the 'missed bus' or 'lost opportunity' thesis. This argues that because of its late accession to the Community and ambivalence about the implications of 'ever closer union', the United Kingdom has never been in a position to influence the shaping of the ground rules. At the level of implementation, Community membership has, in the words of a former Foreign Secretary, David Owen, been a process of 'continuous negotiation' of national and collective interests.[15] That process is, frequently contentious and occasionally acrimonious, as exemplified by the bitter division of opinion between the United Kingdom and its Community partners during 1996 concerning the incidence of BSE in British beef. This came at a particularly difficult time for John Major, who was struggling to maintain his political authority in the face of sustained criticism, from both sides of his party, about his approach to the post-TEU agenda.

## Enlargement

### From six to twenty-seven

For the first 15 years of its existence, the Community comprised the original six signatories: Belgium, the Federal Republic of Germany, France, Italy, Luxembourg and the Netherlands. Membership doubled by the mid-1980s: Denmark and Ireland became Member States under the same Treaty of Accession that admitted the United Kingdom, Greece entered the Community in 1981, and Portugal and Spain in 1986.

Accession is not necessarily a smooth path. Any European State may apply to become a member, but it must be able to assume the obligations of membership. Two of the 1993 'Copenhagen criteria' confirmed that applicants must be democracies which respect human rights, and must operate market economies capable of coping with competition. Greece, Portugal and Spain could not be serious contenders until their dictatorial regimes of the mid-1970s had been replaced, and Turkey's human rights deficit continues to be an obstacle to its admission.[16] Greece's entry was delayed, too, because its economy was for a time considered incapable of sustaining the obligations of membership. By contrast, the applications by Austria and the Scandinavian countries in the 1990s were welcome, first because the strength of their economies meant that they would be net contributors to the Community budget, and second, because they might be expected to oppose the spending ambitions of the poorer countries.[17] Accession also requires unanimity among existing Member States. During the 1960s President de Gaulle twice blocked the United Kingdom's application because he doubted its commitment to the Treaty's aspirations.

The realignment of Europe's geopolitical map following the end of the Cold War raised the question whether the Community's priority should be to widen its membership to include the newly liberated Eastern European countries or to maintain the drive towards political and economic union. Arguments in favour of enlargement point both to the economic and political gains (100 million new consumers together with an overall increase in living conditions for the new Members; more effective action against common problems of crime and illegal immigration, encouraging greater political security and stability) and to the impetus it would give to the reform of the EU's institutional arrangements. Those against highlight the potential for gridlock in decision-making, and the economic problems that will follow from the substantial economic differences between the existing and the candidate countries (eastwards movement of capital and the westwards migration of cheap labour, together with an eastwards flow of EU funds). Disagreement about these issues and about the preference to be given as between enlargement and integration formed a major part of the Maastricht negotiations which preceded the TEU. Finding new allies in the recently elected Nordic countries, who shared its preference for a wider but looser association of nation states, the United Kingdom argued that more was to be gained for Europe by assisting the former communist republics to achieve economic and political independence, than by deeper integration. The difficulties that could readily be anticipated in connection with the negotiations for their accession also held out the prospect of serious dislocation to any plans for closer union. In line with their history, France, Germany and the Benelux countries sought a continuing commitment to political and economic union, arguing that while these countries were in principle welcome to join, more urgent was the strengthening of the Community itself. These fundamental disagreements meant that the TEU was a compromise which postponed the issue of expansion.

During the 1990s a number of former Soviet republics (CEECs: Central and Eastern European Countries) formally applied for membership, bringing the total of candidates in 2001 to 12.[18] The European Council allocated these to one of two groups, reflecting their proximity to the Copenhagen criteria. The 'first wave' comprised

Cyprus, the Czech Republic, Estonia, Hungary, Poland and Slovenia; negotiations commenced in 1998. Negotiations with the second wave, Bulgaria, Latvia, Lithuania, Malta, Romania and Slovakia, commenced in 1999. At the close of 2002, formal invitations to join were agreed for 10 countries. These comprise the six 'first wave' candidates plus Latvia, Lithuania, Malta and Slovakia from the second.[19]

## The economic implications of enlargement

The economic implications for the Community of the accession of new Member States are complex. First, economic strengths and weaknesses are not equally divided. Both within and between Member States there are areas of relative prosperity: northern Italy is highly industrialised, whereas the south is poor and dependent on agriculture and fishing; Ireland is relatively under-industrialised, and some areas of the United Kingdom require significant invest-ment to counter the effects of the decline in its traditional industries. The strength of Spain's fishing fleet was an important factor in the negotiations leading to its accession, and as the *Factortame* litigation in the United Kingdom shows,[20] the threat it posed was not only of an economic nature. Nor do realignments of economic power pose threats only to the existing membership. France, with its substantial Mediterranean economy, and more obviously Italy, benefited from a more pronounced Mediterranean interest in the working out of Community policy during the 1980s. Eastwards enlargement will incorporate countries whose economic circum-stances are generally worse than the poorest of the existing Member States. The CEECs will generate tensions both between themselves and the net contributors in the West, some of whom are, like them, smaller States (such as Benelux and Denmark), and between them and the current net beneficiaries, particularly in the South (the Club Med.) and Ireland, who will seek some 'upward adaptation' to compensate.[21]

Of particular note is the impact of enlargement on the Common Agricultural Policy (CAP). CAP was established in 1962 for the purpose of ensuring food supplies and a fair standard of living for farmers. Given its historic trading preferences within the Common-wealth, the United Kingdom's accession was always going to pose a problem.[22] Continuation of those preferences quickly brought it into conflict with France over the application of CAP to New Zealand lamb, culminating in the trade wars of 1978–80.[23] In the 1980s the accession of Greece and the Iberian countries put pressure on the Community to reorient CAP towards Mediterranean products and, more generally, to assist these Member States' economic development. By contrast, the existing northern Europeans' efforts to curb CAP's excesses was one reason for the Community's insistence on a long transitional period in agriculture preceding the entry of Portugal and Spain. Issues concerning CAP resurfaced with the CEEC applications. In 2002 it cost £27 billion, 45 per cent of the EU budget. Unless reformed, the vast tracts of under-developed agricultural land in Poland, Hungary, Slovenia and Slovakia will add massively to that burden.[24]

Besides their impact on CAP, two further consequences of the accession of CEECs merit note. Their eastern borders will also constitute the external frontier of an EU that, following the Schengen Agreement, has virtually done away with internal controls. They thus pose an external security risk: the price that they will have to pay for admission will include effective border controls to keep out illegal immigrants,[25] drugs and arms imported from yet further east. Secondly, the accession of the CEECs raises the question, how to manage possibly 27 Member States in a structure built for six?

## Integration

### Early developments

During the Community's first ten years many aspects of the Treaty of Rome's principal features were set in place, for example CAP and the customs union, while its institutions and budgetary arrangements assumed a relatively settled shape. The economic progress achieved by the six founding Members was substantially due to the fact that these developments coincided with their own national interests. This functional approach to integration was successful because it sought to introduce common policies on discrete economic sectors which did not require a reduction in national sovereignty. However, largely because of France's absolute refusal to accept the automatic transfer of national agricultural levies to the Community as its 'own resources', further efforts to advance closer union ground to a halt. French grievances were resolved by the Luxembourg Compromise

(1966), which provided that a Member State could block a majority vote on a proposal of the Commission, by pleading that its 'very important interests' were at stake. In such a case, the Council would, within a reasonable time, endeavour to reach a solution which could be adopted by all.

Although the new leaders of the French and German Governments, Georges Pompidou and Willy Brandt, persuaded the Community in 1969 to be more active in achieving closer union, little progress was made over the next 15 years. This was due to factors both external and internal to the Community. First, whereas the 1960s had seen widespread and sustained economic growth, substantial increases in the price of oil in 1973–74 and again in 1979–80 contributed to a worldwide recession. Secondly, progress was hampered by the British budgetary question (BBQ). Because CAP was funded in part by a customs tariff on imports into the Community, the United Kingdom's substantial Commonwealth trade put it at a disadvantage. While its contributions exceeded those made by stronger economies, it received less benefits than those having a greater dependence on agriculture, notably France. The matter was superficially dealt with by the Labour Government's 're-negotiation' during 1974 and 1975, but for Margaret Thatcher it assumed a far greater significance. First, CAP's subsidies offended her political credo, which was to reduce public expenditure. Second, it had become a by-word for expense and fraud. Guaranteed prices encouraged market distortion, over-production and the additional expense of 'intervention' to dispose of butter mountains and wine lakes. The justice in the United Kingdom's case was, however, compromised by the Prime Minister's confrontational approach and strident references to 'my money'. Fuelled by her perception that France and Germany regarded the Community as their club, the BBQ negotiations were both difficult and protracted.

## The Single European Act 1986

Progress towards closer union during the 1970s was therefore modest, with procedural activity acting as a substitute for policy. Encouraged by the successful completion of entry negotiations with Greece and the Iberian countries, the completion of the common fisheries policy, and their resolution at Fontainebleau in June 1984 of the BBQ, the heads of government established a committee to develop ideas agreed that year by EP. Chaired by a former Irish foreign minister, James Dooge, the committee on 'Institutional Affairs' advocated further extension of QMV, an increase in the powers of EP and the completion of the internal market. Reflecting the divisions of opinion that preceded it (Denmark, Greece and the United Kingdom in particular expressing so many reservations that they became known as 'the footnote countries'), the resulting Single European Act 1986 was a diluted version of the 1984 proposals, and, because of ratification difficulties in Ireland and Denmark, did not come into force until 1987.[26]

The Single European Act authorised important extensions in the Community's reach over Member States' affairs: research and technological development, the environment, economic and social cohesion (better known as regional policy), and foreign policy.[27] Its principal ambition was the completion of the internal market by 1 January 1993. This required the removal of all physical, technical and fiscal barriers to the free movement of goods, persons, services and capital, and was strongly backed by the larger and more influential transnational commercial and financial interests.[28] In order to ensure that individual Member States could not obstruct progress, SEA extended QMV to six Articles of the Treaty, including the internal market. While Margaret Thatcher pursued 'one overriding positive goal...to create a single Common Market',[29] she retained substantial reservations about other forms of singularity. Contemplating the implications of the absence of border controls, she observed, 'I was not prepared to give up our powers to control immigration (from non-EC countries), to combat terrorism, crime, and drug trafficking and to take measures on human, animal and plant health...'.[30]

## The Treaty on European Union 1992

### Economic and political union

Since 1957, 'ever closer union' had come to assume a variety of forms which extended well beyond a purely economic community. These were given further expression in the TEU. TEU established that the geographical area covered by the three Communities would constitute the EU, and that the Union would itself comprise three 'pillars'. The first consists of the three original Communities, within which the Treaty of Rome was renamed the European Communities Treaty. The second pillar was established to deal with common foreign and security policies (CFSP), and the third with justice and home affairs (JHA). The second and third pillars lie largely outside the Communities' institutional arrangements; joint action or joint position are determined at inter-governmental level, that is, at the Council of Ministers.

The Treaty also sought to address the increasing sense of the Community's remoteness from its citizens' lives by the inclusion of the principles of proportionality and subsidiarity. Though legally complex, the principle of subsidiarity was simple enough: 'that the EU should act only if the Member States cannot achieve the aim on their own. Proportionality requires that when the EU does act, it should do so as lightly as possible, leaving as much as possible to the Member States themselves'.[31] Secondly, Member States' citizens became European citizens. In addition to their right 'to move and to reside freely within the territory of the Member States', European citizens became entitled to vote or stand in elections to EP, wherever in the Community they happened to reside, and to petition EP and appeal against administrative malpractice to a Community Ombudsman.

From the perspective of the advocates of deeper integration, TEU's most notable achievement was to agree the stages to be completed for economic and monetary union (EMU).[32] The UK Government's approach to the Maastricht negotiations was the promotion of a strong Europe characterised by the shared aims of nation states, with entry into EMU 'when the time is right'. Unlike Margaret Thatcher, John Major was prepared to engage fully in the Intergovernmental Conferences (IGCs), and in the event, he achieved virtually all his aims. The government hailed the elimination of the 'F' word as a considerable triumph of negotiation, which also saw two opt-outs: one on monetary union and a second on the Social Chapter.[33]

But despite winning support across the Conservative Party, John Major had also inherited its entrenched divisions. These became more significant following the April 1992 election as the Conservative majority fell from over 100 to 21. At first, he was able to bridge the divide; the Bill ratifying Maastricht received a comfortable majority in May 1992.[34] However, Denmark's refusal in June to ratify TEU encouraged the Conservative Euro-sceptics to demand a fresh start on Europe. Their objections reached a new intensity when, on 16 September 1992, Britain's inability to maintain sterling within the approved rates forced it to withdraw from the ERM. 'Black Wednesday' was an economic and political disaster. Young comments that it 'was *the* turning point of the Major premiership and a numbing experience for all concerned'.[35] For the Euro-sceptics it merely confirmed the folly of joining the ERM in the first place. There followed, until the 1997 election, five years of ill-tempered and bitter exchanges between the Prime Minister and the Euro-sceptics.[36]

*Two speed Europe*

In readiness for the 1996 Turin IGC at which progress towards EMU was to be reviewed, France and Germany had both accepted that the Community could as well proceed to monetary union by recognising that some Member States would take longer than others to meet the conditions for convergence. Their varying economic circumstances encouraged talk of 'flexible integration' and 'variable geometry'; Euro-code for a two-tier or a two-speed Europe.[37] French and German acceptance of a 'two speed' Europe was born also of their growing impatience with John Major's lack of commitment. His preference was for a 'multi-track, multi-speed and multi-layered' Europe, tolerant of Member States who wished to contribute to and enjoy the benefits of shared ambitions, but who equally did not wish a deeper integration driven by ideology. His pragmatic vision was restated in the 1996 White Paper, *A Partnership of Nations*.[38] Predictably, this pleased few within the Conservative Party. While it discounted any further extension of QMV or the grant of new legislative powers to EP, it was not tough enough for the Euro-sceptics. For the pro-Europe wing, the danger inherent in 'flexibility' was the United Kingdom's progressive isolation from the Community.

But for all the Foreign Secretary's (Malcolm Rifkind) emollient rhetoric about the United Kingdom being both at the heart of Europe (for the benefit of Brussels) and seeking to serve its own national interests wherever possible (for the benefit of the Euro-sceptics), relationships with its European partners became increasingly sour during 1996 as a consequence of the BSE crisis. Driven by concerns that were not entirely political – the loss of a multi-million pound export industry and with consequent pressure from the farming lobby – the government first condemned its partners' decision to ban the export of beef and beef products as unreasonable, threatened various unlawful actions by way of retaliation, and finally, in a re-run of de Gaulle's 'empty chair' policy concerning automatic French CAP contributions, vetoed over 70 unconnected matters requiring unanimity. The beef crisis played squarely into the Euro-sceptics' hands; when ranged alongside the loss of employment in the fishing industry in consequence of the imposition of fishing quotas, the Community could readily be portrayed as pursuing policies inimical to traditional elements of the country's economy. The Cabinet's pro-Europeans were genuinely dismayed by the Commission's decision. John Major's decision to 'paralyse the EU' by use of the 'serial veto' may have pleased the Euro-sceptics, but with a majority in the Commons in single figures, he was effectively trapped by them. Neither did his combative approach succeed. At the Florence summit in June 1996, the government accepted the Commission's proposed 67,000 cull, that there would be no timetable for lifting the ban, and that its lifting would be subject to EU scrutiny.[39] Relations with Europe were as bad as they had been during the BBQ negotiations when led by Margaret Thatcher.[40]

### The Treaty of Amsterdam 1997

The TEU compromise left a number of matters of 'unfinished business' for future decision. These were in part addressed in the Treaty of Amsterdam 1997. With the Maastricht difficulties, coupled with the post-TEU ratification setbacks, still fresh in the collective memory, there was perhaps little stomach for radical change; the most controversial issues associated with enlargement were deferred. But there were changes. These re-allocated matters from the third to the first pillar (free movement of persons) and added new matters to the EC Treaty (equal opportunties, sustainable development). Reflecting its focus on issues of freedom, security and justice, the third pillar was refocused to deal with police and judicial co-operation in criminal matters (PJCC).

The treaty of Amsterdam also extended EP's influence over legislative acts. As noted earlier, the initial conception of EP's role was limited to consultation. Since SEA, however, its role 'has been greatly enhanced as a result of the widened consultation, co-operation, assent and co-decision procedures' established through successive Treaty amendments.[41] The co-operation procedure was introduced by SEA. It applied at first primarily to single market decisions, and is now largely confined to EMU matters. Under Article 252 (TA), where it had formerly enjoyed only a first reading of a Council proposal (acting on a proposal from the Commission), this procedure gives EP a second reading of the 'common position' which the Council has adopted having obtained its opinion. At the second reading, EP has a variety of options, including rejection or amendment. Its views are not dispositive; depending on the extent of any disagreement, enactment requires either a qualified majority in the Council, or unanimity. The co-operation procedure constituted a modest advance in EP's involvement in the making of Community law, disappointing those who wished to see it given a more influential voice. The 'co-decision' procedure is the product of changes introduced by TEU and expanded by TA. It is so called because 'it is designed to prevent a measure being adopted without the approval of both the Council and the European Parliament, and because it places emphasis on the reaching of a jointly approved text'.[42] Here again EP has two readings and a power of negative veto, but it cannot impose its own will. Nevertheless, Article 251 redresses many of the procedural imbalances between the Council and Parliament. Its more assertive role can be seen in the wider context of the mass resignation of the Commission in 1999 following its critical report on fraud and corruption and in its second pillar scrutiny.[43]

**The Treaty of Nice 2001**

Against a background of demands by the candidate states that the EU deliver on its promises,[44] the purpose of the Nice Treaty was to address three primary issues left over from TA (the 'Amsterdam Triangle'): the weighting of votes in the Council of Ministers, the further extension of QMV, and the size and composition of the Commission.[45] The Treaty is to take effect on 1 January 2005.[46] An IGC is planned for 2004 to clarify the division of responsibilities between Brussels and national governments, to simplify the Treaties, to give national parliaments a bigger role in the EU, and to consider whether to make the EU's *Charter of Fundamental Rights*, formally adopted in

December 2000, legally binding. Each one of these, and particularly the last, can be guaranteed to generate controversy.

### Qualified majority voting (QMV)

Representation in the Council of Ministers has never been intended directly to reflect Member States' populations; such a policy would, comparing Luxembourg (400,000) with the unified Germany (82 million) for example, mean no effective representation for the smaller State. The weighting of votes is a compromise between one vote per Member State against an allocation proportional to population size. States' relative positions are reflected in the value that is attached to that allocation. It is not *how many* votes a Member State has to cast that is significant, but their *effect* (when combined with others) on the decision being taken.[47]

In 1993 the Treaty of Rome, which had adjusted voting weights with successive enlargements, valued the largest, France, Germany, Italy and the United Kingdom, at 10; the smallest, Luxembourg, at 2; the total weighting of the 12 Member States being 76. In the commonest instance, where the Council was voting on a proposal from the Commission, the majority had to be at least 54. These procedures meant that the four largest members (40 votes) could not dictate to the others. They also meant that the blocking vote of 23 could be achieved by the votes of two of the largest Member States (20) and one of those weighted at three (Denmark and Ireland). The planned accession of Austria and the Nordic countries in 1995 would have increased the total of votes to 90, the majority to 64 and the blocking vote to 27.[48] The United Kingdom and Spain objected, since its (intended) effect would be to weaken the influence of any one of the largest Member States. But the other 10 were adamant, and faced with this impasse, the 12 agreed to an arrangement which recalled the Luxembourg 'veto'. Proposed by the Greek presidency, the Ioannina compromise would be triggered by 23–26 blocking votes, whereupon the Council would endeavour to negotiate a solution that could be adopted by at least 68 votes.

At Nice the United Kingdom's strategy was to strengthen its position at the expense of the smaller (and newer) Member States.[49] In the case of the Council, this entailed two connected objectives: that its voting weight be increased to reflect more closely population differences between Member States, and, second, that where matters

were decided by QMV, the bigger States' votes would carry more
weight. Unlike Ioannina, this strategy was shared by all four of the
other largest Member States. Taken as a whole, the 'big five' achieved
their ambitions, but not, as expected, without disagreements
between them and the smaller States. The Table below sets out the
voting weights of the existing Member States and the 12 candidate
countries.

| Current | | The 12 candidate countries | |
|---|---|---|---|
| *Member State* | *Voting weight* | *Member State* | *Voting weight* |
| Germany | 29 | Poland | 27 |
| France | 29 | Romania | 14 |
| Italy | 29 | Czech Republic | 12 |
| United Kingdom | 29 | Hungary | 12 |
| Spain | 27 | Bulgaria | 10 |
| The Netherlands | 13 | Lithuania | 7 |
| Belgium | 12 | Slovakia | 7 |
| Greece | 12 | Cyprus | 4 |
| Portugal | 12 | Estonia | 4 |
| Austria | 10 | Slovenia | 4 |
| Sweden | 10 | Latvia | 4 |
| Denmark | 7 | Malta | 2 |
| Finland | 7 | | |
| Ireland | 7 | | |
| Luxembourg | 3 | | |

In terms of their populations, the 'big five' remain relatively under-
weighted. From their perspective, therefore, a key achievement is
that an effective QMV decision in an EU of 27 will require *both*:

- a majority of votes (258 out of 345); *and*
- that that majority represents countries whose combined population amounts to 62 per cent of the EU's overall population.

A blocking vote (88) can be reached, first, by a combination of any
three of the largest Member States (87) plus one only of the smallest.
Alternatively, even if that vote is not achieved, under the 'demo-
graphic bar', any group of States together representing more than
38 per cent of the EU's population can block a QMV decision. This

compensates Germany, which, while having 23 million more citizens than the second most populous Member State, the United Kingdom (59 million), is allocated the same voting weight (29) and thus has the lowest *relative* weight. The 'population safeguard', which is based on absolute and not proportional population values, means that Germany plus the two other largest States (France and the United Kingdom) may exercise a veto on QMV decisions.[50]

On those matters subject to QMV, the government was adamantly opposed to any transfer from unanimity of decisions on Treaty amendments, taxation, border controls, social security, EU revenue raising and defence. Like its predecessors, its position was wholly pragmatic: to agree to QMV where it was in the United Kingdom's interest. Inasmuch as when advocating this position, the Foreign Secretary, Robin Cook, pointed to the occasions on which the United Kingdom's interests had been frustrated by other Member States' exercise of *their* veto, the government might have been thought to want to eat its cake and have it.[51] In the event, the government was obliged to concede the veto on a number of issues, though retaining it on tax and social security.

*Other institutional reforms*

The government was also aligned with the largest States' long-held wish to limit the size of the Commission. The smaller States naturally objected to the proposed departure from the principle of one Member State: one Commissioner. Part of the price that the 'big five' paid for the 're-balancing' of QMV was acceptance of the objectors' position. Each of the 'big five' will have one Commissioner only; thereafter there will be a rota for the other States so that the total of Commissioners does not exceed 27 at any one time. They also accepted an increase in membership of the EP, from 626 to 738. Reflecting the fact that it is the largest Member State, Germany retained its 99 seats; each of the other four accepted a reduction.

## New Labour and the EU: a Europe of nations

The Amsterdam negotiations overlapped the final months of John Major's doomed premiership and Tony Blair's emphatic election success in May 1997. The new Prime Minister at once indicated his intention to give fresh impetus to the United Kingdom's relationship

with the EU. He created a Minister for Europe, announced that the
United Kingdom would sign up to the Social Chapter, and the
Foreign Secretary, Robin Cook, offered a 'mission statement' in which
Britain would be 'a leading player in Europe'. The rhetoric was not,
however, matched by any substantial shift in the United Kingdom's
European objectives. So far from pursuing deeper integration, New
Labour maintained the Conservatives' pragmatic tradition and pressed
hard for progress on eastwards enlargement.[52]

In terms of these objectives, TA was a success.[53] Its formal recognition
that some Member States wish to move at different speeds carried the
inevitable threat that those in the 'fast lane' would, as in the past, set
the rules.[54] The United Kingdom's negotiating stance in the pre-Nice
IGCs was to promote a policy of 'enhanced co-operation'. Member
States who so chose would be permitted to move towards deeper
integration faster than those who chose otherwise, but on condition
that (a) no Member State was precluded from joining the fast lane
later on, and (b) *all* Member States, not just those in the fast lane,
agreed the rules. The justification for this policy, which was supported
by Spain and the Nordic countries, was that it would be unfair to
those seeking to join, to create yet further obstacles to their accession.
In its appeal to the notion that there should be no second class
citizens in the EU, this was, therefore, a policy which simultaneously
reinforced the United Kingdom's pro-enlargement credentials and
restrained other Member States from further integration. Likewise,
Tony Blair hailed the outcome of the Nice Treaty a vindication of his
government's diplomacy.[55] The United Kingdom's position in the
Council of Ministers was enhanced, at least for the time being, and
the Commission's influence reduced a little. On the perennial issue
of closer union, the Treaty accepted the promotion of a 'multi-speed'
Europe in which Member States could participate but without jeopardising their future position on those areas in which they did not.
In this, it may be said that the EU has moved closer to the United
Kingdom's preferred model of a Europe of nation states. This is the
result not of the persuasiveness of the United Kingdom's diplomatic
efforts since its accession, but of the political and economic consequences of 30 years of widening and deepening.

Tony Blair's vision, outlined in his Warsaw speech in October
2000, of the EU as 'a super power but not a super state', built on the
strength and common purpose of nation states, is, in this respect,

strikingly reminiscent of Margaret Thatcher's Bruges speech. Unlike 1988, and against a very different background – the virtual completion of EMU, the creation of the EU and its second and third pillar advances, the implications of further and potential enlargement – his vision of 'a Europe of nations' struck a chord even with the integrationists. Germany, in particular, had become concerned about the impact of eastwards enlargement on its economy. Once admitted, the free movement of persons and capital within an EU containing such Member States as the Czech Republic, Poland and Slovakia, whose substantially lower labour costs were already exacerbating unemployment rates in some eastern *Länder*, would inevitably compromise its recovery from the costs of reunification. Its enthusiasm for enlargement had waned, too, as the cost of the environmental and animal and human health consequences of the intensive farming encouraged by CAP became apparent during the BSE and foot and mouth crises. As a net loser (by some 5 billion Euros), Germany has every incentive to promote its reform, and every disincentive to see its benefits extend eastwards, even as eastwards enlargement shifts the EU's geopolitical balance in its direction. The French President's (Jacques Chirac) maladroit handling of the final draft of the Nice agreement, which deeply alienated the smaller States,[56] reduced relations with Germany to their lowest ebb and underlined the post-Nice differences between France and Germany as to the best way forward.

When Jean Monnet and Robert Schuman presented their vision of a European federation for the preservation of peace, they envisaged a Europe that extended far beyond what was then the border with the Soviet Union. Their goal – the 'finality of Europe' – has been given greater emphasis by the ending of the Cold War, but as we have seen, the integration of the newly liberated Eastern European countries presents problems of enormous complexity. These reduce to two parallel tasks: adapting to the consequences of enlargement, and ensuring that the EU maintains a capacity to act. These tasks must be performed against a backdrop of increasing disenchantment with the EU: a bloated bureaucracy, out of touch with its citizens and in a state of perpetual tension with the individual interests of its members. How to move forward? For its exponents the goal is attainable, but will require a massive concentration of effort. In a highly influential speech given in Berlin in 2000, Joschka Fischer, then German foreign minister, though speaking personally, envisioned a European federation with a European Parliament and a European Government exercising respectively legislative and executive power. This would initially require the formation of a 'centre of gravity' (to include at least France and Germany) to drive a 'core Europe' whose institutional configuration would embed this vision and ultimately provide the basis for political integration between all Member States. Fischer's speech sparked intense debate, not the least of which concerned the fundamental legal issue, about how this arrangement can simultaneously embrace the standard characteristics of a federation while preserving the integrity of its constituent nation states.[57]

For the United Kingdom, talk of a 'centre of gravity' setting the agenda is merely a repeat of earlier integrationists' support for 'two-speed' Europe, in which those who are unwilling or unable to maintain the momentum miss the bus. The government does, however, share the common agenda, which comprised a central aspect of Fischer's speech, that there must first be a solution to the democracy problem, together with a fundamental re-ordering of competencies both horizontally (that is, between the EU institutions) and vertically (that is, between the EU, the nation state and the regions). As Tony Blair said in his Warsaw speech, its citizens must feel that they own Europe, not that Europe owns them.[58] Good governance is the object of the Constitutional Convention agreed at the Laeken summit in December 2001. Chaired by a former French President, Giscard D'Estaing, and with two arch-integrationists as vice-Chairmen, it can confidently be predicted that the debate on its future will, notwithstanding Tony Blair's vision of a streamlined EU with democratic accountability rooted in the nation state,[59] tread familiar ground.

## Notes

In addition to the specific references that follow, the following are useful introductions: L. Cram, D. Dinan and N. Nugent (eds) (1999), *Developments in the European Union*; D. Dinan (1999), *Ever Closer Union? An Introduction to European Integration*; J. McCormick (2002), *Understanding the European Union*; W. Nicholl and T. Salmon (1999), *Understanding the European Communities*. I am grateful to my colleague Dr Jo Hunt for her helpful comments.

1. Denmark and Sweden also opted out of the launch of the Euro.
2. EEC, Article 2 [TEU: Article 2].
3. EEC Treaty, Preamble para. 1.

4. On the Court of Justice, see Chapter 3. In 1975 a Court of Auditors was created whose functions, previously separately exercised by each Community, are to ensure that the Communities' money is properly accounted for.
5. The Treaty Establishing a Single Council and a Single Commission of the European Communities.
6. EEC, Article 4 [TEU: Article 4]. This section deals very briefly with the Community institutions. For more detailed accounts, see P. Craig and G. de Burca (2002), *EU Law: Text, Cases and Materials* and the Community website www.europa.org.
7. To reflect the addition of the second and third pillars, the Council of Ministers was renamed in 1993, the Council of the European Union.
8. Over 80 per cent of EU legislation is co-decided by the Council and the European Parliament; the Government's Reply to the Seventh Report from the Select Committee on the European Union, *A Second Parliamentary Chamber for Europe: An Unreal Solution to Some Real Problems*, HL 48, 2000–01 (February 2002), para. 8.
9. Commission of the European Communities, *European Governance*, COM (2001) 428 final; p. 3.
10. For example, selling fruit and vegetables in metric weight rather than pounds and ounces, *Thoburn v. Sunderland City Council* [2002] EWHC 195.
11. See Chapter 5.
12. For further discussion of the Convention, see Chapter 11.
13. See S. George (1990), *An Awkward Partner: Britain in the European Community*, *passim*; S. Greenwood (1996), *Britain and European Integration since the Second World War*, pp. 158–189; G. Edwards (1993), 'Britain and Europe', in J. Story (ed.) *The New Europe*, pp. 187–227.
14. J. Young (2000), *Britain and European Unity 1945–1999*, pp. 184–202.
15. D. Owen (1991), *Time to Declare*, pp. 277–278.
16. The tensions between the EU and the United States concerning Turkey's admission to the EU that occurred in late 2002 also illustrate the point that membership carries implications well beyond its external borders. Turkey is a member of NATO and is of strategic importance in the war against Iraq that the United States was then contemplating.
17. Norway was part of these negotiations, but in a subsequent referendum, the Norwegian population voted against entry.
18. See P. Balzas (1998), 'Strategies for eastern enlargement of the EU: an integration theory approach'.
19. For further discussion of Enlargement, see Chapter 5.
20. *R. v. Secretary of State, ex p Factortame* [1991] 3 All E.R. 769 (CJEC). See Chapter 3.
21. B. Kerremans (1998), 'The political and institutional consequences of widening: capacity and control in an enlarged Council', p. 100. The impact of their admission will also be felt in the United Kingdom in the allocation of regional aid. Being much poorer, the CEECs' admission will lower the average GDP across the EU. This in turn will mean that the

average within the Objective 1 areas of the UK will rise above the 75 per cent threshold, thus disqualifying them for these funds.

22. It was one of the grounds on which de Gaulle opposed the United Kingdom's entry to the Common Market.

23. See F. Snyder (1990), *New Directions in European Community Law*, pp. 25–26, 76.

24. On CAP, see N. Nugent (1999), *The Government and Politics of the European Community*, Chapter 15.

25. Between 1997 and 2000 the EU contributed 30 million Euro to Hungary to reinforce its border with Romania. See Chapter 9.

26. Given effect in the United Kingdom by the European Communities (Amendment) Act 1986.

27. See E. Regelsberger (1993), 'European political cooperation', pp. 270–291, and Chapter 8.

28. See A. Bressand (1993), 'The 1992 breakthrough and the global economic agenda', pp. 314–327.

29. M. Thatcher (1993), *The Downing Street Years*, p. 553.

30. Ibid.

31. See the Government's Reply to the Seventh Report from the Select Committee on the EU, *A Second Parliamentary Chamber for Europe: An Unreal Solution to Some Real Problems* (HL 48, 2000–01), para. 13.

32. D. Arter (1993), *The Politics of European Integration in the Twentieth Century*, p. 210.

33. See Chapter 6. Denmark secured opt-outs on monetary union and the purchase of second homes, Ireland on abortion.

34. HC Deb, 20–21 May 1992, cc. 264–600.

35. Young, op. cit., p. 161.

36. Ibid., pp. 165–174.

37. A. Watson (1998), 'A two-speed Europe'.

38. Cm. 3181.

39. Despite the Commission's decision to lift the ban in August 1999, France maintained a unilateral, and unlawful, embargo; *Commission of the European Communities* v. *French Republic*, Case C1/00 (19 December 2001).

40. Further evidence of these divisions emerged at the IGC in Dublin in October 1996, where the Government argued for its opt-out on the employment chapter; see Chapter 6.

41. Craig and de Burca, op. cit., p. 76.

42. Ibid., p. 135. Both procedures are complex; see ibid., pp. 129–143 and G. Falkner and M. Nentwich (2000), The Amsterdam Treaty: the Blueprint for the Future Institutional Balance?

43. See further Chapter 8.

44. For Poland, first promised membership by 1995, these postponements were a matter both of disillusionment and anger. Of the newly invited Member States, Poland stands to gain the most from membership; some £4 billion.

45. See further Chapter 6.

46. In its referendum in June 2001, Ireland voted to reject the Treaty.

47. Art. 148(2) [TEU: Article 205]. See Kerremans, op. cit.
48. As noted earlier, Norway subsequently voted against entry.
49. *IGC: Reform for Enlargement: the British Approach to the European Union Intergovernmental Conference 2000* (Cm. 4595).
50. See V. Miller, *The Treaty of Nice and the Future of Europe Debate* (House of Commons Library, Research Paper 01/49), www.parliament.uk/ parliamentary_publications_and_archvies/research_papers.cfm
51. HC Deb, 23 November 2000, cc. 458–459.
52. On one matter – the common currency – there was a break from the past; see Chapter 7.
53. The European Communities (Amendment) Act 1998 which gave effect to TA was comfortably enacted.
54. A. Stubb (2000), 'Negotiating Flexible Integration under the Amsterdam Treaty'.
55. Ratified, by a large majority, in the European Communities (Amendment) Act 2001.
56. The French were accused of re-writing matters that had been agreed, and of introducing new matters that had not been discussed.
57. 'From Confederacy to Federation: Thoughts on the Finality of European Integration.' The speech, together with some of the debates which it prompted, are available at www.iue.it/RSC/symposium.
58. The Prime Minister proposed the creation of a Second Chamber in the European Parliament consisting of representatives from national parliaments; see Seventh Report from the Select Committee on the EU, *A Second Parliamentary Chamber for Europe: An Unreal Solution to Some Real Problems*, op. cit., and the debate on the Report, HL Deb, 11 February 2002, cc. 886–906.
59. HC Deb, 17 December 2001, cc. 19–37.

# 3
# Balancing Supremacy: EU Membership and the Constitution

*Alan Page*

## Introduction

Membership of the European Union has had profound consequences for the UK constitution. At root those consequences stem from the twin ideas of direct effect and supremacy on which Community law – the law of the Union – is based. Direct effect means simply that Community law is capable of conferring rights on individuals, which national courts are obliged to uphold. This is in contrast to most treaties which affect only the states that are party to the treaty and not their citizens. In *Van Gend en Loos*[1] the European Court described the Community as:

> a new legal order of international law for the benefit of which the states have limited their sovereign rights, albeit within limited fields, and the subjects of which comprise not only Member States but also their nationals. Independently of the legislation of Member States, Community law therefore not only imposes obligations on individuals but is also intended to confer upon them rights which become part of their legal heritage.[2]

Supremacy, on the other hand, refers to the fact that Community law takes precedence over conflicting provisions of national law, regardless of whether these were made before or after the Community law in question. In *Costa* v. *ENEL*[3] the European Court held that:

> the terms and the spirit of the Treaty, make it impossible for the states...to accord precedence to a unilateral and subsequent

measure over a legal system accepted by them on a basis of reciprocity. Such a measure cannot therefore be inconsistent with that legal system. The executive force of Community law cannot vary from one State to another in deference to subsequent domestic laws, without jeopardising the attainment of the objectives of the Treaty.[4]

And the European Court subsequently went on to hold that Community law even took precedence over the constitutions of Member States, with the consequence that responsibility for the protection of rights guaranteed by national constitutions fell to the European Court rather than to national courts.[5]

Neither of these 'defining characteristics'[6] of Community law appears on the face of the EC treaty itself. Instead they were both fashioned by the European Court in the early years of the Community's existence. In attributing these characteristics to Community law not only did the Court transform the prospects for its enforcement – by giving individuals a direct stake in its enforcement – it also transformed or 'constitutionalised' the relationship between Member States and the Community. For proponents of the constitutionalism thesis:

> the Community has evolved and behaves as if its founding instrument were not a treaty governed by international law but, to use the language of the European Court, a constitutional charter governed by a form of constitutional law. Constitutionalism, more than anything else, is what differentiates the Community from other transnational systems and, within the Union, from the other "pillars."[7]

When the United Kingdom joined the Communities in 1973, therefore, it did not join a purely economic arrangement, although economic considerations were uppermost: it joined a constitutional arrangement, membership of which would in turn have profound consequences for its own unwritten or, more accurately, uncodified constitution. It is with these consequences that we are concerned in this chapter.

## Parliament 정부

The conventional shorthand way of describing Parliament's position within the constitution before accession was to say that it was 'sovereign'. By this was meant that its legislative competence was unlimited – there was no subject on which it could not legislate – and that the validity or constitutionality of its legislation was not open to challenge in the courts. Acts of Parliament were the highest form of law known to the constitution. Dicey, the most renowned exponent of the doctrine, wrote:

> The principle of Parliamentary sovereignty means neither more nor less than this...namely, that Parliament...has, under the English constitution, the right to make or unmake any law whatever; and, further, that no person or body is recognised by the law of England as having a right to override or set aside the legislation of Parliament.[8]

Thus defined, the sovereignty of Parliament was 'the dominant characteristic of our political institutions', and 'the very keystone of the law of the constitution'.[9]

The origins of the doctrine of parliamentary sovereignty or supremacy as expounded by Dicey may be traced to the 17th century constitutional conflict between the Crown on the one hand and Parliament and the courts on the other. Parliament emerged from that conflict occupying a uniquely powerful position in the constitution. The basis of that position was that its approval, expressed in the form of legislation, was required to change the law and to raise taxes.[10] The combined effect of these requirements was that there were few aspects of domestic policy that did not require the legislatively expressed sanction of Parliament.

Parliament never succeeded in asserting the same degree of control over government in the field of foreign policy. The making and subsequent ratification of treaties, for example, continued to be treated as executive acts. There too, however, Parliament's role in the legislative process – its monopoly of law-making – was protected by the rule that a treaty had first to be incorporated by statute if it was to have the force of law in the United Kingdom.[11] Were the executive not to be obliged to obtain parliamentary approval to incorporating legislation, it would be in a position to alter individual rights and duties without submitting itself to the disciplines, in the form of the need to explain and defend its proposals and to secure the repeated support of a majority for them, inherent in the legislative process.

Membership has emptied the distinction between foreign and domestic affairs of much of its former significance.[12] The consequences for the domestic legal system are set out by the European Communities Act 1972. The key provision is section 2(1), which provides that 'enforceable Community rights', that is, rights which 'in accordance with the Treaties are without further enactment to be given legal effect or used in the United Kingdom', are to be 'recognised and available in law, and ... enforced, allowed and followed accordingly'. The upshot is that, in contrast to the provisions of a treaty, Community legislation has domestic legal effect without any intervening act on the part of Westminster being necessary or indeed, according to the European Court, permissible.[13]

Membership has meant, therefore, that Parliament's approval is no longer a prerequisite of changes to the law. The Community legislature has power to adopt measures that automatically become part of the law applicable in the United Kingdom. Not only that but, as we shall see, where there is a conflict between Act of Parliament and Community law the latter takes precedence. Acts of Parliament are no longer trumps.

Although the European Communities Act gave the force of law to Community legislation in the United Kingdom, it did not seek to impose any restriction on Parliament's legislative competence. There were good reasons for this. The rule that Parliament's legislative competence was unlimited was commonly held to be subject to the exception that no Parliament could bind its successors; were it to have the power to do so, the result would be to limit their (unlimited) legislative competence.[14] An attempt to restrict the legislative freedom of future Parliaments would thus have been of questionable legal effect, as well as politically inflammatory. It was in any case unnecessary. All that was necessary, given that legislation in the United Kingdom is by and large a function of government,[15] was that the government should refrain from promoting legislation inconsistent with the United Kingdom's obligations as a member of the Community. So long as this self-imposed limitation is observed, the result is a reduction in the practical scope of the exercise of Parliament's theoretically unlimited legislative power.

When the Community was first established the boundaries of its legislative competence were relatively narrowly drawn: in *Costa v. ENEL*, the European Court spoke of the Member States having limited their sovereign rights, 'albeit within limited fields'.[16] The loss of law-making power Parliament faced was thus limited. In the 1970s and early 1980s, however, the limits to the Community's competence were eroded to the point at which it could be said that there was nothing on which the Community could not legislate.[17] The Treaty of Maastricht acknowledged the desirability of setting limits to the Community's competence by incorporating the principle of subsidiarity in the EC Treaty.[18] Whether the principle by itself affords sufficient protection of Member States' competences is, however, open to debate. Among the questions to be addressed in the course of the 'deeper and wider debate' called for in the declaration on the future of the Union, annexed to the Treaty of Nice, is how to establish and monitor a more precise delimitation of powers between the Union and the Member States, reflecting the principle of subsidiarity.[19] In the meantime, the potential loss of domestic law-making power remains.

Although the practical scope of the exercise of Parliament's legislative competence has thus been reduced as a result of membership, Parliament has not lost all say in matters concerning the Union. Amendments to the treaties, including the EC Treaty and the Treaty on EU, must be ratified in accordance with Member States' constitutional requirements before they enter into force.[20] In the United Kingdom, as we have seen, ratification is a matter for the executive, but where the obligations to be assumed under a treaty entail changes in domestic law, those changes must be made by statute. Rather than run the risk of Parliament refusing to give its sanction to required changes, and thus of being unable to fulfil obligations assumed under a treaty, the practice is for the executive to refrain from ratifying a treaty until the necessary changes in domestic law have been made by Parliament.[21] As a matter of constitutional practice, therefore, parliamentary approval of any consequential changes to domestic law is a precondition of executive ratification of an amending treaty. It was the need to obtain Parliament's approval that set the scene for the struggle in which the Conservative

Government found itself embroiled over ratification of the Maastricht Treaty.[22]

Under the European Communities Act some consequential changes to domestic law may be made by way of subordinate legislation. Section 1(3) of the Act empowers the government to declare that a treaty is to be regarded as one of the 'Community Treaties' – with the result that rights created by or under the treaty must in accordance with section 2(1) of the Act be given effect in the United Kingdom – by Order in Council approved in draft by both Houses of Parliament. In theory, therefore, it would have been open to the executive to curtail the scope for parliamentary discussion by relying on Orders in Council under section 1(3) of the 1972 Act rather than primary legislation. In practice this has not happened. Since the Maastricht Treaty, which was given by the European Communities (Amendment) Act 1993, the Treaties of Amsterdam and Nice, the enlargement Treaty, and two 'own resources' decisions on financing the Community budget have all been given effect by Act of Parliament – by the European Communities (Amendment) Acts 1998 and 2002, the European Union (Accessions) Act 1994 and the European Communities (Finance) Acts 1995 and 2001.

Parliament's position has also been safeguarded, on the face of it at least, by the introduction of specific safeguards of its position. The prototype of such safeguards is contained in section 6 of the European Parliamentary Elections Act 1978. This provision, which was introduced in response to fears that any increase in the powers of the Strasbourg Parliament would be at the expense of Westminster, fetters the executive's treaty-making power by requiring a treaty which provides for an increase in the powers of the European Parliament to be approved by Act of Parliament before it is ratified by the United Kingdom. Since both the Treaties of Amsterdam and Nice provided for an increase in the powers of the European Parliament, the government was obliged to obtain statutory approval of those Treaties before ratifying them.[23]

The example set by section 6 of the 1978 Act was followed in the European Communities (Amendment) Act 1993, section 2 of which stipulates that no notification is to be given to the Council of Ministers that the United Kingdom intends to move to the third stage of economic and monetary union and join the single currency, unless, *inter alia*, a draft of the notification has first been approved by Act of

Parliament. This safeguard has been deprived of much of its significance, however, by the commitment not to join the single currency without a referendum. Only if the result is not clear-cut, is Westminster likely to have any real say.

Parliament also has a continuing role in the implementation of Community obligations, not all of which are directly applicable in the sense of taking effect without any intervening act on the part of the national legislature being necessary. An efficiency scrutiny set up to examine ways of minimising the burden on business imposed by EC law estimated that over a third of existing UK legislation (including subordinate legislation) arose from an obligation to implement Community law.[24] Most Community obligations are implemented by subordinate legislation, but primary legislation may, and in certain cases must, be used: the Directive on Integrated Pollution, Prevention and Control, for example, was implemented by the Pollution Prevention and Control Act 1999.[25] In contrast to primary legislation that has no Community dimension, however, the scope for amendment is confined by the binding nature of the obligations assumed. As Mitchell observed, the legislature can play

> only a limited and automatic role. It is cut out of any real choice as to substance (which is governed by the directive) and is confined, at most to a technical role more appropriate to a Parliamentary Draftsman. While one can appreciate the reasons for adopting directives one can see the problems of Parliamentary *amour propre* to which they can give rise.[26]

The overall effect of membership has thus been to diminish Parliament's role in the constitution. That role was based, as we have seen, on the fact that its consent was required to raise taxes and change the law; it was its possession of those powers that made it important. Insofar as its consent is no longer required to changes in the law its importance is diminished. Membership has meant the replacement of a power of legislation with an uncertain power of scrutiny.

National parliaments remain important, however, not least because democracy and democratic institutions remain 'firmly wedded to the territorial state'.[27] They therefore appear to offer a means of 'reconnecting' citizens to the Union, but only if, as the House of Commons Scrutiny Committee warns, they themselves are not disengaged from

their own citizens.[28] The challenge is therefore to find a role for
national parliaments in 'the European architecture'; a challenge
acknowledged in the declaration on the future of the Union annexed
to the Treaty of Nice.[29] Carving out an effective role for national
parliaments in the Union is, however, no simple task.[30] What is needed,
one observer suggests, is 'a strategy which recognise[s] the intra-
Community fault line as running not between the Member States
and the Community but between the executive branch operating at
different levels and "counterposed" by a co-ordinated parliamentary
action which [seeks] to maximise and rationalise parliamentary
strength – national and European'.[31] In a 'multi-level system of governance' the solution to the problem of democratic control and
accountability will not be found at a single level.

## The executive

The executive branch, in contrast to Parliament, emerged from the
17th century constitutional conflict with few inherent powers,
dependent on the sanction of Parliament for changing the law,
raising taxes and (later) spending money. Its position was to be
transformed by the rise of representative, and with it, party government, so that by virtue of its command of a majority on which it
could normally rely to vote in its favour it could be confident of getting
what it wanted by way of legislation. Nevertheless it remained the
case that it required parliamentary approval to legislate, to raise taxes
and to spend money.

When the United Kingdom first joined the Communities, the
consequence for the executive upon which most emphasis was placed
was the increased freedom it had acquired to act, in combination
with governments of other Member States, without the domestic
consequences of that action being subject to the need for parliamentary approval or the degree of discussion and scrutiny formerly
associated with the legislative process. As the Select Committee on
European Legislation observed:

> the Executive itself by agreeing with the other Member govern-
> ments to a proposal for legislation makes the law, i.e. has assumed
> the constitutional function and power of Parliament[32]

In this respect the executive had escaped the confines of the 17th century constitutional settlement.

This theme of increased executive freedom was underscored by the vastly increased power of delegated law-making the executive assumed under the European Communities Act for the purpose of implementing Community obligations. Section 2(2) of the Act empowers the government to legislate for the purpose of:

- implementing the Community obligations of the United Kingdom or enabling such obligations to be implemented;
- enabling rights enjoyed or to be enjoyed by the United Kingdom under or by virtue of the Treaties to be exercised, or
- dealing with matters arising out of or related to such obligations or rights (or the operation from time to time of section 2(1)).

Such legislation may include 'any such provision (of any such extent) as might be made by Act of Parliament'.[33] Section 2(2) also provides that in the exercise of other delegated law-making powers regard may be had to the objects of the Communities and to enforceable Community rights, thereby enabling Community obligations to be implemented in the exercise of delegated law-making powers specific to the area in question.[34]

The European Communities Act imposes limits on the power to make delegated legislation in the implementation of Community obligations, which reflect 'a general understanding of what is inappropriate to statutory instruments'.[35] Under Schedule 2 to the Act the power conferred by section 2(2) may not be used to make provisions:

- imposing or increasing taxation;
- having retrospective effect;
- sub-delegating the power to legislate, other than a power to make procedural rules for courts or tribunals; or
- creating new criminal offences punishable with more than two years' imprisonment or, on summary conviction, with more than three months' imprisonment or a fine exceeding the statutory maximum.[36]

Where these restrictions apply, primary legislation must be used.

Where subordinate legislation is used, the scope for parliamentary discussion is at the discretion of the government. Schedule 2(2) to the Act provides that an instrument made under section 2(2) shall be subject to annulment by resolution of either House unless a draft has been approved by each House before it was made. Therefore, unless the government invites Parliament to approve an instrument, there is no guarantee that it will be discussed, since it has become extremely difficult to find time to debate instruments subject to negative resolution procedure.[37] This has prompted criticisms of substantial obligations being imposed without parliamentary debate; the Joint Committee on Statutory Instruments, for example, has criticised the use of negative resolution procedure for instruments involving considerable sums of expenditure or substantially amending Acts of Parliament.[38]

While readily understandable, this criticism in a sense misses the point, which is that the substance of the implementing legislation is effectively determined by the substance of the obligations to which effect is being given. The scope for discussion and rejection of instruments is accordingly limited.[39] The point applies with equal force to primary legislation implementing EU obligations, including those arising under the second and third pillars. In the debate on the Anti-terrorism, Crime and Security Bill, Lord Kingsland speculated that one of the reasons why the government was seeking power to implement third-pillar obligations by means of secondary legislation was because it had 'concluded that whether decisions made by the Council of Ministers at the third pillar are implemented by delegated or primary legislation matters not a jot. Once the framework decision is taken, the nature of the obligation on the member state is so strict and severe that the room for national parliamentary manoeuvre is zero'.[40] It is not clear therefore that increasing the scope for the parliamentary discussion of subordinate legislation implementing Community obligations would serve any purpose beyond perhaps reminding MPs of their lack of voice in the Community legislative process.

The section 2(2) power is confined to the implementation of Community obligations. It does not extend to the implementation of second or third pillar obligations. In the aftermath of September 11, however, the government took power in the Anti-terrorism, Crime and Security Act to implement third pillar measures (police

and judicial co-operation in criminal matters) by secondary legislation.[41] The House of Lords Delegated Powers and Regulatory Reform
Committee questioned, however, whether 'an emergency bill, which
is expected to pass through all its stages in both Houses of Parliament
within some three weeks, [was] a proper vehicle for making profound
changes to the way in which a significant category of European legislation is incorporated into the law of the United Kingdom'.[42] In the
face of widespread criticism, the government narrowed the range of
measures the power could be used to implement and agreed that it
should run for six months only, to 30 June 2002. It is unlikely
however, that the question of the implementation of second and third
pillar obligations by secondary rather than primary legislation will
not recur.

Membership, however, is not just about increased executive
freedom to act: it is also about its subjection to constraints, not all of
which are, inevitably, to its liking. As Daintith explains:

> The effect of such constraints may sometimes be to rule out
> consideration of substantive policy choices at national level alto-
> gether; if they are to be pursued at all, they must be pursued at
> Community level... No less often, the impact of Community
> membership is to impose special restrictions on instrument choice
> at state level: Community legal norms may require the use of given
> instruments of policy at state level (e.g. the use of production
> quotas in agriculture, or of direct control instead of reliance on
> self-regulation), or may determine the acceptable content of given
> instruments if a state decides to use them (as by the operation of
> non-discrimination rules).[43]

Moreover, as a result of the doctrine of direct effect, many of these
constraints are enforceable by individuals in proceedings before
domestic courts. In combination with the doctrine of supremacy,
this gives the Treaties a 'bindingness' matched by few, if any, other
international instruments.

As we have seen, the doctrines of direct effect and supremacy were
laid down in the early years of the Community's existence.[44] The
response of Member States to the possibility of finding themselves
subject to obligations, which in contrast to other international
obligations they could not easily avoid, was to seize control of the

decision-making process. In Hirschman's terms increased voice compensated for the loss of (selective) exit.[45] Henceforth they would be bound only by those obligations to which they consented. The shift to qualified majority voting that took place after the Single European Act, however, threatened to upset this equilibrium by opening up the possibility of a state being bound against its will by the majority vote of its partners.

Under the last two Conservative Governments, attitudes towards the EU were strongly coloured by this possibility. Ministers saw themselves and their policy-making powers as confined within an 'iron triangle' formed by EU requirements and restrictions, by increasingly powerful pressure groups, and by judicial review.[46] More recently, however, much of the heat has been drawn from this issue, partly as a result of the intergovernmental character of the second and third pillars, which removes the possibility of states being bound against their will, and partly also of the realignment of legislative agendas which took place under the Santer Commission, the predecessor of the present Commission, with its commitment 'to do less, but to do it better'. The executive branch has thus recovered much of the position it appeared to be in danger of losing at the time of the Maastricht Treaty.

The picture we have of the effect of membership on the executive is therefore mixed. On the one hand, it is a picture of an executive whose capacity for autonomous action is much diminished. The forum for decision-making on an immense range of issues, from trade to agriculture, from competition to consumer protection, from transport to energy, is now European rather than national. On the other hand, it is an executive whose freedom of action in relation to Parliament is increased; which in turn puts a premium on the latter's capacity to exercise effective oversight of the executive in the absence of any formal role in EU decision-making.

## The courts

The 17th century constitutional settlement was a victory not just for Parliament but also for the courts. The courts, however, occupied a subordinate position to Parliament. In Bacon's famous phrase they were 'lions under the throne'. Consistent with their subordinate position their task in relation to Acts of Parliament was limited to interpreting and applying them. The positive meaning of the doctrine of parliamentary sovereignty, Dicey wrote, is that that 'any Act of Parliament, or part of an Act of Parliament, which makes new law, or repeals or modifies an existing law, will be obeyed by the courts'.[47] The courts could not therefore refuse to obey or give effect to an Act of Parliament; nor because it was the supreme law – the highest form of law known to the constitution – could they hold an Act of Parliament to be invalid.

> it is fundamental to our (unwritten) constitution that it is for Parliament to legislate and for the judiciary to apply and interpret the fruits of Parliament's labours. Any attempt to interfere with primary legislation would be wholly unconstitutional.[48]

Community law, however, envisages a wider role for the courts. In particular it envisages that in cases of conflict the courts will give effect to Community law over conflicting provisions of national law, regardless of the fact that it may take the form of an Act of Parliament. In the *Simmenthal* case,[49] which first alerted many UK lawyers to the constitutional significance of membership, the European Court stated:

> A national court which is called upon, within the limits of its jurisdiction, to apply provisions of Community law is under a duty to give full effect to those provisions, if necessary refusing of its own motion to apply any conflicting provision of national legislation, even if adopted subsequently, and it is not necessary for the court to request or await the prior setting aside of such provisions by legislative or other constitutional means.[50]

This was in a case in which an order to repay charges levied contrary to Community law had been challenged on the grounds that under the Italian constitution only the Italian Constitutional Court had the authority to declare the Italian law under which the charges had been levied unlawful.

From a UK constitutional point of view, ensuring the primacy of Community law over national law was seen as a much less tractable problem than that of ensuring that effect was given to Community law. The 'stumbling block'[51] in the eyes of most commentators was the doctrine of the sovereignty of Parliament which, as we have seen, was commonly understood as meaning that no Parliament could bind its successors, and that the courts were powerless to review the validity of an Act of Parliament. Since effect could only be given to Community law in the United Kingdom by means of an Act of Parliament, one difficulty anticipated by some commentators was that the courts might treat a later Act of Parliament which was inconsistent in its application with Community law as impliedly repealing the provisions of the Act giving effect to Community law. Another was that, faced with a conflict between Community law and an Act of Parliament the courts would regard themselves as bound to give effect to the Act.

The European Communities Act sought to forestall these difficulties by enjoining the courts to interpret and apply domestic law in a manner consistent with Community law. Section 2(4) of the Act provides that '...any enactment passed or to be passed...shall be construed and have effect subject to the foregoing provisions of this section': those provisions include section 2(1), which gives the force of law in the United Kingdom to those provisions of Community law which, under the Treaties, are to be given legal effect without further enactment.[52] The Act did not therefore attempt to deny Parliament the power to enact legislation that ran contrary to Community law. As was pointed out above, such a provision would have been of questionable legal effect as well as politically inflammatory. Instead, it sought to deny effect to such legislation by controlling the way in which the courts construe and give effect to it.

Although section 2(4) appears to open up the possibility of effect being denied to conflicting statutory provisions, the preferred approach of the courts to conflicts between Community law and statutory provisions has been to resolve them by interpretative means rather than by denying effect to the inconsistent provisions. In *Garland* v. *British Rail Engineering Ltd*,[53] Lord Diplock took as his starting point the basic principle of statutory construction that where the words of a statute relating to the United Kingdom's treaty obligations were 'reasonably capable' of bearing a meaning consistent with those obligations, they should be given that meaning. This principle, he said, applied with special force to Community obligations, and he went on to question whether, in view of the direction as to the construction of enactments 'to be passed' contained in section 2(4) of the 1972 Act, anything short of 'an express positive statement' in a later Act that Parliament intended to legislate in defiance of Community law would justify a court in interpreting that statute in a manner inconsistent with Community law, 'however wide a departure from the prima facie meaning of the language of the provision might be needed in order to achieve consistency'.[54]

In pursuance of this approach the courts have shown themselves to be willing to supply the omission of the legislature (and of the executive) by in effect re-writing implementing legislation in order to achieve its stated purpose. In *Pickstone* v. *Freemans plc*[55] the House of Lords was faced with a question of the construction of the Equal Pay (Amendment) Regulations 1983, which had been made in order to repair shortcomings in the Equal Pay Act revealed in enforcement proceedings before the European Court. On a literal interpretation they failed to do so. The House of Lords held, however, that in order that their 'manifest purpose' might be achieved and effect given to the 'clear but inadequately expressed intention of Parliament' certain words were to be read into them 'by necessary implication'.[56] To interpret the Regulations otherwise, Lord Keith said, would mean that the United Kingdom had failed 'yet again' fully to implement its obligations, a failure which it was plain Parliament could not possibly have intended.[57]

In *R* v. *Secretary of State for Transport, ex parte Factortame*,[58] however, the courts found themselves faced with a dispute that could not be solved by interpretative means. The Merchant Shipping Act 1988 introduced a new system of registration for British fishing boats with the aim of stopping Spanish fishermen 'quota hopping', that is gaining access to UK quotas under the common fisheries policy by the simple device of re-registering their boats as British. To prevent this the Act required boats entered on the new register to be British owned, a requirement which Spanish owners and operators whose boats were registered under the old register argued discriminated against them contrary to Community law. In judicial review proceedings they sought an order restraining the Secretary of State from enforcing the Act against them pending a ruling by the European Court on its compatibility with Community law. The House of Lords held that as a matter of national law the courts had no power to suspend the effect of an Act of Parliament, but referred to the European Court the question whether Community law empowered or obliged a national court to provide effective interim protection of rights claimed under Community law. The Court replied that if the only obstacle to the granting of relief in order to protect directly effective Community rights was a rule of national law prohibiting it from doing so, the national court must as a matter of Community law set that rule aside. The House of Lords then took the unprecedented step of restraining the Secretary of State from applying the Act pending a ruling on its compatibility with Community law by the European Court.[59]

Parliamentary reaction to the European Court's ruling was predictably hostile. Richard Shepherd described it as setting aside our constitution 'as we have understood it for several hundred years';[60] while the Prime Minister shared with Teddy Taylor his concern that it was 'a dangerous development' for the Court to take on 'the power to suspend sections of laws passed by this Parliament'.[61] But for Lord Bridge the suggestion that this was 'a novel and dangerous invasion' by a Community institution of the sovereignty of the UK Parliament was misconceived:

If the supremacy within the European Community of Community law over the national law of member states was not always inherent in the EEC Treaty it was certainly well established in the jurisprudence of the European Court of Justice long before the United Kingdom joined the Community. Thus, whatever limitation of its sovereignty Parliament accepted when it enacted the European Communities Act 1972 was entirely voluntary. Under the terms of the Act of 1972 it has always been clear that it was the duty of a United Kingdom court, when delivering final judgment, to override any rule of national law found to be in conflict with any directly enforceable rule of Community law. Similarly, when decisions of the European Court of Justice have exposed areas of United Kingdom statute law which failed to implement Council directives, Parliament has always loyally accepted the obligation to make appropriate and prompt amendments. Thus there is nothing in any way novel in according supremacy to rules of Community law in areas to which they apply and to insist that, in the protection of rights under Community law, national courts must not be inhibited by rules of national law from granting

interim relief in appropriate cases is no more than a logical recognition of that supremacy.[62]

*Factortame* thus resolved what was undoubtedly the most difficult
question arising out of membership by making it clear that the
courts accepted the supremacy of Community law, and would
accordingly decline to give effect to Acts of Parliament if to do so
would conflict with Community law.

The potential of judicial review of Acts of Parliament on grounds
of incompatiblity with Community law was demonstrated in the
subsequent *EOC* case.[63] At issue in the case was the compatibility of
the 'threshold' provisions of the Employment Protection (Consolidation) Act 1978 with Community law. These provisions set the
thresholds above which workers qualified for protection against
redundancy and unfair dismissal. The House of Lords accepted that
the thresholds set by the Act discriminated against women, who
were more likely to fall below the thresholds than men, and granted
a declaration to that effect. A striking feature of the case was that the
House of Lords declined to avoid the issue by addressing the Secretary
of State's reasoning rather than the Act itself.[64] Nor did it feel it
necessary to seek a preliminary ruling on the matter from the
European Court.

There have been no cases of comparable significance since the *Factortame* and *EOC* cases. In the recent *Metric Martyrs* case,[65] however,
Lord Justice Laws took the opportunity to 'clarify' the relationship
between EU and domestic law in what may turn out to be a landmark decision. In his view the 'correct analysis' of the relationship
involved and required four propositions:

1. All the specific rights and obligations which EU law creates are by
   the ECA incorporated into our domestic law and rank supreme:
   that is, anything in our substantive law inconsistent with any of
   these rights and obligations is abrogated or must be modified to
   avoid the inconsistency. This is true even where the inconsistent
   municipal provision is contained in primary legislation.
2. The ECA is a constitutional statute: that is, it cannot be impliedly
   repealed.

3. The truth of (2) is derived, not from EU law, but purely from the
   law of England: the common law recognises a category of constitutional statutes.
4. The fundamental legal basis of the United Kingdom's relationship
   with the EU rests with the domestic, not the European, legal powers.
   In the event, which no doubt would never happen in the real world,
   that a European measure was seen to be repugnant to a fundamental
   or constitutional right guaranteed by the law of England, a
   question would arise whether the general words of the ECA
   were sufficient to incorporate the measure and give it overriding
   effect in domestic law.[66]

Lord Justice Laws considered that the balance struck by those four
propositions gave full weight both to the proper supremacy of
Community law and to the proper supremacy of the UK Parliament.
The supremacy of *substantive* Community law was guaranteed by
propositions (1) and (2); the supremacy of the legal *foundation* within
which those substantive provisions enjoy their primacy by propositions (3) and (4). 'If this balance is understood, it will be seen that
these two supremacies are in harmony, and not in conflict.'[67]

Constitutional interest in the case lies principally in the fourth
proposition identified by Lord Justice Laws. As the limits to the
Community's competence have become less certain, the constitutional
courts of some Member States, including those of Germany and
Italy, have indicated that there are nevertheless limits beyond which
they may not be prepared to accept the supremacy of Community
law. In the United Kingdom, however, it had tended to be assumed
that once the supremacy of Community law over Acts of Parliament
had been accepted there would then be no grounds on which the
courts might resist the intrusion of Community law.

Once it has been accepted that Community law prevails over later
Acts of Parliament, does it make sense to wonder about conflicts
between EC law and substantive *constitutional* law? If Parliament
can enact any laws whatsoever without constitutional shackles,
then should not the same liberty now be recognised (a fortiori) to
the Community legislator?[68]

What Lord Justice Laws' judgment suggests is that this assumption may be false. The possibility cannot be excluded therefore that effect may be denied to a Community measure in the United Kingdom because it is repugnant to the constitution.

The *Metric Martyrs* case may also shed light on a key question left open by the *Factortame* case, namely how would the courts respond in the (unlikely) event of Parliament enacting legislation in defiance of Community law, which made it plain that effect was to be given to its provisions over conflicting provisions of Community law? In an earlier case Lord Denning had suggested that:

> If the time should come when our Parliament deliberately passes an Act with the intention of repudiating the Treaty or any provision in it or intentionally of acting inconsistently with it and says so in express terms then I should have thought that it would be the duty of courts to follow the statute of our Parliament.[69]

In the absence of a fundamental constitutional clash of the kind identified by Lord Justice Laws, however, it may well be that the courts would decline to give effect to such legislation, unless the government also intended to withdraw from the Union. Short of withdrawal, however, it would not be able to pick and choose among the obligations with which it complied by securing the enactment of legislation that required the courts to give effect to its provisions over Community law.[70]

Membership has thus increased the role of the courts in the constitution. Whereas traditionally their role was confined to interpreting and giving effect to the law as made by Parliament, they now have the power to deny effect to that law where it conflicts with Community law. Only in the event of legislation being enacted which explicitly states that effect is to be given to its provisions over Community law is there any question of effect to being denied to Community law, and, in the absence of a threat to fundamental rights of the kind envisaged by Lord Justice Laws, even that must be considered uncertain.

## Notes

1. Case 26/62 [1963] ECR 1.
2. [1963] ECR 12.

3. Case 6/64 [1964] ECR 585.

4. [1964] ECR 597.

5. Case 11/70 *Internationale Handelsgesellschaft* [1970] ECR 1125.

6. De Witte, 'Direct effect, supremacy and the nature of the legal order', in Craig and De Burca (eds), *The Evolution of EU Law*, Oxford: Oxford University Press, 1999, p. 177.

7. Weiler, *The Constitution of Europe*, Cambridge: Cambridge University Press, 1999, p. 221.

8. Dicey, *An Introduction to the Study of the Law of the Constitution*, London and Basingstoke: Macmillan, 10th edn, 1959, pp. 39–40.

9. Ibid, pp. 39, 70.

10. Case of Proclamations (1611) 12 Co. Rep. 74; Bill of Rights 1689, Art. 4.

11. *A-G for Canada* v. *A-G for Ontario* [1937] AC 326.

12. Cooper, *The Post-Modern State and the World Order*, London: Demos and The Foreign Policy Centre, 2nd edn, 2000.

13. *Variola* v. *Amministratzione Italiana delle Finanze* [1973] ECR 981.

14. Dicey, op. cit., pp. 64–70; *Ellen Street Estates Ltd* v. *Minister of Health* [1934] 1 KB 590.

15. Miers and Page, *Legislation*. London: Sweet and Maxwell, 2nd edn, 1990, pp. 5–7.

16. [1964] ECR 585 at 593.

17. Weiler, op. cit., pp. 39–63.

18. Article 5 EC.

19. Declaration 23, para. 5.

20. Article 48 TEU.

21. HC Deb, 15 February 1993, c. 31; HL Deb, 28 February 1996, c. 1556.

22. Ware, *Westminster and Europe*, pp. 261–296; and Rawlings, 'Legal politics: the United Kingdom and ratification of the Treaty on European Union', *Public Law*, 1994, pp. 254–278, 368–391.

23. European Communities (Amendment) Act 1998, s. 2; European Communities (Amendment) Act 2002, s. 3. In *R* v. *Secretary of State for Foreign and Commonwealth Affairs, ex parte Rees-Mogg*, the Divisional Court rejected a claim that by ratifying the protocol on social policy annexed to the Maastricht Treaty the government would be in breach of section 6 of the 1978 Act: [1994] 1 All ER 457.

24. Department of Trade and Industry, *Review of the Implementation and Enforcement of EC Law in the UK* (1993), Introduction, para. 1.

25. And see below, pp. 45–47. In a 1998 study Page estimated that 92 per cent of Community obligations had been implemented by statutory instrument: 'The impact of European legislation on British public policy making: a research note' (1998) 76 *Public Administration*, pp. 803–809.

26. Mitchell, 'British law and British membership' (1971) 6 *Europarecht*, p. 106.

27. Cooper, op. cit., pp. 20–21.

28. Thirtieth Report from the Select Committee on European Scrutiny 2001–02, HC 152–xxx, *European Scrutiny in the Commons*, paras 3, 24.

29. Declaration 23, para. 5.

30. Thirty-third Report from the Select Committee on European Scrutiny, 2001–02, HC 152–xxxiii, *Democracy and Accountability in the EU and the role of National Parliaments*.
31. Weiler, op. cit., p. 277.
32. Second Report from Select Committee on European Secondary Legislation 1972–73, HC 463, para. 34.
33. European Communities Act, s. 2(4).
34. Excluding this provision, Community obligations might be considered to be extraneous matters that ministers were obliged to ignore.
35. Mitchell, Kuipers and Gall, 'Constitutional aspects of the Treaty and Legislation relating to British Membership' (1972) 9 *Common Market Law Review*, p. 140.
36. Sched. 2, para. 1(1).
37. *Making the Law. The Report of the Hansard Commission on the Legislative Process*, London: The Hansard Society, 1993, paras 364–384; and Blackburn and Kennon, *Griffith and Ryle on Parliament*, London: Sweet and Maxwell, 2nd edn, 2003, paras 9-018–9-024.
38. First Special Report from Joint Committee on Statutory Instruments, 1977–78, HC 169, HL 51, para. 36.
39. See above; there is of course no scope for the amendment of subordinate legislation, though instruments may be withdrawn and revised in response to points made.
40. HL Deb, 3 December 2001, c. 596.
41. ss. 111–112.
42. Seventh Report from Select Committee on Delegated Powers and Regulatory Reform, HL 45, 2001–02, para. 12.
43. Daintith, 'Regulation', in *The International Encyclopaedia of Comparative Law*, Vol. xvii, 'Law, State and Economy', Tubingen: Mohr, 1997, para. 51.
44. In Cases 26/62, *Van Gend en Loos* [1963] ECR 12 and 6/64 *Costa* v. *ENEL* [1964] ECR 585.
45. Hirschman, *Exit, Voice and Loyalty – Responses to Decline in Firms, Organisations and States*, Cambridge MA: Harvard University Press, 1970. For the argument, see Weiler, 'The Transformation of Europe'.
46. Willetts, 'The perils of political power', *Financial Times*, 30 January 1997.
47. Op. cit., p. 40.
48. *R* v. *Secretary of State for Transport, ex parte Factortame* [1989] 2 CMLR 353 at 397, per Lord Donaldson, M. R.
49. *Amministratzione delle Finanze dello Stato* v. *Simmenthal Spa (No. 2)* [1978] ECR 629.
50. [1978] ECR at 645–646.
51. Mitchell, 'The Sovereignty of Parliament and Community Law: The stumbling block that isn't there' (1979) 55 *International Affairs*, pp. 33–46.
52. Section 3(1) of the Act also provides that any question as to the meaning or effect of any of the Treaties, or as to validity, meaning or effect of any Community instrument, is to be treated as a question of Community law to be determined either by the European Court or in accordance with the principles laid down by it.

53. [1983] 2 AC at 751.
54. [1983] 2 AC at 771.
55. [1989] AC 66.
56. [1990] 1 AC at 554, per Lord Keith of Kinkel.
57. [1989] AC at 111–112. For the parliamentary proceedings on the Equal Pay (Amendment) Regs (SI 1983/1794), see HC Deb, 20 July 1983, cc. 480–500, and Clark, *Diaries*, London: Weidenfeld and Nicolson, 1993. See also *Litster* v. *Forth Dry Dock and Engineering Co Ltd* [1990] 1 AC 546.
58. [1990] 2 AC 85.
59. *R* v. *Secretary of State for Transport, ex parte Factortame (No. 2)* [1991] 1 AC 603.
60. HC Deb, 20 June 1990, c. 926.
61. HC Deb, 21 June 1990, c. 1108.
62. [1991] 1 AC at 658–659.
63. *R* v. *Employment Secretary ex p Equal Opportunities Commission* [1995] 1 AC 1.
64. Craig, 'Report on the United Kingdom', in Slaughter, Sweet and Weiler (eds), *The European Court and National Courts – Doctrine and Jurisprudence*, Oxford: Hart Publishing, 1998, p. 217.
65. *Thoburn* v. *Sunderland City Council* [2003] QB 151.
66. At para. 69.
67. At para. 70, original emphasis.
68. De Witte, op. cit., pp. 204–205.
69. Macarthys v. Wendy Smith [1979] 3 All ER 325 at 329.
70. Craig, op. cit.

## Works cited

Clark, *Diaries*, London: Weidenfeld and Nicolson, 1993.

Cooper, *The Post-Modern State and the World Order*, London: Demos and The Foreign Policy Centre, 2nd edn, 2000.

Craig, 'Report on the United Kingdom', in Slaughter, Sweet and Weiler (eds), *The European Court and National Courts – Doctrine and Jurisprudence*, Oxford: Hart Publishing, 1998, p. 217.

Daintith, 'Regulation', in *The International Encyclopaedia of Comparative Law*, Vol. xvii, 'Law, State and Economy', Tubingen: Mohr, 1997.

Department of Trade and Industry, *Review of the Implementation and Enforcement of EC Law in the UK* (1993).

De Witte, 'Direct effect, supremacy and the nature of the legal order', in Craig and De Burca (eds), *The Evolution of EU Law*, Oxford: Oxford University Press, 1999.

Dicey, *An Introduction to the Study of the Law of the Constitution*, London and Basingstoke: Macmillan, 10th edn, 1959.

Griffith and Ryle, *Parliament*, London: Sweet and Maxwell, 1989.

*Making the Law: The Report of the Hansard Commission on the Legislative Process*, London: The Hansard Society, 1993.

Hirschman, *Exit, Voice and Loyalty – Responses to Decline in Firms, Organisations and States*, Cambridge MA: Harvard University Press, 1970.

Miers and Page, *Legislation*. London: Sweet and Maxwell, 2nd edn, 1990.

Mitchell, 'British law and British membership', 6 *Europarecht*, 1971, p. 106.

Mitchell, 'The Sovereignty of Parliament and Community Law: the stumbling block that isn't there', 55 *International Affairs*, 1979, pp. 33–46.

Mitchell, Kuipers and Gall, 'Constitutional aspects of the Treaty and legislation relating to British membership', 9 *Common Market Law Review*, 1972, p. 140.

Page, 'The impact of European legislation on British public policy making: a research note', 76 *Public Administration*, 1998, pp. 803–809.

Rawlings, 'Legal politics: the United Kingdom and ratification of the Treaty on European Union, *Public Law*, 1994, pp. 254–278, 368–391.

Ware, 'Legislation and ratification: the Passage of the European Communities (Amendment) Act 1993', in Giddings and Drewry (eds), *Westminster and Europe: The Impact of the European Union on the Westminster Parliament*, London: Macmillan, 1996, pp. 261–296.

Weiler, *The Constitution of Europe*, Cambridge: Cambridge University Press, 1999.

Willetts, 'The perils of political power', *Financial Times*, 30 January 1997.

# 4
# Parliamentary Scrutiny of Policy and Legislation: The Procedures of the Lords and Commons

*Priscilla Baines*

The purpose of this chapter is to describe how the mechanisms for scrutinising European Union matters in the two Houses evolved following the Maastricht Treaty in 1992. Those mechanisms have always depended mainly on the use of the traditional methods of select committees, oral statements and debates. This chapter concentrates on the major issues surrounding the work of the scrutiny committees in each House from 1992 until the end of the 1997–2001 Parliament, but takes account of reviews of the scrutiny process by the two scrutiny committees early in the 2001 Parliament.

At the start of the 1992 Parliament, the scrutiny processes in both Houses were well-established. The two primary scrutiny instruments – the Commons European Legislation Committee and the Lords European Communities Committee (hereafter described as the Commons Committee and Lords Committee) – had changed their basic methods of operation remarkably little since they were first set up in 1974.[1] The Parliaments that started in 1992 and 1997 saw few outward changes in the scrutiny processes but there was continuing evolution and development, partly driven by the committees' own desire to improve the operation of the scrutiny mechanisms, but also by the need to respond to EU developments, especially the provisions of the Maastricht and Amsterdam Treaties, and the second and third pillars created by the Maastricht Treaty.

From the committees' inception in 1974, the scrutiny procedures in both Houses, but particularly the Commons, have been kept under regular review. After 1992, both Committees' desire to ensure fully effective scrutiny procedures led to a series of reviews, often driven by shared concerns about enhancing the effectiveness of national parliaments throughout the EU. Some of the reviews led to immediate changes but more often, especially those by the Commons Committee, they were part of an iterative process that fed into reviews by other committees and a process of incremental change.

## Review of scrutiny procedures – the Commons

Following a report in 1994–95 on the 1996 inter-governmental conference (IGC) which described the system as being in 'deep crisis',[2] the Commons Committee reviewed its own work in a detailed report in 1995–96,[3] to which the government replied in December 1996.[4] That report also formed the basis of a Procedure Committee report in 1996–97 (to which there was no formal government response) which concentrated mainly on perceived gaps and weaknesses in the scrutiny process, making an explicit effort to move away from the European Legislation Committee's concerns about the minutiae of its work.[5]

As part of a general commitment to modernising the House of Commons, the Labour Party's 1997 manifesto contained a specific provision to overhaul the process of scrutinising European legislation. A report on *The Scrutiny of European Business* by the newly created Modernisation Committee in the first session of that Parliament was based largely on a memorandum from the Commons Committee that picked up business left unfinished in the Procedure Committee report, plus another by the President of the Council (Mrs Ann Taylor) that repeated the manifesto commitment to 'the principle of effective scrutiny by Parliament of European Union business'. Despite the promised 'overhaul', the report proposed no radical changes but its endorsement of most of the proposals by both the Procedure Committee and the European Legislation Committee for strengthening the scrutiny process led to some significant changes.[6]

The government responded to the report in a White Paper which repeated the manifesto commitment to greater involvement by national parliaments in the EU but observed that 'The present scrutiny arrangements are generally accepted as having served their purpose reasonably well' and that 'The UK Parliamentary scrutiny system compares favourably with arrangements in many other EU member states.' Nevertheless, those arrangements had not kept pace with the need to 'ensure comprehensive Parliamentary oversight of developments in the EU and to make transparent and understandable the process by which EU policy and legislation are made'. The Modernisation Committee's relatively limited proposals were seen as providing the mechanisms required to enable both Houses 'to carry out proper oversight business' under all three pillars of the EU.[7] They were agreed following a short debate in the House of Commons on 17 November 1998.

In 2001–02, the Commons Committee published a further review against the background of the priority given by the government in the Convention on the Future of Europe to developing the role of national parliaments. The report concluded, like its predecessors, that '(the) general principles of the scrutiny system are largely sound' although it recommended further adjustments to make the system more open and accountable.[8] The government response remarked that 'The Committee's engagement on EU matters is a strength for the United Kingdom and for the EU as a whole.'[9] Following that reply, the Leader of the House, Robin Cook, gave oral evidence to the Committee about the scrutiny process on 5 November 2002.[10]

## Review of scrutiny procedures – the Lords

The House of Lords scrutiny procedures have been subject to fewer detailed examinations, although the Lords Committee has consistently pressed government departments to meet their obligations under the scrutiny process. Early in the 1992 Parliament the Committee conducted a detailed inquiry into second and third pillar scrutiny,[11] followed in 1997 by a further report on third pillar scrutiny.[12] In 1998–99, the Committee on Procedure of the House published a short report on the Committee's terms of reference, its name and the need for the House of Lords to have its own scrutiny reserve resolution.[13] In 2001–02, the Committee turned to what had previously been largely Commons territory in a short report on the operation of the scrutiny reserve in relation to provisional agreement in the Council of Ministers.[14]

Late in the 2001–02 session, the Lords Committee initiated a wide-ranging review of scrutiny procedures. As with the Commons

Committee's similar review, its genesis lay in a desire to contribute to the examination of the role of national parliaments being undertaken by the Convention on the Future of Europe. It was also formally triggered by a recommendation, made as part of a wider review of the House's working methods by the so-called 'Leader's Group' and the Procedure Committee, that the Committee itself should review the European scrutiny work of the House. That review was completed in December 2002, the Committee having examined the scrutiny machinery in other EU Member States and taken evidence from the chairman of the Danish European Affairs Committee, often seen as a model for other member states because of its tight controls over Ministers' actions in the European Council. There were sixty recommendations on how the system could be strengthened[15] and the government responded in March 2003.[16]

## Post-Maastricht: the co-decision procedure

Before those reviews had occurred, both Committees had to adjust to the complexities of the post-Maastricht co-decision procedure. The procedure was based on the previous co-operation procedure but was intended to make the European Parliament a more equal partner with the Council of Ministers in the EU's legislative processes and allowed more opportunities for amendments to be introduced.[17]

The Commons Committee recognised immediately that the procedure would make the EU's legislative procedures more complex and scrutiny by national parliaments more difficult in important policy areas. In a special report in December 1993, the Committee concluded that the scrutiny process needed to be altered to take account of amendments to proposals after their initial deposit with the two Committees. It recommended that the Committee should be kept informed of developments via Supplementary Explanatory Memoranda, with an amendment to the scrutiny reserve resolution to bring 'crucial stages' of the co-decision procedure within its scope.[18]

Delays in ratification of the Maastricht Treaty meant that the co-decision procedure did not come into operation until November 1993, while the government's reply to the special report was delayed until July 1994.[19] The government's suggested 'wait and see' approach was accepted by the Committee. Meanwhile, the Lords Committee's 1994–95 report on the 1996 IGC expressed considerable doubts about the procedure, seeing it as 'over-complicated and flawed', while any extension of co-decision must involve some diminution of the role and influence of national parliaments. Specific Treaty changes were suggested to make it more difficult for the European Parliament to cause legislation to go through 'without thorough and careful investigation'.[20]

In its 1995–96 review, the Commons Committee recognised that co-decision was likely to become the EU's principal legislative procedure, which led to a repeated recommendation that the scrutiny reserve resolution should be amended to take account of the key stages in the procedure.[21] The Amsterdam Treaty subsequently provided for a simplified version of co-decision to become the normal legislative route and initially informal scrutiny arrangements operated, with the Conservative Government agreeing to behave in negotiations on proposals under co-decision as if they were already subject to the formal constraints. The Leader of the House also offered to table appropriate amendments to the scrutiny reserve resolution, although that was not done before the 1997 election.[22]

The Commons Committee's memorandum to the Modernisation Committee in 1997–98 referred again to the complexities of the procedure and the difficulties for national parliaments in keeping up with the various stages of consideration during which proposals might be heavily amended.[23] These difficulties were acknowledged by the Modernisation Committee, which recommended, and the government accepted, the long-sought amendment of the scrutiny reserve resolution to take account of the revised procedure.

The Nice Treaty in 2000 further amended the co-decision procedure so that when the Council adopted legislation by qualified majority voting, it did so by co-decision with the European Parliament. This change potentially added significantly to the procedure's complexity and meant that, as the Lords Committee noted in its 2002 report, final texts after the procedure was used often differed considerably from the original version, but the EU's procedures still contained no provision for scrutiny by national parliaments. The Committee urged the Convention on the Future of Europe to revise the procedure to allow a greater opportunity for national parliamentary scrutiny. The UK Government was also urged to ensure better provision of information on matters subject to the co-decision procedure at its various stages.[24]

The Commons Committee's 2002 report also drew attention to the particular risk of scrutiny reserve overrides in respect of legislative proposals under the co-decision procedure.[25] The government attributed the problem to co-decision's often being 'a fast-moving process', but agreed to seek ways of getting useful information to the Committee more rapidly, while also seeking more rapid consideration by the Committee when required.[26] The Committee also commented unfavourably on how the procedure in practice meant that it was often difficult for anyone outside the EU institutions, including national parliaments, to track what was happening and seek in public to influence those involved, especially in relation to legislation, a view that the government shared.[27]

## Post-Maastricht: the second and third pillars

The inclusion of the second and third pillars in the Maastricht Treaty had significant potential implications for the parliamentary scrutiny process, partly because of the importance of the topics they covered but also because those topics were legally outside Community competence, so work within them would not lead to the adoption of Community law under existing legislative procedures. Incorporating scrutiny of second and third pillar matters was therefore expected to require some adjustments to the scrutiny processes in both Houses. For the Commons, there were also issues surrounding the division of responsibilities between the European Legislation Committee and two departmental select committees (Foreign Affairs and Home Affairs), while the question of the scope of the European Legislation Committee's order of reference needed to be resolved in relation to its powers to consider all types of second and third pillar documents.

Initially, the Conservative Government was noticeably reluctant to meet the desire of both scrutiny committees to deal with second and third pillar matters in the same way as other EU matters. The Foreign Affairs Committee had quickly recognised the potential difficulties in holding ministers to account for decisions reached intergovernmentally under the second pillar but urged that the government should consult the House before important decisions were taken on proposals under the Common Foreign and Security Policy (CFSP). Similarly, the House would need to ensure that any actions or new legislation in the home affairs field received at least the same degree of scrutiny as legislation under the Community pillar and the Government should consult the House before important decisions were taken under the third pillar.[28]

In response, the government made few concessions to the need for parliamentary scrutiny of second and third pillar matters. It would do no more than make available to the House the 'first full text' to be tabled of any convention or proposals which, if agreed, would require UK primary legislation 'and also other documents of significance'. The government justified this approach by arguing that much CFSP business would be fast moving and subject to the normal confidentiality and security considerations of foreign policy. Parliamentary involvement in CFSP issues would therefore mirror the arrangements for other foreign policy issues, although certain CFSP documents might fall within existing scrutiny guidelines. Similarly, the government proposed 'to keep Parliament informed' of work in the area of justice and home affairs. The relationship between the European Legislation and Home Affairs Committees might require further consideration by the House authorities.[29]

This guarded approach was also adopted by the Home Office in a memorandum to the Home Affairs Committee (HAC) that suggested that the documents to be made available to the House should, as far as possible, be analogous to those covered by the terms of reference of the Scrutiny Committee, but excluding proposals that related to 'security arrangements or operational matters [where] publication could prejudice the effectiveness of the intended action'.[30] The Home Secretary (Kenneth Clarke) told the Committee on 21 April 1993 that the government had not reached a final view on the arrangements for Parliament to examine the work on the 'Intergovernmental Pillars', but both he and the Foreign Secretary thought that Parliament should be given more documents and conduct more systematic scrutiny than had been the case in the past. Mr Clarke disagreed with the HAC chairman (Sir Ivan Lawrence), who clearly saw third pillar matters as the HAC's province of the Home Affairs Committee, while also recognising a role for the European Legislation Committee.

The Lords Committee's order of reference already allowed scrutiny of both second and third pillar matters but the Committee decided in 1993 to conduct an inquiry into the second and third pillars. The report concluded unequivocally that work under the intergovernmental pillars should be supervised by national parliaments and that the key to effective supervision was to obtain the right documents in time to influence the outcome. Acquiring documents subject to inter-governmental negotiation was, however, much more difficult than acquiring draft Community legislation. The Committee accepted the Home Secretary's proposal to provide Parliament with the first full text of any convention or proposal which would, if agreed, require later primary legislation in the United Kingdom, and other documents of significance. It suggested three tests for the submission of documents: significance, particularly where the rights or duties of individuals might be affected; the eventual need for UK legislation; and the imposition of legally binding commitments on the United Kingdom. Documents that qualified under any of these tests should be provided to Parliament, with no distinction between those relating to the second and third pillars.

The Committee accepted that, while the need for speedy decision should not restrict disclosure, the need for secrecy might restrict what could be disclosed to Parliament. The same tests should be applied to CFSP decisions, although in that area there might be fewer documents. The government should ensure that, wherever possible, agreement was not given to any proposal until parliamentary scrutiny had taken place. Qualified majority voting had speeded up the process of reaching agreement and required the Committee to be more flexible, so considerations of speed did not mean that the reserve should not apply to second and third pillar matters. The Committee also proposed revised terms of reference for itself that specifically included the second and third pillars.[31]

The government's response acknowledged the need to find 'arrangements for parliamentary involvement which best reflect the different natures of the two pillars and the pre-eminent role which national parliaments should play in accountability in these areas', but otherwise made minimal concessions to the Committee's desire for comprehensive scrutiny. It disagreed that the two pillars should be treated in the same way, mainly because of confidentiality and timing issues raised by second pillar matters. CFSP documents that fell within existing scrutiny guidelines should be deposited and the government would consider making available to Parliament at an early stage the few CFSP documents that were not subject to confidentiality considerations and met at least one of the Committee's three criteria. The suggestion that such documents might be subject to a scrutiny reserve was, however, rejected out of hand. Parliament might have a limited role in relation to third pillar matters but the government would go no further than the Home Secretary's original offer to provide 'whenever possible' the 'first full text', while the suggestion of a scrutiny reserve was again rejected, mainly because decisions might have to be reached quickly.[32]

In a debate on 12 April 1994, the chairman of the Lords Committee, Lord Boston of Faversham, acknowledged that the Home Secretary, Michael Howard, had 'responded positively' to the Committee's general approach in agreeing to provide third pillar documents 'more or less in line with our criteria' but he and the Committee had been 'a little disappointed' (as were other speakers) that the Government was willing to deposit so few second pillar documents. He also hoped that the Government would 'at least keep an open mind' about extending the scrutiny reserve to third pillar documents. Replying for the government, Baroness Chalker of Wallasey underlined the government's commitment to finding appropriate arrangements for parliamentary supervision of work under the inter-governmental pillars, but reminded the House of the need to take account of 'the substantively different' nature of that work. The government would keep the position under review and did not necessarily rule out future change.[33]

## Slow progress

For the remainder of the 1992 Parliament, both Committees tried to make further progress. They both considered second and third pillar scrutiny in reports in 1994–95 on the 1996 IGC, the Commons Committee noting that there was still 'much to be done',[34] while the Lords Committee described its own involvement in the CFSP as 'negligible' although involvement in third pillar matters had been more satisfactory as the Home Secretary had implemented his undertakings to supply documents.[35] In its 1995–96 review, the Commons Committee saw the case for effective and systematic national Parliamentary scrutiny of the second and third pillars as even stronger than when the Lords Committee reported in 1993, since for both pillars a clear democratic deficit remained.[36]

The 1996–97 Procedure Committee noted 'widespread dismay' that activities under the second and third pillars were 'outside the normal mechanisms of democratic scrutiny and control'. Activity under those pillars might not fit altogether neatly into the existing scrutiny system, but broadly similar treatment should be given to most European documents, legislative or not. The House should have had the opportunity to debate several of the matters agreed under the two pillars, and such opportunities would have arisen had the scrutiny system been applied as then proposed.[37]

In July 1997, the Lords Committee reconsidered third pillar scrutiny, following significant practical difficulties in relation to proposals under third pillar procedures, particularly frequent delays in depositing documents and the previous government's 'unduly restrictive' view of what constituted the first full text of those proposals. The Home Office had considered that the criteria for depositing third pillar documents had worked satisfactorily, and that in practice documents had been deposited in accordance with the Committee's wishes, rather than within the government's rather more restrictive criteria. The Committee concluded, however, that more formal guidelines were needed for the deposit of those documents, with less discretion for government departments, while the Commons Committee's mandate should be extended to third pillar matters and a scrutiny reserve for third pillar proposals was essential.[38]

## A new approach – the Modernisation Committee

The Leader of the House's memorandum to the Modernisation Committee marked a significant change in the government's approach. It accepted the need for more effective parliamentary scrutiny of second and third pillar documents, particularly by the House of Commons, and that the scrutiny reserve should apply to documents deposited for scrutiny under both inter-governmental pillars. The European Legislation Committee repeated its predecessor's view that there was no conflict between the roles of the two departmental select committees with interests in those areas (Foreign Affairs and Home Affairs): it was 'axiomatic' that the work of systematic scrutiny and sifting should be carried out by the European Legislation Committee.

The Modernisation Committee urged acceptance of the government's proposal without delay, while the government's White Paper admitted the lack of parliamentary oversight of second and third pillar matters, particularly in the Commons, under the post-Maastricht scrutiny arrangements. In the short debate on the Committee's report on 17 November 1998, the extension of the scrutiny process to the second and third pillars was approved with remarkably little discussion. On 6 December 1999, the Lords Committee's terms of reference were also revised to include specific references to the second and third pillars, at the same time as the House of Lords adopted its own scrutiny reserve resolution to apply to the second and third pillars.[39]

Both Committees experienced considerable practical difficulties in dealing with second and third pillar matters. The Lords Committee's 1997 report documented numerous problems with the Home Office over the timely deposit of third pillar proposals and other scrutiny problems. Early in 1998, these difficulties led the Committee to conduct a short inquiry, explicitly to inform the House, into government departments' experiences of dealing with the third pillar, against the background of the complexity of third pillar procedures and the difficulty of keeping track of business transacted under that pillar.[40]

Post-1998, third pillar proposals caused even greater difficulties for the Commons Committee and for government departments, especially the Home Office, than they had for the Lords Committee. This led to numerous complaints about the Home Office's poor performance in meeting the Committee's requirements and an appearance by a Home Office Minister at a session of oral evidence before the Committee early in the 2001 Parliament.[41] Subsequently, the existence of fewer explicit complaints suggested that pressure from the two Committees had led to some improvements in the Home Office's performance.

Other problem areas remained, particularly in relation to second pillar matters. In a 1999–2000 Procedure Committee inquiry into scrutiny of treaties, the Commons Committee Chairman, Jimmy Hood, described how lengthy confidential negotiation processes meant that often the first document officially available for scrutiny was the text of the final agreement. That was much too late for Parliament to have any real influence, and often left very little time for scrutiny because the parties were anxious to ratify the treaty. His Committee had had to develop informal means of keeping up with the negotiating process. In other second pillar areas, the Committee had had to accept that most of the substantive inquiries should be conducted by departmental select committees.[42]

Before 1999 and its new terms of reference, the Lords Committee conducted very few inquiries into second pillar matters, mainly because of the lack of any documentary basis for such work. In 2001, the Committee argued that parliamentary oversight of the CSFP remained weak, and looked specifically to the 2004 IGC for improvements in second pillar scrutiny.[43] Late in the 1997–2001 Parliament more second pillar documents were being deposited but, like the Home Office, the Foreign and Commonwealth Office obviously had problems in handling the practical realities of routine EU scrutiny processes in either House.

## The Committees' terms of reference

The two Committees had had very different experiences over their terms of reference. From 1974, the Lords Committee had had very broad terms of reference which had allowed in-depth inquiries into general policy areas as well as into individual documents and specific legislative proposals. Before Maastricht, it had also conducted inquiries into topics that were to become second and, more particularly, third pillar matters. Until pressure for systematic scrutiny of second and third pillar matters arose after Maastricht, there was little need for change.

By contrast, from its inception the Commons Committee had conducted a war of attrition over its terms of reference, driven by the Committee's desire for an inclusive approach to its scrutiny responsibilities and to ensure that the documents deposited covered the full range of EU activities. That process continued throughout the 1992 Parliament, mainly but not exclusively in relation to second and third pillar matters. The Committee's 1995–96 review sought to widen its terms of reference to include 'related matters', which would have allowed consideration of institutional and procedural change. In addition, its terms of reference did not include Commission legislation, Council working documents, negotiating mandates or agreements with third countries or organisations, and submissions to the Council from individual Member States, as well as second and third pillar matters.[44]

The Modernisation Committee 'fully supported' the European Legislation Committee's desire to examine institutional and procedural change and, with some hesitation, accepted the other recommendations. The 1998 White Paper accepted that scrutiny arrangements had not kept pace with the need to ensure comprehensive parliamentary oversight of EU developments and to make EU policy-making and legislative processes 'transparent and understandable'. It proposed extending scrutiny on the lines sought, referring to 'proposals for European legislation and other important documents covering all three areas of EU activity', subject to requirements of confidentiality.[45] The proposals were approved on 17 November 1998, when the Commons Committee's name was also changed. The Committee itself had argued in the 1995–96 review that its name no longer reflected the significant non-legislative element of its work. After various suggestions were rejected by the Procedure Committee and the Modernisation Committee, the Modernisation Committee's recommendation of the 'European Scrutiny Committee' was finally approved.

By 1998–99, the Lords Committee was concerned that its terms of reference still made no specific provision for second and third pillar scrutiny. The Select Committee on Procedure recommended in November 1999 that the Committee's terms of reference should be updated so that it could 'consider European Union documents and other matters relating to the European Union', with a definition of 'European Union documents' that would include the second and third pillars as well as all other policy proposals. The same report recommended that the Committee's name should be changed to the 'Select Committee on the European Union', since 'The Committee's title no longer reflects the scope of its work.'[46] Both changes, and the adoption of a House of Lords scrutiny reserve on the same lines as that of the House of Commons, were agreed after a short debate on 10 November 1999.

## The scrutiny reserve

Until 1999, scrutiny procedures in both Houses were underpinned by the Commons scrutiny reserve resolution of 1990. The existence of the scrutiny reserve has always been seen as a key feature of the scrutiny process as it constrains ministers from agreeing to EU legislative proposals until parliamentary scrutiny is completed. The need to ensure that the reserve covered the full range of documents to be deposited was an enduring concern to the Commons Committee, resolved only with the adoption of the Modernisation Committee's proposals in 1998.

As the Commons Committee noted in 1995–96, if business was properly organised, the scrutiny reserve should in theory never have to be used. In practice, the use of the reserve was usually the result of either the unpredictability of Council business or the failure of UK departments to keep abreast of EU developments. There were three specific areas of concern. The few occasions when the reserve had been lifted by accident had a disproportionate effect on confidence in the system. There had also been occasions when Ministers had failed to explain as soon as they should why they had agreed to proposals that had not been cleared, while in some cases, notification of agreement to uncleared proposals had been given after the event.

Both the Procedure Committee and the Modernisation Committee acknowledged the European Legislation Committee's concerns about the scrutiny reserve. The Procedure Committee considered that the resolution should lay an explicit duty on ministers to inform the relevant committee of confidential proposals and explain the need for confidentiality. Ministers should also explain why agreement had had to be given to a proposal before scrutiny was completed. The Modernisation Committee considered – and the government agreed – that the 1990 resolution should be amended in parallel with the terms of reference of the Committee and extended to legislation made by the co-decision procedure, by 'political agreement' (informal decisions by Ministers before final adoption by the Council of Ministers), as well as to pre-legislative documents, and documents submitted to European Councils. The changes were approved on 17 November 1998.

The Commons Committee examined the operation of the scrutiny reserve in its 2002 review, following concerns about the frequency of breaches, particularly by the Home Office and the Department of Trade and Industry. The Committee had developed the practice of calling in Ministers who breached the scrutiny reserve resolution and at the time of the report had done so three times.[47] It did not, however, favour a statutory scrutiny reserve, considering that it was more important to concentrate on the Council's operations, and how national scrutiny reserves were treated in the Council.[48] In its response, the government repeated that it took seriously its obligations not to override the scrutiny process except in 'particular and unavoidable circumstances' and would 'share the reasoning behind any such decision when asked to by the Committee'.[49]

The House of Lords' concerns about the scrutiny reserve arose specifically in relation to second and, more particularly, third pillar matters. In 1997, the Committee noted that, unlike in 1993, the Home Secretary had indicated his willingness to consider a parliamentary scrutiny reserve for third pillar matters and again concluded that a formal reserve was essential for effective scrutiny of the third pillar. The adoption by the House of Lords of its own scrutiny reserve, in almost identical terms to that of the House of Commons, followed a Procedure Committee proposal in November 1999. It was agreed on 10 November 1999 and welcomed by the Chairman of the European Scrutiny Committee (Lord Tordoff) who concluded that it would allow the committee to 'maintain the degree of flexibility in the subjects we discuss that this House has always had. Therefore I believe that we are in a stronger position than another place to deal with this legislation'.[50]

The existence of its own scrutiny reserve did not mean that the Lords Committee experienced no problems in relation to overrides of the reserve, particularly by Home Office Ministers in respect of third pillar matters. In June 2002, the Committee also drew attention to a problem originally noted by the Commons Committee:[51] how the resolution was potentially being undermined by the practice of reaching 'provisional agreement' on a text in the Council which meant that the scrutiny reserve could, in effect, be overridden.[52]

## Post-Maastricht

### The IGCs at Amsterdam and Nice

Both Lords and Commons Committees paid close attention to the IGCs for which the Maastricht and Amsterdam Treaties provided, focusing in particular on the operation of the EU's institutions and how they related to the work of national parliaments. This interest reflected increasing public concern about the need to enhance the accountability of the EU's legislative processes. The Commons Foreign Affairs Committee also reported regularly on the IGCs and forthcoming new treaties, having decided in March 1994 to add

monitoring of the CSFP and institutional developments in the EU
and preparation for the 1996 IGC to its permanent agenda.[53]

### The role of national parliaments

The Commons Committee's first IGC report in July 1995 contained
a section on 'Democracy and efficiency', prompted by the Committee's long-standing concern with the mechanics of the scrutiny process, and with the Community institutions' failure to conduct their
business so that national parliaments could play their proper part.
The Maastricht Declaration 13 on the Role of National Parliaments
and Declaration 14 had been 'a sham' (a view shared by the Lords
Committee) and 'something more (was) required' of the 1996 IGC.
The main role of national parliaments was in respect of their own
governments, but accountability required that they should also give
'detailed, demanding and timely scrutiny' to both draft legislation
and other EU documents.

There were two main criticisms of the EU's law-making, both
shared by the Lords Committee: the Council's willingness to discuss
legislation on the basis of an unofficial text, which prevented national
parliaments from carrying out their proper scrutiny functions; and
the lack of a minimum period of notice for legislation to be considered
in the Council, with the result that the Council often considered
versions tabled at the last minute, without time for prior consideration
by national parliaments. The only solution was a Treaty requirement
of minimum notice of four weeks between the official text of
a document being available 'in every national capital' and a Council
decision on the document.[54]

The Lords Committee concentrated on the institutions and decision-
making processes in an expanding EU and on the functioning of
the two new pillars of the Maastricht Treaty. It considered how
national parliaments could become more effective, many witnesses
having regarded the relationship between national parliaments and
Community institutions as a crucial problem. Like its Commons
counterpart, it rejected the idea of a second chamber, since national
parliaments could most effectively contribute to the EU's legislative
process by 'exercising timely pressure' on their own governments.[55]

The Commons Committee returned to the role of national parliaments in 1997 when it noted that the government had accepted the
proposal for a minimum four-week period of notice for any text with

legislative implications and formally tabled an amendment to the draft Treaty. That had been followed by a Draft Protocol from the Presidency, seen as a substantial improvement over Declaration 13, although some way short of the Committee's recommendations and the government's formal proposal. A six-week notice period was eventually incorporated in the Amsterdam Treaty – more than the Committees had originally sought and a reward for their persistence, with noticeable benefits to the scrutiny process.[56] That Treaty also contained a provision requiring EU Green and White Papers to be forwarded to national parliaments, an important step in ensuring that the scrutiny process could start at an early stage in policy developments.

The 2000 IGC was dominated by the forthcoming enlargement of the EU with a limited, mainly enlargement-related, agenda. During the 1999–2000 session the Commons European Legislation and Foreign Affairs Committees and the Lords Committee conducted specific inquiries into the 2000 IGC[57] but as the IGC agenda did not include the role of national parliaments, that issue was not specifically considered.

Soon after the 2001 election, the Lords Committee returned to the role of national parliaments in an inquiry that followed the Prime Minister's proposal for a new body composed of members of national parliaments and widespread concerns about the 'democratic deficit' in the EU, as well as other aspects of national parliamentary scrutiny. The Committee accepted the existence of the 'democratic deficit' and that there were areas such as the CFSP where oversight was weak, but concluded that there were major constitutional and practical obstacles for a second chamber in solving those problems, preferring strengthening national parliamentary scrutiny of national governments as a more significant way forward.[58]

The Commons Committee also returned to the subject early in the 2001 Parliament, revisiting its earlier concerns in a long report in June 2002. That inquiry was conducted in the context of the EU's widely acknowledged problems in respect of democracy and accountability and the Laeken Declaration's recognition that EU citizens wanted better democratic scrutiny. The report discussed at length how the role of national parliaments could be strengthened but, like the Lords Committee, it rejected the idea of a second chamber which would not, it considered, achieve the objectives set for it.[59]

## The role of COSAC

Within the context of the role of national parliaments, both committees
examined several times the role of the Conference of Community and
European Affairs Committees (COSAC), which acquired an enhanced
status in the Amsterdam Treaty, particularly in relation to legislation.
This enhanced status was intended to give national parliaments a
greater role in the decision-making process and enable them to contribute more to the drafting of EU legislation, although the protocol
also provided that 'Contributions made by COSAC shall in no way
bind national parliaments or prejudice their position.'

The Commons Committee was never over-enthusiastic about COSAC
and in its 1995 consideration of the Amsterdam IGC argued that it had
been most successful when it considered the technique and practice
of parliamentary control and scrutiny rather than engaging in
'inconclusive political debate'.[60] The same arguments were made in
the 1995–96 report on *The Role of National Parliaments in the European
Union*, which saw the main disadvantage of the regular meetings as
that each Conference was 'very much the Presidency country's show . . .
[with] too many Ministerial set-pieces'.[61] The Lords Committee saw
COSAC as a 'useful forum' for the exchange of views, ideas and
experience, particularly on scrutiny mechanisms, but no more than
that.[62] The Commons Committee was sceptical about a French proposal that COSAC should take on wider responsibilities in relation to
subsidiarity and second and third pillar matters. It nevertheless
accepted that it might not win the arguments and urged that
whatever roles COSAC might undertake, 'they should not be to the
detriment of the valuable technical exchanges on Scrutiny matters'.[63]

Early in the 2001 Parliament both the Lords and Commons
Committees returned to COSAC's role in the context of proposals for
a second chamber and the need to enhance the role of national
parliaments. The Lords Committee urged that COSAC should return
to acting as a practical forum for the exchange of views about
national parliamentary approaches to EU issues,[64] while the Commons
Committee argued that the opportunities COSAC could provide were
'largely squandered'. However, it could, and should, be made more
effective, so that it could 'help to resolve one of the problems facing
national parliaments which actively scrutinise EU legislation, which
is that many national parliaments do not' and should draw up
minimum standards of parliamentary scrutiny.[65] The government's

response welcomed the Committee's interest in making COSAC effective, but left further initiatives for COSAC itself within the framework of the Convention on the Future of Europe – perhaps an indication of the government's own scepticism about the organisation.[66]

## The Scrutiny Committees in action: the Commons

The Committees' workloads increased significantly after 1992: the Commons Committee's 1995–96 review showed that between 800 and 1000 documents were considered each year in the mid-1990s, while the average in the early 2000s was between 1100 and 1300 a year. This growth reflected partly the increase in draft legislation in the second and (especially) third pillar areas after 1998, but also the growth in pre-legislative scrutiny (of Green and White Papers), the effects of the co-decision procedure, which generated increasing numbers of amended proposals, often very fast-moving, and the continuing flow of draft legislation in all policy areas. The breadth of subject matter considered had always been wide and tended to grow, particularly with the addition of third pillar material; much of it also became very technical. The result was considerable pressure to keep up with the flow of paper and both Committees depended heavily on input from their officials.

The increase in the volume of paper to be processed led to little change in either Committee's pattern of work. The Commons Committee usually met weekly, producing around thirty reports in a normal session. Meetings were generally short and attendance, at between 60 and 70 per cent, not normally high, other than when oral evidence was taken from Ministers. By contrast, turnover among the Committee's membership was generally below the average for select committees in both Parliaments and it had the same chairman (Jimmy Hood, Member for Clydesdale) throughout. After the 1998 changes, and like the Lords Committee, the Committee started to devote increasing efforts to pre-legislative scrutiny (of Green and White Papers), pre- and post-Council scrutiny (following a suggestion by the Modernisation Committee) and to such tasks as reviewing the Commission's annual work programme.[67] As the annual report on 2002 showed, in the 2001 Parliament the Committee became considerably more pro-active, with higher attendance, longer meetings and many more sessions of oral evidence from Ministers.

Since its inception in 1974, the Committee had been concerned about practical obstacles to the scrutiny process. The external obstacles, arising mainly from the methods of proceeding in the Commission and Council, were described and documented at length in 1994–95 in the first report on the 1996 IGC.[68] The government's response acknowledged the substance of the Committee's complaints but contained no commitments to further action[69] and the Committee returned to the attack in 1995–96. That report also examined the Committee's 'internal problems' – the 'increasingly worrying' difficulties caused by government departments' handling of scrutiny business – listing *'some* of the lapses' that had been identified since the start of the previous session.[70]

The government's response shared the Committee's concerns about the availability and transmission of documents from Community institutions. The Foreign and Commonwealth Office had already undertaken to try to secure improvements, including the minimum notice period eventually incorporated in the Amsterdam Treaty. Concerns about the clearance of unofficial versions of texts were also acknowledged. The 'internal problems' caused by failings of some government departments were taken 'very seriously' and the attention of the relevant departments had been drawn to the Committee's strictures so that procedures could be tightened.[71]

The Procedure Committee saw many of these difficulties as 'facts of life' and explicitly directed its attention elsewhere.[72] The European Legislation Committee's evidence to the Modernisation Committee of 'handling and scrutiny failures by Departments' was accepted as showing (again) that 'more vigorous efforts' had to be made by government departments if the recommended reforms were to be fully effective. The Modernisation Committee recommended that government departments should appoint a senior official to be responsible for the oversight of scrutiny business.[73] It also supported the suggestion, originally made in 1995–96 by the then Shadow Leader of the House (Ann Taylor) to the Commons Committee[74] and subsequently endorsed by the Procedure Committee,[75] for a national parliament office in Brussels. Such an office, staffed by parliamentary officials, would act as a forward observation post for the House and as the 'eyes and ears' of the European Legislation Committee. Its establishment was approved by the House in November 1998 and it came into operation in November 1999.

The 1998 White Paper explicitly acknowledged that effective scrutiny by Parliament depended on efficient operation of procedures by all concerned and that correct operation of the scrutiny system by government departments was 'a priority for the Government'.[76] The Commons Committee found significant improvements in 2002, attributed to the appointment in most departments of scrutiny co-ordinators as recommended by the Modernisation Committee, although some 'practical difficulties'. remained.[77] There were still cases where deposit of documents, submission of explanatory memoranda and provision of information were delayed. Mostly, the Commission was to blame but on occasions it was the fault of government departments. The National Parliament Office, which among other things provided weekly briefings to support the detailed work of the Commons Committee, was seen as a successful innovation that had contributed significantly to the effectiveness of the scrutiny process.[78] It also provided a high level of support to the work of the Convention on the Future of Europe.

## The Scrutiny Committees in action: the Lords

Like its Commons equivalent, the Lords Committee's *modus operandi* continued post-Maastricht with relatively little outward change, although the implementation of the Jellicoe Committee's recommendations, made shortly before the 1992 election, led to an initial reduction in the overall level of activity. That Committee considered that the European Communities Committee should adjust its working methods and sub-committee structure to make it more flexible, with fewer sub-committees and fewer peers involved in the work of the Committee, to allow the House to undertake committee work in other areas. The 'rotation rule' should in future allow peers to serve for no more than three rather than five sessions on a committee or sub-committee. Membership of sub-committees should not exceed twelve and poor attenders should not be reappointed. The Committee should exercise its scrutiny functions 'with greater speed and more selectivity' to keep up with the Community's fast-moving legislative processes, although the highly valued more considered reports into wider areas of Community policy should continue.[79]

The Jellicoe Committee's report was debated on 3 June 1992, when the Leader of the House (Lord Wakeham) welcomed the recommendations to make the European Communities Committee more flexible, as well as the suggested reduction in the number of sub-committees. Some speakers, especially members of the European Communities Committee, doubted the wisdom of reducing the size of the Committee at a time when more rather than less activity might be expected from the Community. For similar reasons, several speakers, including Baroness Serota, chairman of the Committee in the previous Parliament, and Lord Aldington, chairman since 1989 of Sub-Committee A, also questioned the recommended reduction in the number of sub-committees. After the debate, the Jellicoe Committee's recommendations were referred to the Procedure Committee.

The Procedure Committee's report in July 1992,[80] soon after the election, endorsed most of the Jellicoe Committee's main recommendations, including the appointment of a Liaison Committee, and welcomed a government undertaking to respond in writing to all European Communities Committee reports within two months of publication. The proposed change in the 'rotation rule' should be amended from three years' service to four years, while the suggested ceiling of twelve members for sub-committees was endorsed, as was the proposal that poor attenders should not be reappointed. The Procedure Committee's report was agreed after a short debate on 9 July 1992.

The Liaison Committee was appointed on 16 July 1992 and its first report recommended five European Communities sub-committees because of the post-Maastricht volume of scrutiny work. In a debate on 7 December 1992, the Leader of the House (Lord Wakeham) recognised the strength of feeling about the Jellicoe recommendations about the European Communities Committee, but also the need for resources to support other committee work. The subsequent debate became a *cause célèbre* in which Lord Aldington, who was about to relinquish the chairmanship of Sub-Committee A, moved an amendment to the report to remove the proposed limit on the number of sub-committees, thereby allowing the main Committee to appoint whatever number it chose. The majority of the speakers in the debate supported the amendment, but the vote was a tie (106:106) so the amendment was lost and the report's recommendation of five sub-committees prevailed.

It soon became clear that, with only five sub-committees, the Committee was struggling. In 1994 the Liaison Committee recommended a sixth sub-committee to look at the 1996 IGC and that the number of sub-committees to be appointed thereafter would be 'a matter for further review'. The European Communities Committee remained exercised by the increasing volume of scrutiny and on 16 July 1996, the House agreed to a Liaison Committee recommendation that it should be able to appoint six sub-committees for an experimental period of two years from the beginning of the following session, after which the position would be reviewed.[81] There were no further changes in the sub-committee structure during the 1997–2001 Parliament.

The allocation of work between the various sub-committees had always posed occasional difficulties and the Committee's review at the end of 2002 examined its structure, the number of sub-committees and the allocation of subjects between them.[82] It concluded that there was a case for more sub-committees, since there was a growing amount of work to be done. The Committee did not, however, want more sub-committees unless there were enough members willing to serve on them so that they could function effectively. It would therefore propose a plan for re-structuring the sub-committees' work, based on 'a practical assessment' of the requirements for scrutiny in different policy areas.[83]

## Departmental select committees

For almost all the period considered here, the Lords Committee and its sub-committees remained the principal focus of committee activity in the House of Lords and there was no scope for conflict about responsibility for scrutiny of EU matters. In the Commons, however, the existence of departmental select committees gave rise both to opportunities for co-operation and to potential overlap or conflict, as in relation to second and third pillar matters, but most departmental select committees remained reluctant to consider EU matters.

All the various reviews recognised the difficulties of involving departmental select committees in EU scrutiny. In 1995–96, the Commons Committee acknowledged the constraints but sought a more active role for departmental select committees in scrutinising EU proposals.[84] The Procedure Committee saw it as 'sad' that departmental select committees showed so little interest but concluded that specific procedural incentives were needed to encourage select committees to be involved in EU matters. It recommended that the Liaison Committee (consisting of all select committee chairmen) should give 'authoritative guidance on the value which the House would place on select committees assisting more in the examination of the policy implications of European documents'. Standing Orders for departmental select committees should allow them to examine the implications of EU documents for the departments they scrutinised, while the European Legislation Committee should be given explicit power to refer documents to a departmental select committee, and to record the fact in the same way as recommendations for debate were recorded.[85]

The Modernisation Committee acknowledged individual select committees' jealousy of the right to determine their own programmes and was cautious about adopting too prescriptive an approach, despite government support for greater involvement. Its recommendations, which the government accepted, were limited to procedural changes that would provide a framework for greater involvement, but no compulsion, and including power for the European Legislation Committee to refer documents to departmental select committees for advice, with a deadline for a reply. These changes were agreed on 17 November 1998.

The European Scrutiny Committee's 2002 report referred to the earlier 'varying degrees of gloom' about greater involvement of departmental select committees in EU matters. The power to refer documents to a departmental select committee for advice was 'unusually strong' for one select committee to have over others but had been used only sparingly since 1998. The Committee welcomed the suggestion by the Chairman of the Trade and Industry Committee of the scope for greater involvement by departmental select committees, especially through examining European Green and White Papers and the implementation of EU legislation. The Liaison Committee was also invited to consider two proposals: the inclusion of consideration of EU Green and White Papers in the list of common objectives of select committees; and, for those committees with much EU legislation within their subject areas, the appointment of a European rapporteur with a watching brief on EU developments and whom the European Scrutiny Committee could consult, or supply with information.[86]

In June 2002, the Liaison Committee's guidance to select committees on core objectives and tasks included the examination of policy proposals from the UK Government and the European Commission in Green Papers and White Papers, 'and to inquire further where the Committee considers it appropriate', guidance that the government welcomed in its response to the Committee's report, as it 'should encourage all committees to consider the European dimension to their work'.[87]

## Debates

The ability of the two committees to recommend debates has always been seen as a key element of the scrutiny system, although it is ironic that in the Commons in particular there has been continuing concern at the lack of interest in most debates on EU matters. The Commons Committee commented in 1995–96 that 'Debate ... allows the House to express a view, and it requires Ministers to set out and defend in a wider forum the policy on which they have already given evidence to us.'[88] In 2002, the Committee saw the dialogue with, and the effect of its reports and the debates it recommended on, ministers and their departments, 'as among the most important aspects of the scrutiny system'.[89] For the House of Lords, there is only one possible forum for debate on EU documents – the floor of the House – but since the 1990 changes the House of Commons has had the choice between referring documents for debate on the floor of the House or in a European Standing Committee (and before that to a Standing Committee on European Community Documents).

In the House of Lords, about 40 per cent of the EU Committee's reports were normally recommended for debate and it was rare for the debate not to happen, so there were between ten and fifteen debates, of varying length, in the course of a normal session. There were, however, often long delays before time could be found, so debates were not necessarily particularly topical by the time they happened. They were normally on 'take note' rather than substantive motions and tended to be insiders' occasions, dominated by members of the Committee itself, or the relevant sub-committee. In its 2002 review, the Committee argued that better arrangements were needed so that more debates happened in prime time, and more quickly, while better planning and more advance notice of debates would be welcomed. Government responses to reports should be made within six weeks of publication of the report, while debates should be held within eight weeks of publication.[90]

For the Commons, there were long-running procedural issues related to debates on EU documents. Since 1990, when the government had insisted on automatic referral of all documents for debate to a European Standing Committee, for a debate to take place on the floor of the House, it had to be 'de-referred'. In its 1995–96 review, the Commons Committee explained how it had always indicated whether a document should be further considered in committee or on the floor, but for a debate to take place on the floor the initiative for a 'de-referral' motion had to remain with the government. The Committee had been sparing in its recommendations for debates on the floor but of those recommendations only 15 per cent had been so considered. It was the government's responsibility to find time for scrutiny debates and the Committee argued that debates on the most important documents should take place on the floor. The Committee also considered that 'Take note' motions might fulfil the technical requirements of scrutiny but the main purpose of the process was to enable the House to express a view on a document. The bland motions that the government favoured neither encouraged Members to attend nor generated a lively debate, making the scrutiny process less focused and reducing accountability.[91]

By the time the 1996–97 Procedure Committee reported, there had been a series of episodes in connection with European Legislation Committee recommendations for debates. The Procedure Committee shared the concerns about the government's unwillingness to provide time on the floor of the House even for debates on important documents. It drew particular attention to an occasion in November and December 1996 when the government had sought to disregard a European Legislation Committee recommendation for a debate on the floor on three documents related to Economic and Monetary Union. The European Standing Committee had been unable to agree on a resolution on the documents and 'the whole issue dominated a two-day debate ... in advance of the December Dublin 1996 EU Summit'.[92] The Procedure Committee found it 'disturbing' that the recommendations of the European Legislation Committee should be so little regarded: EU documents recommended for debate on the floor should not stand referred automatically to committee, and should require a referral motion, open to effective objection by forty Members, should the government wish to hold the debate in standing committee.

## Motions on the floor

A further problem arose in relation to motions tabled when documents were considered on the floor of the House following consideration by a European Standing Committee. The Procedure Committee had observed in 1991 that when a document that had been debated in Standing Committee was subsequently tabled for approval on the floor of the House, the government could table a different motion from that agreed by the Committee. This 'loophole' could 'make a mockery of the scrutiny process' and waste the Standing Committee's time and effort.[93] The government had previously rejected this argument on the grounds that a motion for consideration on the floor should be tabled by the government, in a form with which the government could agree.

The Procedure Committee, supported by the European Legislation Committee, reopened the argument in 1996–97. The problem arose only rarely, but the outcome of committee proceedings should not be 'swept under the carpet' if the system was to retain credibility,[94] a view shared by the Modernisation Committee.[95] It was, however, clear 'that the present Government, like the previous Government, is unlikely to view [the European Legislation Committee's] proposals with favour'. The Committee admitted defeat since a simple reiteration of previous proposals was unlikely to lead to practical improvements in the scrutiny of European business.[96] Some hope of change 'in due course' was held out but when the Commons Committee conducted its 2002 review, those hopes had not been realised. The Committee still saw the procedures as undermining the credibility of the scrutiny process and considered that, in the light of the Government's desire to improve the ways in which the House dealt with European business, the issue should be reopened. It suggested how the Committee's motions might be given greater importance[97] but, once again, the government disagreed.[98]

## The number of committees

The number of European Standing Committees had caused difficulties ever since they were first set up in 1991, as had generally poor attendance and lack of media interest in their work. In 1995–96, the European Legislation Committee suggested that more committees would make workloads more even and reduce backlogs of documents awaiting debate.[99] The Procedure Committee acknowledged the difficulties in getting Members to serve on the committees, attributing poor attendance to the large number of meetings and 'indigestible range of unconnected subjects' they had to consider. It recommended at least four committees of ten to twelve Members each to handle the expected increase in workload in the next Parliament and provide the benefits of specialisation and continuity.[100] The Modernisation Committee agreed that more standing committees were desirable and proposed five committees.[101] The government agreed that 'the usual channels' should consider increasing the number of committees, and whether permanent Members should be nominated for a whole Parliament.[102]

In the event, only three committees were appointed in 1998 and in 2002 the European Scrutiny Committee again remarked on poor attendance and lack of attention to debates. It sought ways to encourage Members to attend and the media to cover proceedings on EU matters, again recommending five committees, as well as steps to ensure greater involvement by members of departmental select committees.[103] The government rejected the suggestion of five committees, since it had already proved impossible to introduce the number of committees and degree of specialisation that the Modernisation Committee had recommended.[104] When the Leader of the House (Robin Cook) gave evidence to the Committee on 5 November 2002, he argued that if there were willing volunteers to serve on the Committees, the whips would be happy to nominate them; the problem was the lack of willing volunteers – possibly as good a description as any of the attitude of the majority of Members to most EU matters.[105]

## Conclusions

It has become almost a truism in some quarters that the Westminster arrangements for scrutiny of EU activities are among the most effective and a success story for both Houses, but particularly for the House of Lords. To quote only two examples, the Jellicoe Committee in 1992 found widespread support for the Committee's 'unique ability to carry out selective but in-depth and objective inquiries' and noted that 'No other parliamentary assembly in other Member States made a comparable contribution', concluding that its achievements and reputation were 'remarkable'.[106] Similarly, in May 2002, the Leader's Group in the House of Lords remarked that 'The Lords European Union Committee is widely regarded as one of the best national parliamentary scrutiny systems in the European Union member states.'[107] The Lords Committee also quoted in its 2002 review the Leader of the House's view that 'our work was extremely important and well regarded in Europe'.

The Leader's Group nevertheless drew attention to suggestions by speakers in a recent debate of concern about the need for better over-sight of European legislation. The Lords Committee also remarked that its work had 'less significance in the UK Parliament' than else-where and quoted other witnesses who had similar doubts about the Committee's overall impact. The Committee itself recognised that from its own perspective the scrutiny process could be significantly improved.[108] These reservations explain at least partly why, in its 2002 review, the Lords Committee looked so closely at the prin-ciples as well as the practice of the process and made numerous recommendations for change.

The various reviews of the Commons scrutiny processes have generally given the basic mechanisms a clean bill of health even while emphasising the need for improvements in matters of detail. Having described the scrutiny system in 1994–95 as being in 'deep crisis', the Commons Committee's 1995–96 review saw much of the criticism of the system as unfounded and unfair because it was ill-informed.

> The British system in fact compares extremely well with others in the Union. Many Parliaments carry out little or no systematic examination of legislative proposals or other documents.[109]

The Procedure Committee in 1996–97 also gave a robust defence of the operation of the process, arguing that there was little to be gained by wholesale change in the basic system:

> much of the criticism of the present system of scrutiny and debate is based on an imperfect grasp of what actually happens at the moment, let alone of the realistic prospects for change. The work of the [European Legislation Committee] is grossly undervalued and underused. Its weekly reports ... provide a wealth of information

on all documents which it regards as of legal or political importance. ... It is very easy to underestimate the degree of influence exercised by the ELC[110]

The committees' scrutiny procedures have evolved, mostly deliberately, so that they complement rather than compete with each other. Those procedures have remained robust and resilient in response to increasingly complex EU procedures and a growing volume of EU activity. The committees' work may be seen as a shared endeavour by Parliament as a whole to scrutinise a particularly intractable area of legislative and, increasingly, other government activity. They have cooperated successfully to pursue many common concerns, in particular over the need to ensure transparency in relation to EU matters, and that government departments make information available to them, and to the public, systematically and reliably, especially through the timely and comprehensive provision of documents. Since in both Houses the scrutiny process has remained primarily document based, their continuing emphasis on what might otherwise appear to be insignificant procedural and administrative details related to the supply of documents by both the EU institutions and government departments is wholly justified.

The Commons Committee's exhaustively recorded battles in the 1990s over the mechanics of scrutiny may have appeared to concentrate unduly on process rather than substance but, like the Lords Committee's regular correspondence with Ministers, they represented a major effort to ensure that government departments observed the principles of accountability to Parliament and that the Committees, and Parliament as a whole, received the information they needed to do their work. The improvements that the Commons Committee found in 2002 were, however, achieved only by constant vigilance and persistence, especially on the part of the Committees' staff. The Committees' experiences in the admittedly complex policy areas of the second and third pillars illustrate very clearly the dependence of the scrutiny process on a high level of co-operation, and administrative efficiency, on the part of government departments – co-operation and efficiency that have not invariably been forthcoming.

Successive governments may have repeatedly and explicitly supported the principles of the scrutiny process, but they have in practice been reluctant to concede the usually limited changes or improvements that the various committees have sought. Any change has been hard-won, achieved mainly by persistence and vigilance. Individual government departments have also frequently failed to deliver their side of the bargain by not following correct procedures. Since the Commons' 1998 changes, which were originally government-driven, there have been detectable improvements but the impression remains that for some departments the parliamentary scrutiny process is a nuisance and an obstacle to progress.

The scrutiny process also depends heavily for its success on the observance by the government of the day of the scrutiny reserve. Without the reserve, the scrutiny process would have no teeth (although the majority of other Member States still have no equivalent requirement). The continuing tension between the need to observe the terms of the reserve and ministers' desire not to have their freedom of manoeuvre in negotiations unduly restricted is an almost unavoidable consequence of the system. The Conservative Government's initial approach to parliamentary scrutiny of second and third pillar matters illustrated the strength of some ministers' (and officials') fears of the possible effects of exposure to those processes on their negotiating positions in what were seen as particularly sensitive policy areas.

Successive adjustments to the Commons scrutiny process have ensured that it has kept up with changes within the EU, but its procedures often appear enclosed and inward-looking. In this respect it differs significantly from the Lords Committee, with its emphasis on conducting inquiries in public, routinely taking evidence from external sources, and generally more open procedures. The Commons Procedure Committee recognised in 1996–97 that the Committees' successes in routinely processing ever-growing volumes of paper often go unnoticed but acknowledged that the nature of the Lords Committee's reports is such that its work often attracts more widespread interest, especially outside Parliament, and is more informative than that of the Commons Committee. The Commons Committee's apparently mechanistic procedures mean that it relatively infrequently considers substantive issues and its work mostly attracts little interest. It can be correspondingly difficult for its members to engage in its activities, although attendance improved significantly in the 2001 Parliament with the Committee's more proactive approach and more frequent sessions of evidence from Ministers. The apparent inconsistency between the Committee's declared desire for an effective scrutiny system, with more widespread interest in its work and in the debates it recommended, and its members' lack of engagement may have begun to change.

No amount of tweaking of the scrutiny process will remove the fundamental reality that in the period under consideration the United Kingdom was only one among twelve (in 1992) and later fifteen Member States, all seeking to protect their own positions. There are also inherent difficulties in trying to make national parliaments, with their widely varying procedures and different constitutional contexts, more effective individually and collectively at holding governments or the EU institutions to account, as the struggles to find an effective role for COSAC showed.

The Foreign Affairs Committee in 1992–93 and the Lords Committee in 2001–02 commented in remarkably similar terms on the difficulty of finding a uniform system throughout the EU for holding ministers to account in their national parliaments on decisions reached inter-governmentally.[111] More generally, national parliaments still face considerable obstacles in becoming more effective in relation to the EU: 'any European initiatives in this area run up against the problem that different national parliaments have very different roles, powers and prerogatives' and operate in very different ways.[112] As the Commons Committee observed in 2002, 'One of the problems facing national parliaments which actively scrutinise EU legislation is that many national parliaments do not.'[113] Within the increasingly complex variable geometry of the EU's decision-making processes, assessing the effectiveness of national scrutiny mechanisms is inherently difficult. In the later chapters of this book we will examine how the system has operated at Westminster in some important policy areas. In making an assessment, much will depend upon how influence has been exercised at key stages in those processes. That such influence is often behind the scenes and with little tangible evidence of results means it is notoriously difficult to measure. But that difficulty should not inhibit us from making the attempt nor prevent from concluding that the process is worthwhile.

## Notes

1. The history of the establishment of the two Committees and their work from 1973–74 is described in detail in the earlier edition of this book – see Chs 4 and 5 in *Westminster and Europe*. There is a convenient summary of

the current operation of the Commons scrutiny system by the European Scrutiny Committee in *European Scrutiny in the Commons* Thirtieth Report HC 152-xxx, 2001–02; and of the Lords system in the European Union Committee's *Review of Scrutiny of European Legislation* First Report HL Paper 15, 2002–03.

2. European Legislation Committee, *The 1996 Inter-Governmental Conference: the Agenda; Democracy and Efficiency; the Role of National Parliaments* Twenty-fourth Report HC 239-1, 1994–95, para. 8

3. Twenty-seventh Report HC 51-xxvii, 1995–96.

4. First Special Report HC 140, 1996–97.

5. Select Committee on Procedure *European Business* Third Report HC 77, 1996–97.

6. Select Committee on Modernisation of the House of Commons *The Scrutiny of European Business* Seventh Report HC 791, 1997–98.

7. *The Scrutiny of European Union Business* Cm. 4095; November 1998.

8. *European Scrutiny in the Commons* Thirtieth Report HC 152-xxx, 2001–02.

9. Second Special Report HC 1256, 2001–02.

10. HC 1298, 2001–02.

11. *House of Lords Scrutiny of the Inter-Governmental Pillars of the European Union* Twenty-eighth Report HL Paper 124, 1992–93.

12. *Enhancing Parliamentary Scrutiny of the Third Pillar* Sixth Report HL Paper 25, 1997–98.

13. Fifth Report from the Select Committee on Procedure of the House HL Paper 116, 1998–99.

14. *The Scrutiny of European Union Business – Provisional Agreement in the Council of Ministers* Twenty-third Report HL Paper 135, 2001–02.

15. *Review of Scrutiny of European Legislation* First Report HL Paper 15, 2002–03. This report contains a useful summary of the scrutiny mechanisms in other Member States. See also *European Affairs Committees – the Influence of National Parliaments on European Policies* European Centre for Parliamentary Research and Documentation for a more detailed comparative analysis.

16. *Government Responses* Twentieth Report HL Paper 99, 2002–03.

17. For more details of the extension of the scope of the European Parliament's involvement, see the Foreign Affairs Committee *Europe after Maastricht* Second Report HC 642, Part XII, 1992–93.

18. *Scrutiny after Maastricht* HC 99, 1993–94.

19. Published with Committee's Second Special Report *Parliamentary Scrutiny of the Co-Decision Procedure* HC 739, 1993–94.

20. *1996 Inter-Governmental Conference* Twenty-first Report HL Paper 105, 1994–95, para. 251; this report describes in detail the co-decision procedure as adopted in the Maastricht Treaty.

21. Twenty-seventh Report HC 51-xxvii, 1995–96.

22. Seventh Report HC 791, 1997–98 Appendix 1 Memorandum by the Select Committee on European Legislation.

23. The procedure was described by the Committee in 1997 as 'hideously complicated' – see report on *The Draft Protocol on the Role of National Parliaments* Thirteenth Report HC 36-xiii, 1996–97, para. 34.

24. *Review of Scrutiny of European Legislation* HL Paper 15, 2002–03, paras 32–35.
25. *European Scrutiny in the Commons* Thirtieth Report HC 152-xxx, 2001–02, para. 56.
26. *European Scrutiny in the Commons: Government Observations on the Committee's Thirtieth Report of Session 2001–02* HC 1256, 2001–02, paras 19–20.
27. *Democracy and Accountability and the EU and the Role of National Parliaments* Thirty-third Report HC 152-xxxiii, 2001–02, paras 88–93; Government response Third Special Report HC 1257, 2001–02, para. 10.
28. Foreign Affairs Committee *Europe after Maastricht* Second Report HC 642, 1992–93.
29. *Europe after Maastricht* Observations by the Secretary of State for Foreign and Commonwealth Affairs Cm. 2287; July 1993.
30. Minutes of evidence of the Home Affairs Committee on Inter-Governmental Cooperation in the Fields of Justice and Home Affairs, 21 April 1993, HC 625-I, 1992–93 (the Committee made no report).
31. HL Paper 124, 1992–93, paras 49–50.
32. Cm. 2471; February 1994.
33. 12 April 1994, HL Deb, cc. 1489–1500.
34. *The 1996 Inter-Governmental Conference: the Agenda; Democracy and Efficiency; the Role of National Parliaments* Twenty-fourth Report HC 239-I, 1994–95, para. 136.
35. *The 1996 Inter-Governmental Conference* Twenty-first Report HL Paper 105, 1994–95, paras 270, 280.
36. Twenty-seventh Report HC 51-xvii, 1995–96, paras 65–98.
37. *European Business* Third Report HC 77, 1996–97, para. 44.
38. House of Lords Select Committee on the European Communities *Enhancing Parliamentary Scrutiny of the Third Pillar*, Sixth Report HL Paper 25, 1997–98.
39. 10 November 1999, HL Deb, c. 1352.
40. *Dealing with the Third Pillar: the Government's perspective* Fifteenth Report HL Paper 73, 1997–98.
41. Minutes of evidence 31 October 2001, HC 325, 2001–02.
42. *Parliamentary Scrutiny of Treaties* Second Report HC 210, 1999–2000.
43. *A Second Parliamentary Chamber for Europe* HL Paper 48 2001–02, paras 44–45, 67–69.
44. Twenty-seventh Report HC 51-xxvii, 1995–96, Part III.
45. Cm. 4095, para. 7.
46. Fifth Report from the Select Committee on Procedure of the House, HL Paper 116, 1998–99.
47. *European Scrutiny in the Commons* Thirtieth Report HC 152-xxx, 2001–02, para. 53; see also *The Committee's Work in 2002* HC 63-viii, 2002–03, para. 7.
48. *European Scrutiny in the Commons* Thirtieth Report HC 152-xxx, 2001–02, paras 51–57.
49. European Scrutiny Committee Second Special Report HC 1256, 2001–02.
50. HL Deb, 606, c. 1358.
51. See, for example, HC 152-i, 2001–02, para. 47.

52. *The Scrutiny of European Union Business – Provisional Agreement in the Council of Ministers* Twenty-third Report HL Paper 135, 2001–02, para. 13.
53. Foreign Affairs Committee *European Union: Preparations for the 1996 Inter-Governmental Conference* Third Report HC 401, 1994–95, paras 1–2.
54. *The 1996 Intergovernmental Conference: the Agenda, Democracy and Efficiency, the Role of National Parliaments* HC 239, 1994–95.
55. *1996 Intergovernmental Conference* HL Paper 105, 1994–95.
56. *The Draft Protocol on the Role of National Parliaments* HC 36-xiii, 1996–97.
57. European Scrutiny Committee Seventeenth Report HC 23-xvii, 1999–2000; and *2000 Inter-Governmental Conference-government observations on the Committee's Seventeenth Report of 1999–2000* First Special Report HC 803, 1999–2000; Foreign Affairs Committee *Developments at the Intergovernmental Conference* Sixth Report HC 384, 1999–2000; and House of Lords European Union Committee *The 2000 Intergovernmental Conference* Eleventh Report HL Paper 92, 1999–2000.
58. *A Second Parliamentary Chamber for Europe: an Unreal Solution to Some Real Problems* HL Paper 48, 2001–02.
59. *Democracy and Accountability in the EU and the Role of National Parliaments* Thirty-third Report 2001–02, HC 152-xxxiii-I–II.
60. *The 1996 Inter-Governmental conference: the Agenda, Democracy and Efficiency, the Role of National Parliaments* Twenty-fourth Report HC 239-I, 1994–95.
61. Twenty-eighth Report HC 51-xxviii, 1995–96, Part III.
62. *1996 Inter-Governmental Conference* Twenty-first Report HL Paper 105, 1994–95, paras 306–307.
63. *The Draft Protocol on the Role of National Parliaments* Thirteenth Report HC 36-xiii, 1996–97.
64. *A Second Parliamentary Chamber for Europe: an Unreal Solution to Some Real Problems* HL Paper 48, 2001–02, para. 75.
65. *Democracy and Accountability in the EU and the Role of National Parliaments* Thirty-third Report HC 152-xxxiii, 2001–02.
66. Third Special Report HC 1257, 2001–02 para. 29.
67. For an up to date account of the work of the Commons Committee, see its first annual report for 2002, published in January 2003 – *The Committee's Work in 2002* Eighth Report HC 63-viii, 2002–03.
68. *The 1996 Inter-Governmental Conference: the Agenda; Democracy and Efficiency; the Role of National Parliaments* Twenty-fourth Report HC 239-I and II 1994–95.
69. Cm. 3051; November 1995.
70. *The Scrutiny of European Business* Twenty-seventh Report HC 51-xxvii, 1995–96.
71. First Special Report HC 140, 1996–97, paras 13–16.
72. Third Report HC 77, 1996–97 para. 8.
73. *The Scrutiny of European Business* Seventh Report HC 791, 1997–98, paras 45–47.
74. HC 51-xxvii, 1995–96, Q. 96 and 105.
75. HC 77, 1996–97, para. 68–71.

76. *The Scrutiny of European Business* Cm. 4095; November 1998, para. 10.
77. Thirtieth Report HC 152-xxx, 2001–02, para. 44.
78. Ibid., paras 45–47.
79. Report from the Select Committee on the Committee Work of the House, HL Paper 35-I, 1991–92.
80. First Report HL Paper 11, 1991–92.
81. HL Deb, c. 742.
82. For a useful description of the Committee at work, see C. S. Kerse 'Parliamentary Scrutiny of the Third Pillar', *European Public Law*, Vol. 6 No. 1 March 2000.
83. First Report HL Paper 15, 2002–03, paras 104–106.
84. Twenty-seventh Report HC 51-xxvii, 1995–96, para. 248.
85. HC 77, 1996–97, para. 61.
86. Thirtieth Report HC 152-xxx, 2001–02, paras 81–87.
87. European Scrutiny Committee *European Scrutiny in the Commons: Government Observations on the Committee's Thirtieth Report of Session 2001–02* Second Special Report HC 1256 2001–02, para. 6.
88. HC 51-xxvii, 1995–96, para. 167.
89. Thirtieth Report HC 152-xxx, 2001–02, para. 64.
90. *Review of the Scrutiny of European Legislation* First Report HL Paper 15, 2002–03, para. 148.
91. Twenty-seventh Report HC 51-xxvii, 1995–96, para. 171 and Table VII.
92. More details of this incident are given in the Sixth Report from the European Legislation Committee HC 64-vi, 1996–97; see also Procedure Committee *European Business* Third Report 1996–97, HC 77.
93. Ibid., quoted in para. 198.
94. Ibid., paras 22–23.
95. *The Scrutiny of European Business* Third Report HC 791 1997–98, para. 28.
96. Ibid., para. 29.
97. *European Scrutiny in the Commons* Thirtieth Report HC 152-xxx, 2001–02, paras 71–73.
98. *European Scrutiny in the Commons: Government Observations on the Committee's Thirtieth Report of Session 2001–02* Second Special Report HC 1256, 2001–02, para. 29.
99. *The Scrutiny of European Business* Twenty-seventh Report HC 51-xxvii, 1995–96, paras 205–208.
100. *European Business* Third Report HC 77 1996–97, paras 33–34.
101. *The Scrutiny of European Business* Seventh Report HC 791, 1997–98, paras 19–26.
102. *The Scrutiny of European Business* Cm. 4095; November 1998, para. 7.
103. *European Scrutiny in the Commons* Thirtieth Report HC 152-xxx, 2001–02, paras 67–74.
104. *European Scrutiny in the Commons: Government Observations on the Committee's Thirtieth Report of Session 2001–02*, HC 1256, 2001–02, para. 27.
105. Oral evidence by the Leader of the House to the European Scrutiny Committee, 5 November 2002, HC 1298, 2001–02, Q. 18.

106. HL Paper 35-I, 1991–92, para. 66.
107. Report of the Committee on Working Practices of the House of Lords (chaired by Lord Williams of Mostyn) HL Paper 111, 2001–02.
108. *Review of Scrutiny of European Legislation* HL Paper 15, 2002–03.
109. Twenty-seventh Report HC 51-xxvii, 1995–96, para. 16.
110. *European Business* Third Report HC 77, 1996–97.
111. *Europe after Maastricht* Second Report HC 642-I, 1992–93, para. 95.
112. *A Second Parliamentary Chamber for Europe* Seventh Report HL Paper 48, 2001–02, para. 67.
113. *Democracy and Accountability in the EU and the role of National Parliaments* Thirty-third Report. HC 153-xxxiii-I, 2001–02. Introduction page 9 and paras 152–153.

# 5

# Governance, Institutional Reform and Enlargement

*Vaughne Miller and Carole Andrews*

## Introduction

In the aftermath of the events of 1989 and the end of the Cold War, former Communist states in Central and Eastern Europe, and also those with a tradition of neutrality, felt able to apply for EU membership. The Maastricht Treaty had given new impetus and direction ahead of enlargement during the 1990s and it was hoped that the new European Union would eventually embrace Eastern Europe and have a stabilising effect on the new democracies there. In 1996 and 2000 Intergovernmental Conferences (IGCs) were launched to amend the Treaties in order to prepare the EU for enlargement by introducing new institutional and decision-making arrangements in fulfilment of the requirements of earlier Treaty amendments and to amend existing institutional arrangements where weaknesses had been acknowledged. Without reform, it was thought, the EU's institutions and legislative processes might founder with enlargement, but this reorganisation should also connect with European citizens and remove public confusion and apathy.

The Treaty of Rome has been amended four times since 1957, three times in the last decade alone. The Treaties of Amsterdam and Nice, like their Maastricht predecessor, included a provision on the timing of the next IGC. The 'institutionalisation' of the IGC process has been justified largely by the enlargement process and the need for institutional reform to cope with expansion. However, by the 2000 IGC, the almost relentless timetable for the European reform process had left 'only nineteen months in sixteen years free from treaty-linked activities'.[1] The period of the 1992 and 1997 Parliaments coincided with two rounds of EU enlargement negotiations and two IGCs.

At Westminster EC/EU Treaty amendment has traditionally generated heated, emotional debate. The debates in 1986 on the Single European Act and in 1992–93 on the Maastricht Treaty were about the political and constitutional enormity of the changes brought about by membership of the EC/EU and its increasingly wide-ranging institutional powers, perceived as encroaching on a thousand years of British parliamentary sovereignty. There has perhaps been an element of 'IGC-fatigue' at Westminster since the tumultuous passage of the Maastricht Bill. Certainly, the passage of the two EC (Amendment) Bills in 1997/98 and 2001/02 was relatively smooth compared with the legislative process to implement the Maastricht Treaty. Neither the Amsterdam nor the Nice Bill produced the procedural jockeying that Maastricht had done, when the final vote on the Treaty became a vote of confidence in the Government.[2] They were less controversial, but presented an opportunity to challenge the Government about specific issues, such as agricultural subsidies or immigration control.

The political profile of the Westminster Parliament changed significantly over the last two Parliaments. The Conservative Government, internally divided over Europe and with a narrow parliamentary majority of 21, was replaced in 1997 by a largely pro-European Labour Government with a considerable parliamentary majority of 178. The new political composition of the Commons, and the significantly reduced rebellious 'Eurosceptic' minority, made it easier for the Government to adopt controversial EC proposals and Treaty amendments.

## The EFTA enlargement

Broadly speaking, there was all-party support for EU enlargement in both the 1992 and 1997 Parliaments. The Major and Blair Governments were both enthusiastic about enlargement. The decision to open negotiations with the European Free Trade Association (EFTA) countries was taken during the UK Presidency of the EU in December 1992, under the Conservative Government, while the subsequent enlargement process was launched in March 1998, during the UK Presidency of the EU under Labour.

By the start of the 1992 Parliament applications for EC membership had been submitted by three members of the EFTA – Austria, Sweden and Finland. Norway (also in EFTA) applied in December 1992. Negotiations opened in early 1993 and were generally unproblematic. The EFTA countries had already adopted most Single Market legislation under the European Economic Area Agreement. Their accession would have a positive effect on the EU's financial balance, as most would be net contributors to the Community budget. They had broadly similar political, economic and cultural backgrounds, and close commercial and financial links with the Community. Difficulties emerged, however, over weighted votes in the Council of Ministers. The Conservative Government claimed the credit in March 1994 for securing at the informal European Council in Ioannina, Greece, the 'Ioannina compromise' on the formation of a blocking minority (covered in Chapter 2, p. 20).

The *European Union (Accessions) Bill* to authorise implementation of the Accession Treaty completed most of its parliamentary stages in June/July 1994 and received Royal Assent on 3 November 1994.[3] Foreign Secretary Douglas Hurd claimed: 'No Government have argued as forcefully as ours that the EU should open its doors. No other leaders have argued as strongly as the Prime Minister and Baroness Thatcher that Europe is not an exclusive club.'[4] Shadow Foreign Secretary John Cunningham welcomed the prospective members with their 'strong traditions of good government'.[5] Sir Russell Johnston, for the Liberal Democrats, was also supportive, but warned that enlargement would place great strains on the existing institutional framework and reform must be addressed urgently before the 1996/97 IGC.[6] Although there was virtually unanimous support for enlargement on both sides of the House, there was a lively and wide-ranging debate, with the participation of many leading pro- and anti-EU MPs, on issues such as deepening and widening, the effects of enlargement on the EU's institutional arrangements, preparation for the 1996/97 IGC and the longer-term prospects for future enlargement.

## The 1996 Intergovernmental Conference

Maastricht had marked a new stage in the process of European co-operation, bringing together twelve Member States under a single umbrella called the EU and introducing subsidiarity. Governance issues

such as democratisation and accountability, efficiency and transparency, dominated the IGC agendas in 1996/97 and 2000.

The agenda for the Amsterdam IGC included weighted votes in
Council, the qualified majority voting (QMV) threshold, the size of
the Commission and other institutional measures (e.g. QMV extension)
to ensure the EU's effective operation with enlargement Imagery
drawn from construction, geometry, gastronomy and transport were
used to describe the future organisation of the EU as it expanded.
Terms to characterise differentiation included 'Europe à la Carte',
'concentric circles', 'variable geometry', 'two-tier', 'hard core', 'multi-
speed' and 'multi-track'.[7] This led both existing Members, including
the United Kingdom, and the candidate states to express concerns
about marginalisation or relegation to second-class membership. The
British Government submitted proposals to the preparatory IGC
Reflection Group on the Court of Justice, QMV, subsidiarity, the role
of national parliaments and the Court of Auditors.

The Amsterdam IGC began under the Conservative Government
and finished under Labour, which entered the final stages of the
Conference after winning the 1997 general election. John Major set
out his vision of a 'flexible', 'multi-layered' Europe in a speech in
Leiden in September 1994, emphasising that there should be no
'hard core' or 'two-tier' development. Following recommendations
by the Commons Foreign Affairs and EC Committees and the Lords
EC Committee,[8] the Major Government published a White Paper on
12 March 1996,[9] in which it set out its views on the future EU, keeping
its options open by stating that it would not be bound by them. Its
position on institutional matters included:

- No change in the pillar structure.
- No extension of QMV.
- QMV votes to be related more closely to population.
- No new powers for the European Parliament (EP).
- A greater role for national parliaments.
- Further entrenchment of subsidiarity.
- Greater use of flexibility.
- Improvements in functioning of the European Court of Justice (ECJ).[10]

The Government also enunciated for the first time the view that the
major net contributors as a group should not be capable of being

out-voted in the Council of Ministers.[11] It rejected the argument that unanimity would be incompatible with effective decision-making in an enlarged Union,[12] and sought a more equitable system of weighted Council votes which took more account of the size of Member States, not allowing a group of small states to out-vote a large State such as the United Kingdom on an issue of national importance.

Sovereignty was the major issue in Westminster debates on the Amsterdam IGC. The Government emphasised the importance of the nation state and the undesirability of 'massive constitutional upheaval'.[13] It wanted the Commission to be more accountable to the Council of Ministers,[14] the roles of all the institutions to be 'clearly defined' and to perform their tasks better, rather than reach out for more.[15] The Major Government had claimed the credit for the inclusion of the Subsidiarity Article (3b) at Maastricht but there had been criticism of the lack of clear guidelines for the application and monitoring of the principle. Now the Government called for a stronger guarantee of national competence.

The new Labour Government was also cautious about increased QMV and it did not support the flexibility arrangements promoted by its predecessors. Reversing the Conservatives' hard-won opt-out from the Social Protocol, the Government agreed to the incorporation of 'Social Chapter' provisions into the EC Treaty, as well as British participation in elements of the Schengen agreement. The extension of QMV was relatively small (only four articles, although eleven new QMV articles were introduced) and the re-weighting of votes was deferred. The change of government in the latter stages of the IGC process gave rise to some jostling for credit, seen in John Major's comments on Mr Blair's statement on the Amsterdam Council:

> Is not the reality that this outcome – which is very welcome – was achieved by negotiations conducted by the last Government, and that what the Prime Minister has done is apply his usual jackdaw technique of picking up other people's property and claiming credit for it?[16]

The Amsterdam and Nice IGC processes were generally more open than the Maastricht one, particularly in the provision of documentation to Parliament.[17] The 1996–97 documents were made available in the form of deposited Conference documents. The Internet was in its

infancy in the UK Parliament during 1996, with most users on the
Parliamentary Estate linked up via the Parliamentary Data and Video
Network (PDVN), but most MPs untrained in its use. *Europa*, the EU's
portal website, was established in February 1995 but did not yet provide
comprehensive IGC documentation.

While the IGC process might have stood up to scrutiny, the EC
legislative process did not. Before the launch of the IGC the Commons
Scrutiny Committee had drawn attention to the problems of ensuring
effective scrutiny of Commission proposals received with very short
notice, and proposed a minimum period of notice for legislation to
be considered in the Council.[18] The Committee wanted a minimum
period of four weeks' notice between an official text being made
available and a decision being taken in Council. The Conservative
Government had 'floated (the idea) in the Study Group', attracting EU
interest and sympathy. In his June statement the new Prime Minister,
Tony Blair, implied a British, if not a personal, success when he said:

> The House will also be interested to know that the treaty contains
> provisions to strengthen Parliament's ability to scrutinise European
> legislation properly, by laying down a minimum six-week period
> for documents to be available.[19]

The IGC addressed institutional weaknesses but failed to reach agreement in three main areas which became known as the 'Amsterdam
leftovers': the size of the Commission, weighted votes in the Council
and QMV extension. Although loosely termed an 'enlargement IGC',
the Amsterdam process resulted in only modest institutional changes
to facilitate enlargement. Several proposals put forward during 1996–97
were finally abandoned in favour of a Treaty Protocol on the institutions, postponing controversial institutional changes to the next IGC.

## The Amsterdam Treaty at Westminster

The *European Communities (Amendment) Bill* to implement the
Amsterdam Treaty received Royal Assent on 11 June 1998.[20] In the
Second Reading debate in the Commons on 12 November 1997
the Opposition expressed concern about the loss of power from
Westminster as a result of more decision-making by QMV, arguing that
enlargement had been sidelined for the sake of deeper integration

and none of the reforms necessary for enlargement (e.g. CAP reform) had been tackled.[21] The Liberal Democrats thought the Treaty contained only 'modest achievements' on institutional reform. Foreign Secretary Robin Cook supported QMV extension to prevent an enlarged EU from facing paralysis over petty issues. He implied that the Opposition's objections signalled their failure to recognise benefits that the candidate states themselves had recognised.

During the debate which followed, Angela Browning, an Agriculture Minister in the previous Conservative Government, described passionately her experience of losing accountability to Parliament as a result of QMV:

> I have to admit that it is an excruciating experience to appear, as a Minister, before a Committee of this democratically elected House – with Hon. Members on both sides asking probing questions on the issue involved – and having to tell the Committee how negotiations are going and what we are seeking to gain, while knowing all the time that, if we are out-voted under qualified majority voting, the concerns of the Committee will not matter a fig. We have no power: power has gone from this Parliament, and power is going from this Parliament, because that is how qualified majority voting works in practice.[22]

## Enlargement to the East

The wider, more complex and more extended enlargement process, involving ten Central and Eastern European countries (CEECs),[23] Cyprus and Malta, began early in the 1997 UK Parliament, with the publication in July 1997 of the European Commission's major policy document on enlargement, *Agenda 2000*, and the Commission's Opinions on the membership eligibility of the applicant states, based on the Copenhagen criteria. The Luxembourg European Council in December 1997 decided to open accession negotiations with the first, best prepared group of applicants (Czech Republic, Estonia, Hungary, Poland, Slovenia and Cyprus), and the enlargement process was formally launched in March 1998, under the UK Presidency. In February 2000 negotiations were opened with a second group of applicants (Bulgaria, Latvia, Lithuania, Romania, Slovakia and Malta)[24]. The Gothenburg European Council in June 2001 set the objective of completing negotiations by the end of 2002 with candidates that were ready, to enable them to participate in the 2004 EP elections.

The CEEC enlargement 'is of a different order of magnitude from any that has happened in the past. It is a challenge of momentous consequence'.[25] Their accession was expected to add substantially to the EU's budgetary costs and would require major political, economic and administrative adjustments by the former Communist states to comply with the *acquis* and other conditions of EU membership. Whereas the more straight-forward negotiations with the EFTA applicants were completed in just over a year, the CEEC round of negotiations would probably take over five years for the most advanced candidates.

In a *Financial Times* article in September 2000 Tony Blair and Swedish Prime Minister Goran Persson argued for a more dynamic approach to the enlargement negotiations and Blair's speech in Warsaw in October 2000 underlined the British Government's position as a champion of enlargement. Britain therefore strongly supported the Commission's November 2000 Strategy Paper, which was endorsed at the Nice European Council in December 2000, and welcomed the new momentum in negotiations under the Swedish Presidency's 'road map' in the first half of 2001.

For the Conservatives, pre-enlargement reform of the Common Agricultural Policy (CAP), not institutional reform, was the major issue, because of the cost implications of enlargement if it remained unreformed.[26] The Opposition emphasised the EU's failure to reform the CAP as part of its anti-EU platform in the run-up to the 2001 general election, which coincided with the foot-and-mouth crisis in the already depressed UK farming industry. While the Government agreed that CAP reform was necessary, it did not want to delay enlargement for this purpose.[27] Foreign Secretary, Robin Cook opposed making CAP reform a condition of enlargement, 'Otherwise, those who oppose agricultural reform will find that that is a basis on which to oppose enlargement.'[28]

The Government provided Parliament with information on the enlargement process in a transparent and fairly systematic way. As enlargement is always on European Council agendas, it was covered in the Prime Minister's oral statement on the summits. Statements on meetings of the General Affairs Council in the form of Written Answers included summaries of progress in the accession negotiations.

The EU Committees in both Houses received documents relating to enlargement, including the annual progress reports on each candidate state and the accompanying European Commission summary/strategy paper, and these were available to Members in the Vote Office. Periodically, Foreign and Commonwealth Office (FCO) Written Answers summarised progress in the negotiations, in terms of chapters of the *acquis* opened and closed by each candidate state.[29] Following a request by the Foreign Affairs Committee (FAC), the Foreign and Commonwealth Office agreed to send the Committee a six-monthly progress report on enlargement[30] and a quarterly updated chart, showing the state of play in the negotiations.

The usual avenues were open to Members to raise enlargement issues in debates and parliamentary questions (PQs). In the Commons, proceedings on the 1994 Accessions Bill[31] were the only debates on enlargement in Government time on the floor of the House during the 1992 and 1997 Parliaments, but the subject was raised during the twice-yearly European affairs debates[32] and in some foreign affairs debates on the Queen's Speech.[33] Only one Commons backbencher used an 'adjournment' debate to raise enlargement issues. The newly elected Conservative Member, Andrew Tyrie, did so in June 1997 in what was in fact his maiden speech.[34] The position of individual EU candidate states was occasionally discussed during more general adjournment debates on the countries concerned, particularly in the cases of Cyprus and Turkey,[35] and some documents on enlargement were debated in European Standing Committees.[36]

In the Lords enlargement issues were raised occasionally on the floor of the House in debates on the Queen's Speech and other foreign affairs debates. The Liberal Democrat peers, Lord Wallace of Saltaire and Lord Avebury, introduced short debates on the commitment to embark on a major enlargement soon after the conclusion of the 1996/97 IGC[37] and on the political accession criteria.[38] However, the main debates on enlargement were based on those reports of the Lords EU Committee.[39]

The most detailed examination of the enlargement process and its implications was carried out by Select Committees, which took wide-ranging evidence, monitored progress and highlighted key issues arising from the negotiations. The Lords EU Committee produced five reports during the 1992 and 1997 Parliaments, either on enlargement in general[40] or on specific aspects, such as the CAP,[41] the financial consequences of enlargement,[42] and external frontier controls.[43] All were the subject of debates on 'take note' motions on the floor of the House. In the 1997 Parliament the FAC also produced two reports on enlargement,[44] and the Commons Scrutiny Committee commented on European documents on enlargement regarded as politically or legally important. Enlargement issues were discussed at evidence sessions given by the Foreign Secretary to the FAC before each European Council, and in the complementary evidence given by the Europe Minister to the Lords EU Committee after each European Council.

The Select Committee reports on enlargement were a valuable source of information for Parliament and for the wider public. For example, the report of the Lords EU Committee on *Enlargement and EU external frontier controls*,[45] was commended by both Government and Opposition.[46] By comparison, the Commons FAC reports on enlargement received less exposure, because they were not debated.

## The 2000 Intergovernmental Conference

Another 'enlargement IGC' was launched in 2000 to tackle the 'Amsterdam left-overs' and institutional changes linked also to governance and the way the Union operated in general. Much of the pre-Amsterdam debate on institutional reform was replayed four years later during the preparatory stages of the 2000 IGC. The Government set out its position in a White Paper[47] just as the Conference opened in February 2000, and did not diverge from this. It made no further contributions to the IGC preparatory stage[48] and in parliamentary debates and replies directed Members to the White Paper, to Mr Blair's Warsaw speech in October 2000 and the Government's Response to the FAC Report on *Developments at the Intergovernmental Conference 2000*.[49] There were very few non-negotiable positions and few UK alternatives to proposals on the table, so when its conditions were largely met at Nice, the Government was confident in claiming before the Commons that the Conference had been a success for Britain, as well as for the EU and applicant states.

In July 1999 the Commons European Scrutiny Committee (ESC) began an inquiry into the 2000 IGC, initially limited to the three outstanding institutional issues and the defence initiative.[50] The extension of QMV was of major interest.[51] The Portuguese Presidency had proposed 39 Articles for transfer to QMV and 8 for partial transfer.

The succeeding French Presidency, which concluded the IGC, proposed 46 Articles for QMV. The British Government's position was to reject any attempt to impose QMV on decision-making in the areas of Treaty amendment, border controls, taxation, social security, defence and revenue-raising, but to consider extending QMV on a case-by-case basis where it might be in Britain's interest.[52] The ESC was dissatisfied with this position, arguing that it was not sufficient to take up a stance of case-by-case negotiation in the national interest in the hope that out of the clash of fifteen national interests might emerge some coherent and operationally efficient extension of QMV.

> We are again disappointed that the UK Government has not seen fit to offer any view on (the Commission's) criteria nor propose any alternatives of its own.... It would at least be a starting point if the UK Government could make clear.... which Articles, in its view, will in all probability remain subject to unanimity and which, in all probability, will be passed to QMV.[53]

The FAC also undertook an inquiry into the IGC, reporting without recommendations in October 2000.[54] In response, the Government reiterated the views set out in the White Paper, adding that its own proposal for an increased number of Vice Presidents in a reduced Commission had 'attracted the most support' in Europe.[55] The Government was not always very forthcoming with information. Of some 105 Commons questions during the course of the IGC, around 30 were answered by a reference to the February 2000 White Paper.[56] Once the Government had responded to the FAC Sixth Report on the IGC, parliamentary answers also referred to this Command Paper.[57]

By the 2000 IGC all IGC submissions were available on the *Europa* site, as the Government indicated in numerous parliamentary answers. All CONFER/2000 documents were kept by the Commons Library and some IGC preparatory documents (draft treaty texts in particular) were officially deposited. While the provision of documents was not a problem in 2000, there was parliamentary concern about the Government's failure to provide information on the complexities of the institutional issues. The FAC, unhappy about the lack of Government information on the implications of Nice, concluded in its Report, *European Union Enlargement and Nice Follow-up* that it is of the utmost importance that the Foreign and Commonwealth Office, and the Government, keep this Committee, its successor Committee, and the House as a whole closely informed about all aspects of its policy towards the next IGC so that there can be greater understanding of the implications of the next IGC than there has been of some of those in the past.[58]

The Government agreed to ensure that the House as a whole, and the FAC in particular, were 'fully informed about all the aspects of policy' towards the 2004 IGC.[59] (We shall see?)

## The Nice Bill

The Nice Bill received its Commons Second Reading on 4 July 2001 and Royal Assent on 26 February 2002.[60] The debates were uneventful, with predictable contributions concerning the erosion of national sovereignty through further QMV extension and the loss of a UK Commissioner. When Ireland voted against the Nice Treaty in June 2001, the Bill's passage was not suspended, pending a resolution of the Treaty rejection, as with Denmark in 1992. EU leaders expressed disappointment, but there was no urgent, collective effort to find alternatives to put to the Irish electorate, as there had been in 1992. The British and Irish Governments suffered a momentary loss of face, when, having promoted Nice as an enlargement Treaty, they conceded that new members could, after all, accede without it. The large Labour parliamentary majority meant there was no threat to the Government's intention to ratify Nice. Neither could a small group of backbenchers gain leverage over the Government, which the Opposition might seek to turn to its advantage in relation to wider or non-EU-related, issues.

## Internal institutional reforms

Institutional reforms not requiring Treaty amendment were also the subject of debate and consideration at Westminster during the period of the 1992 and 1997 Parliaments. The mass resignation of the Commission in March 1999 provided the backdrop for debate on Commission corruption, competence and accountability, and mechanisms for monitoring the use of EU funds. Although turnout in the

EP elections in 1994 and 1999 was poor, in the late 1990s EP election arrangements received some attention as the Gibraltar lobby campaigned for the rights of Gibraltarians to vote in them.[61]

## The Commission

The European Commission's role and methods are poorly understood in Westminster and often appear insidious. 'Eurosceptics' such as Austin Mitchell and Sir Teddy Taylor and Lords Bruce of Donington and Pearson of Rannoch assiduously probed both Conservative and Labour Governments about Commission powers and accountability. The Liberal Democrats raised Commission mismanagement at an Opposition Day debate on Europe on 13 January 1999. David Heathcoat-Amory (Conservative)[62] said that fraud and mismanagement were 'endemic in the European Union at all levels, and in the European Commission in particular', pointing to the 'scandalous waste' documented in the Court of Auditors' annual reports.[63] The Leader of the House, Margaret Beckett, refused a request from Conservative Alan Clark for a debate on Commission corruption.[64] Once the decision was taken to establish the 'Committee of the Wise' to investigate Commission fraud and nepotism, the Government declined to comment on specific allegations made about particular Commissioners, on the grounds that the matter was under investigation.[65] Mr Blair tried to put a positive gloss on the event. A new Commission President:

> should be the opportunity to push through root-and-branch reform of the Commission, its mandate and its method of operation.... The new President of the Commission must be a political heavyweight, capable of providing the Commission with leadership and authority.[66]

The Opposition leader, William Hague, called for an emergency summit to 'restore public confidence in European institutions'.[67] His reform proposals included a binding code of conduct for the appointment of senior officials and EP powers to sack individual Commissioners guilty of misconduct. Peers criticised the Council's decision to establish the new anti-fraud office (OLAF) within the 'lame duck' Commission instead of with the Court of Auditors, where it would have 'full independence'.[68]

In July 1999 the Commons Public Accounts Committee published a report entitled *Financial Management and Control in the European Union*,[69] which drew on the results of a fact-finding mission in April 1999 to those EU institutions responsible for the management and oversight of the EC budget. The Committee recommended a clearer division of responsibilities of Commissioners and Commission staff; individual accountability within the Commission and to the EP; enhanced accountability of Member States for Structural Funds; greater transparency in project and programme administration and in staff recruitment and whistleblowing procedures; better Commission follow-up of ECJ and EP recommendations; and greater transparency in the work of OLAF. The Committee also urged the Government to ratify the Convention and Protocols on the Protection of the European Community's financial interests, which it did in September 1999.

Between the revelations of Commission fraud and the resignation of the Commission, the Lords European Communities Committee published a report on Commission delegated decision-making powers, *Delegation of Powers to the Commission: reforming Comitology*.[70] For sceptics, this complex system of delegated legislation was perceived as a way of adopting vast amounts of EC legislation 'by the back door'. The Report concluded that the new Comitology decision[71] should enhance EP involvement in delegation, simplify the procedures and inject greater transparency.[72] The Report was debated in the Lords in June 1999 and in recommending the Report to the House, the Committee Chairman, Lord Hope of Craighead, underlined 'the role which we see in this matter for the national Parliament' and for an improved national scrutiny role for the Committee.[73]

## The European Parliament

The EP gained powers incrementally from Maastricht to Nice, as the EU attempted to address its 'democratic deficit'. Amsterdam reduced the proliferation of legislative procedures, largely abolishing the co-operation procedure, extending EP assent and extending and simplifying co-decision.[74] Although there were national concerns that the EP would use its new powers to increase its influence over the legislative process, evidence showed that the EP exercised its ultimate power of veto sparingly.[75] Nor was legislative efficiency seriously compromised by co-decision, as some had feared, although it caused problems for national scrutiny procedures.

Given MEPs' poor attendance, the extent to which co-decision adds legitimacy is perhaps questionable. UK media coverage of the MEPs' 'expenses scandal' in 1998 prompted questions in Westminster about the EP's cost, MEPs' pay and allowances.[76] MEPs' attendance and conduct were raised at the Cardiff European Council in June 1998 under the UK Presidency, when Mr Blair urged the EP to speed up the introduction of new rules to curb abuse of the system.

Commitment to a uniform electoral system for EP elections originates with the Treaty of Rome but has been slow to come to fruition. In July 1998 the EP adopted a Resolution on a draft electoral procedure incorporating common principles for the election of MEPs.[77] Under the Belgian EU Presidency in 2001 the Council agreed on the substantive proposals (including a UK contribution on EP voting rights for Gibraltarians).[78] The Presidency noted that, as all unresolved issues were now settled, the conditions for political agreement to amend the 1976 Act on direct universal suffrage had been met.[79] Tony Blair had said as Shadow Home Secretary that a Labour Government would reform the UK voting system for the EP[80] and both Labour and the Liberal Democrats supported a Proportional Representation (PR) system based on regional lists. In the United Kingdom the change was implemented by the *European Parliamentary Elections Act 1999* and applied in the elections in June of that year.

The role of national parliaments in the EU was not mentioned in the EC Treaties until the TEU included a Declaration (No. 13) on their role. The EP is not accountable to national parliaments and the Treaty does not require it. Where links have developed, they have been on a bilateral, co-operative basis. In some countries (e.g. Belgium, Germany and Greece), the European Affairs committees comprise both national and EP parliamentarians. In the United Kingdom mixed MP/MEP committees were allegedly under consideration by John Major's Government but have not been established. Measures introduced to improve links have generally been informal. In the Commons members of the ESC and departmental select committees made increasing use of opportunities to visit and liaise with EP counterparts.[81]

On a more formal basis, since 1992 several British MEPs have appeared before the Lords EU Committee. In July 1994 John (now Lord) Tomlinson and Terry Wynn gave evidence to the Lords Committee regarding financial control and fraud.[82] Wynn returned in March 1999 on the subject of financing the EU.[83] From the 1999 EP, Caroline Jackson spoke about the European Food Agency in May 2000.[84] Andrew Duff, Christopher Beazley, Simon Murphy and Richard Corbett gave evidence on the 2000 IGC,[85] and in April 2001 Christopher Heaton-Harris spoke about reform of the Court of Auditors.[86]

Until April 2002 UK MPs were entitled to one annual paid visit to the EU institutions or to a Member State parliament.[87] PQs in 1995 and 1996 gave details of the numbers of MPs availing themselves of this facility,[88] which averaged 66 per year, and the costs of subsidising visits.[89] The lack of PQs since then could indicate either that visits are now taken for granted or little interest in the relationship. The take-up has not been any greater in recent years. There were 65 visits in 1998–99, 61 visits in 1999–2000, 72 in 2000–01 and 80 in 2001–02 (until the end of March 2002).[90] There was a move from individual curiosity to wider parliamentary involvement. Interest in the EP increased in terms of time spent at the EP by Westminster MPs (and vice versa), although the number of references to EP reports in PQs decreased over the two Parliaments. Nevertheless, EP reports and opinions were on occasion used as a basis to hold the Government to account in sensitive areas such as health and agricultural policy.[91]

The Conference of Bodies specialising in Community Affairs (COSAC),[92] includes delegations from national parliaments and the EP. There was little interest in the activities of COSAC among British parliamentarians, although its role was considered by the Commons European Legislation Select Committee (European Scrutiny Committee since November 1998) in July 1996.[93] Proposals to transform COSAC into a second EP chamber were not supported at Westminster, although the Labour Government supported the idea of a new institution representing national parliaments. In 1998 Robin Cook (then Leader of the House) discussed the idea of a stronger link between national parliaments by means of a new European forum to examine subsidiarity questions.[94]

In a speech in Warsaw in October 2000, Tony Blair supported the idea of a second EP chamber to review the EU's work, particularly to 'help provide democratic oversight at a European level of the common foreign and security policy'.[95] However, the Lords EU Committee, in its November 2001 Report,[96] did not favour the Prime Minister's proposal. It considered that 'a second EP chamber would not solve the democratic deficit, could come into conflict with the existing EP and would be difficult to involve in treaty revision'.[97] It was for national parliaments to ensure the accountability of their ministers and to monitor subsidiarity. COSAC, it concluded, was an opportunity missed, and should primarily focus on scrutiny issues rather than general debate.[98] The Committee did, however, support:

- appropriate co-operation between national parliaments and with the EP;
- increasing informal co-operation between national parliamentarians in the CFSP;
- similar co-operation in examining the Commission's Work Programme;
- the Prime Minister's proposal for a charter of competencies, although basing any such document on a political, rather than a legal, text would be problematic;

Although the EP as an institution may have gained in stature at Westminster, there was no development of any real public understanding of its work or importance. The overall EU turnout of 49.4 per cent in the 1999 elections was the lowest since direct elections began in 1979. In the United Kingdom it was even lower, at around 24 per cent, which caused concern at Westminster[99] and gave rise to a Home Office Review of voter turnout.[100]

## Conclusion

In July 2001 the Commission's White Paper on *European Governance*[101] examined problems the EU faced in connecting with its citizens. This had been acknowledged on numerous occasions, particularly during the IGCs, after negative EU referendums and EP elections with ever-lower turnouts. Enlargement to include new, enthusiastic members would, it was believed, provide the impetus to remedy this. The Commission Paper proposed that reform of European governance should be a requisite part of the broader debate on the future of Europe. Peter Hain welcomed the Paper as 'an important initiative in the effort to make the EU's institutions more efficient, effective, transparent and accountable',[102] particularly the practical ideas not necessitating Treaty change. The European Scrutiny Committee applauded the

Commission's 'refreshing frankness',[103] supporting proposals for parliamentarians to provide leadership in the future of Europe debate and for speeding up the legislative process (provided adequate time was allowed for parliamentary scrutiny), but expressing reservations about other institutional proposals.

The Blair Government maintained that it wanted progress in both EU deepening and widening, rather than widening in order to curtail deepening, yet it was cautious throughout its first term about some of the EU's most ambitious projects, such as Economic and Monetary Union and the relationship between the EU and NATO. With regard to parliamentary involvement in the European process, although Parliament was generally well informed by Government on progress in the accession negotiations, and although key issues were addressed by Select Committees, there was not much evidence of full parliamentary engagement in some of the major financial issues relating to enlargement, which would come into focus in the final stages of the accession negotiations. The flow of information from Government to Parliament on the progress of enlargement was generally systematic and transparent. Scrutiny of the issues by Select Committees, especially in the Lords, was effective, but there was no evidence of intensive interest among Members generally in debates. While select committees carried out some wide-ranging and informative inquiries on governance issues and proposed Treaty amendments, Parliament as a whole was not always kept informed about the implications of these matters, something which the Government pledged to remedy for the 2004 IGC.

This situation may raise questions about Parliament's desire or need to be informed about EU developments, given its limited influence over the adoption of EC legislation and the ratification of treaties. Parliament's role has been essentially to monitor and scrutinise, but it has rarely, with the exception of the debates on the Maastricht Treaty, displayed much interest in the detail of European issues. Parliament needs to be informed in order to pressurise the Government and to stir up public interest. Is Parliament likely to be effective in this (or does the media often have a greater role)? While PQs have forced the Government to outline its basic position, it is only in the Select Committees that a more thorough examination of European policies and the Government's views on them has been possible.

The European Council in Laeken in December 2001 adopted a Declaration on the Future of Europe, establishing a 'Convention' which would bring together representatives of national governments and parliaments in the Member States and candidate states, the EU institutions, non-government organisations and the general public, to prepare an institutional and constitutional reform of the EC Treaties in the form of a European constitution. In its Working Group discussions and Plenary debates the Convention has kept alive governance issues, such as reform of the Council, the pillared structure of the Union and the role of national parliaments. The Westminster Parliament might be faced with an opportunity for greater input into European affairs and the EU's legislative processes, if proposals agreed at the Convention on the role of national parliaments in the future European architecture are introduced. The timely and comprehensive provision of information to Member States will be vital if national parliaments are to have more influence in these processes. This will no doubt affect the way in which EU matters are considered at Westminster, although it might not give rise to greater interest in EU issues among parliamentarians generally.

## Notes

1. *Common Market Law Review*, Vol. 37, No. 4, August 2000, footnote to guest editorial, Philippe De Schoutheete, 'The Intergovernmental Conference', p. 845.
2. The Maastricht Second Reading vote was 336 to 92, while the Motion of confidence in the Government's Europe policy, following defeat in the vote on the Social Protocol Resolution, was 339 to 299. In the Amsterdam Second Reading the House divided 392 to 162. At Third Reading the Division was 370 to 145. In the Nice Treaty Second Reading, the House divided 385 to 148 and at Third Reading 392 to 158.
3. The accession treaty was agreed in March 1994 and signed at the Corfu European Council in June 1994. Norway's application was withdrawn following the negative referendum. The other three candidates acceded on 1 January 1995.
4. HC Deb, 11 July 1994, c. 687.
5. Ibid., cc. 695–696.
6. Ibid., c. 715.
7. See also Douglas Hurd, speeches in Inverness and Warsaw in May 1994; Michael Howard, *Independent* 4 June 1994 and Malcolm Rifkind, HC Deb, 24 October 1996, c. 135.
8. Foreign Affairs Committee Third Report, *European Union: Preparations for the 1996 Inter-Governmental Conference*, HC 401, 1994–95; Select Committee on

European Legislation Twenty-fourth Report, *The 1996 Inter-Governmental Conference: the Agenda, Democracy and Efficiency, the Role of National Parliaments*, HC 239-I, 1994–95; Lords Select Committee on the European Communities Twenty-first Report, *1996 Inter-Governmental Conference*, HL Paper 105, 1994–95.

9. Cm. 3181, para. 19.
10. Adapted from FAC Third Report, 1995–96, *The Intergovernmental Conference*, 23 July 1996, para. 17.
11. Cm. 3181, para. 24.
12. Ibid.
13. Douglas Hurd, Institut Français des Relations Internationales, Paris, 12 January 1995.
14. Ibid.
15. Ibid.
16. HC Deb, 18 June 1997, c. 317.
17. The Maastricht process was described by Helen Wallace as 'a document negotiated in a room without windows', 'European Governance in Turbulent Times', *Journal of Common Market Studies*, Vol. 31, No. 3, 1 September 1993, p. 296.
18. *Select Committee on European Legislation*, Twenty-fourth Report, 1994–95, *The 1996 Inter-Governmental Conference: the Agenda; democracy and efficiency; the role of national parliaments*, 17 July 1995.
19. HC Deb, 18 June 1997, c. 315.
20. Bill 71 1997/98; HL Bill 62 1997/98; HL Bill 116 1997/98; Bill 193 1997/98; HL Bill 123 1997/98; CAP 21 1998.
21. HC Deb, 12 November 1997, c. 923.
22. Ibid., c. 956.
23. Bulgaria, Czech Republic, Estonia, Hungary, Latvia, Lithuania, Poland, Romania, Slovakia and Slovenia.
24. Turkey was declared eligible for accession in 1997 was recognised as a candidate in 1999, but could not open negotiations because it had not fulfilled the political criteria for accession.
25. Lords European Community Committee, Tenth Report, 25 November 1997, HL Paper 41, Part 2, para. 10.
26. For example, see Francis Maude, then Shadow Foreign Secretary, HC Deb, 15 June 2000, c. 1140.
27. The Berlin European Council, March 1999, on the financial perspective for 2000–06, decided that there was sufficient provision for enlargement to go ahead.
28. HC Deb, 23 January 2001, c. 798.
29. HC Deb, 16 November 2001, c. 924W.
30. The first such report was published as a memorandum in the FAC's Fifth Report, 3 April 2001, HC 318, 2000–01.
31. Second Reading, HC Deb, 11 July 1994, cc. 263–372; Remaining stages, 13 July 1994, cc. 1044–1104.
32. HC Deb, 2 July 1992, cc. 976–1059; 24 November 1992, cc. 758–842; 16 May 1994, cc. 556–647; 21 June 1995, cc. 355–448; 7 December 1995,

cc. 506–593; 4 December 1997, cc. 513–569; 11 June 1998, cc. 1242–1284; 3 December 1998, cc. 1081–1140; 25 May 1999, cc. 178–259; 1 December 1999, cc. 314–404; 15 June 2000, cc. 1122–1210; 23 November 2000, cc. 451–540.

33. Commons: HC Deb, 8 May 1992, cc. 276–296, 307–346; 17 November 1994, cc. 133–228; 24 October 1996, cc. 129–226; 27 November 1998, cc. 438–512. Lords: HL Deb, 17 November 1994, cc. 26–140; 16 November 1995, cc. 24–122; 28 October 1996, cc. 114–220; 15 May 1997, cc. 29–134; 26 November 1998, cc. 133–230; 18 November 1999, cc. 25–168.

34. HC Deb, 18 June 1997, cc. 270–277.

35. For example, Whitsun (Spring) adjournment debate on Cyprus, HC Deb, 26 May 1994, cc. 420–429; Wednesday adjournment debates on Cyprus, HC Deb, 29 October 1997, cc. 817–836; 28 October 1998, cc. 251–271. See also Lords debate on unstarred question on human rights in Turkey, HL Deb, 18 July 1997, cc. 1164–1186.

36. For example, Enlargement: accession negotiations, European Standing Committee B, 10 May 1994; Enlargement of the EU, European Standing Committee B, 26 April 1995; Relations with Central and Eastern Europe, European Standing Committee B, 24 May 1995.

37. HL Deb, 13 March 1996, cc. 851–856.

38. HL Deb, 20 December 2000.

39. For example, Debate on the Tenth Report of the European Communities Committee on the Financial Consequences of Enlargement, (HL 41, 1997/98) HL Deb, 4 December 1997, cc. 1509–1569; Debate on the Twenty-first Report of the European Communities Committee on Enlargement of the EU: Progress and Problems (HL 118, 1998/99), HL Deb, 7 December 1999, cc. 1191–1243; Debate on the report of the European Union Committee on Enlargement and EU External Frontier Controls (HL 110, 1999/2000), HL Deb, 9 March 2001, cc. 482–506.

40. *Enlargement of the Community*, First Report 1992–93, HL Paper 5; *Enlargement of the EU: Progress and Problems*, Twenty-first Report 1998–99, HL Paper 118.

41. Twelfth Report 1995–96, HL Paper 92.

42. Tenth Report 1997–98, HL Paper 41.

43. Seventeenth Report, 1999–2000, HL Paper 110.

44. *European Union Enlargement*, Third Report 1998–99, HC 86; *European Enlargement and Nice Follow-up*, Fifth Report 2000–01, HC 318.

45. Seventeenth Report 1999–2000, HL Paper 110.

46. HL Deb, 9 March 2001, c. 497.

47. *IGC: Reform for Enlargement: the British Approach to the European Union Intergovernmental Conference 2000*, Cm. 4595; February 2000.

48. The White Paper is the only UK contribution on the *Europa* site.

49. Cm. 4893, 30 October 2000, Government Response to FAC Sixth Report, *Developments at the Intergovernmental Conference 2000*, HC 384, 1999–2000.

50. ESC, Seventeenth Report, 1999–2000, *The 2000 Inter-Governmental Conference*, HC 23-xvii; HC 97-I-iv; HC 942-I (1998–99), 15 May 2000.

51. Of some 145 PQs relating to the IGC and the Nice Treaty, more than a third concerned the extension of QMV. For example, see HC Deb, 21 December 2000, cc. 341–343W, HC Deb, 16 January 2001, c. 166W, HL Deb, 5 February 2001, c. WA80, HL Deb, 20 March 2001, c. 150WA.
52. Statement by Robin Cook, HC Deb, 15 February 2000, and White Paper on the IGC.
53. ESC, Seventeenth Report, 1999–2000, *The 2000 Inter-Governmental Conference*, HC 23-xvii; HC 97-i–v; HC 942-i (1998–99), 15 May 2000.
54. HC 384, FAC Sixth Report, 1999/2000.
55. Cm. 4893, *Developments at the Intergovernmental Conference 2000*, FCO Response, October 2000.
56. Nine of these referred indirectly to the White Paper by way of a reply to a question from John Redwood on 30 October 2000.
57. Cm. 4893.
58. FAC Fifth Report, *European Union Enlargement and Nice Follow-up*, HC 318, 10 April 2001, from: http://pubs1.tso.parliament.uk/pa/cm200001/cmselect/cmfaff/318/uc318i02.htm.
59. Government Response to the FAC Report, Cm. 5198; July 2001.
60. *European Communities (Amendment) Act 2002*, c. 3, 2002.
61. This sudden surge in interest in EP elections at Westminster followed a European Court of Human Rights judgment in the case of Gibraltarian, Denise Matthews. The Court ruled that she was entitled to vote in EP elections, which meant that the Government had to find a way of including Gibraltar as a UK constituency for EP elections. *Matthews* v. *UK*, Application No. 24833/94, judgment of 18 February 1999, at: http://hudoc.echr.coe.int/hudoc/ViewRoot.asp?Item = 0&Action = Html&X =829144912 &Notice = 1&Noticemode = 2&RelatedMode = 0.
62. Mr Heathcoat-Amory, broadly 'Eurosceptic', is one of the UK's national representatives at the Convention on the Future of Europe.
63. HC Deb, 13 January 1999, c. 382.
64. HC Deb, 21 January 1999, c. 1024.
65. HC Deb, 26 February 1999, c. 493W.
66. HC Deb, 16 March 1999, c. 887.
67. Ibid., c. 888.
68. Lord Shaw of Northstead (Conservative), HC Deb, 18 June 1999, c. 628.
69. Committee of Public Accounts, Twenty-ninth Report, HC 690, 1998–99, 7 July 1999.
70. HL Select Committee on European Communities, Third Report, 1998–99, HL 23, 2 February 1999. The Lords Committee considered Comitology in a report on the 1996 IGC, *1996 Inter-Governmental Conference*, Twenty-first Report, 1994–95, HL Paper 105, para. 295, concluding that it was not convinced the system was seriously at fault.
71. Declaration 31 of the Amsterdam Treaty called on the Commission to submit by end 1998 a proposal to amend the 1987 comitology decision (Decision 87/373/EEC).
72. HL 23, para. 16, Conclusions.
73. HL Deb, 18 June 1999, c. 624.

74. Whereas under co-operation, if the EP opposed a proposal, the Council could still approve it by unanimity, co-decision gave the EP an ultimate right of veto in certain circumstances.
75. Since the introduction of co-decision in November 1993, there have been some 400 co-decision procedures and the procedure has failed to produce a result on just four occasions: in 1994 the Council sought to reintroduce its common position after a failed conciliation and the EP plenary rejected it; in 1995 an agreement reached in conciliation (with a tight majority) was rejected by the plenary; in 1998 the Council anticipated the provisions of Amsterdam and allowed a proposal on the Security Committee (problem of comitology) to lapse and did not try to reintroduce its common position after failure to reach agreement in conciliation; and in 2001 the plenary rejected a deal reached in conciliation on the Takeovers directive with the vote being a tie (the proposal was therefore not adopted). See Conciliation Committee Annual Reports at http://www.europarl.eu.int/code/ Information/activity_en.htm
76. For example, HL Deb, 15 July 1998, cc. 26–27WA, HC Deb, 19 May 1999, c. 1060, HL Deb, 27 July 1999, cc. 129–130WA.
77. Resolution 10331/98, EP Doc A4–0212/98, 15 July 1998, OJC 292, 21 September 1998, p. 66.
78. Gen. Sec. 6150/02, 20 February 2002.
79. Presidency Note, 21 February 2002, 6472/02. At the time of writing EC Drafts 6151/02; 6472/02; 6151/02, 14 March 2002, were awaiting approval in Council.
80. Labour Party Conference pledge in 1993.
81. Figures for Select Committee visits to the EU institutions can be found in the Sessional Returns. See also HC 152-xxxiii-I, ESC, Thirty-third Report, *Democracy and Accountability in the EU and the Role of National Parliaments*, 21 June 2002.
82. HL 75, 1993/94, House of Lords European Communities Select Committee, Twelfth Report.
83. HL 36, 1998/99, Lords European Communities Select Committee Sixth Report, *Financing of the EU: who pays and how?* 2 March 1999.
84. HL 66, 1999/2000, Lords Committee Seventh Report, 16 May 2000.
85. HL 92, 1999/2000, HL Eleventh Report, 25 July 2000.
86. HL 63, HL Twelfth Report, 3 April 2001.
87. In April 2002, Members, entitlement was increased to three visits per year and included the parliaments of the candidate states.
88. 31 Members from 1 January 1992 to 31 March 1992. 88 Members in year ending 31 March 1993. 75 Members in year ending 31 March 1994. 68 Members in year ending 31 March 1995: HC Deb, 18 April 1995, c. 1W.
89. HC Deb, 3 December 1996, c. 601W.
90. Records of visits supplied by the House of Commons Fees Office.
91. For example, HC Deb, 9 December 1992, c. 697W and HC Deb, 11 January 1994, c. 235W on the transport and storage of spent nuclear fuels and plutonium, HC Deb, 16 March 1994, c. 679W on public health monitoring, HC Deb, 21 June 1995, c. 246W landfill of waste, HC Deb, 18 July 1995,

c. 1021 on the health effects of nuclear testing, HC Deb, 20 November 1996, c. 552W on sustainable development, HC Deb, 18 March 1997, on genetically modified organisms, HC Deb, 20 July 2000, c. 256W on the transport of nuclear waste, HC Deb, 3 May 2001, cc. 714–715W on crowd control technologies.

92. The acronym stems from its French title, the Conférence des Organes Specialiseés dans les Affaires Communautaires.

93. HC 51-xxviii, 1995/96, European Legislation Select Committee, Twenty-eighth Report, *Role of National Parliaments in the European Union*, including discussion of COSAC, 18 July 1996.

94. *New Statesman*, 14 August 1998, p. 11.

95. FCO website at: http://www.fco.gov.uk/news/speechtext.asp?4913.

96. HL Paper 48, 2001–02, *A Second Parliamentary Chamber for Europe: an unreal solution to some real problems*, 27 November 2001.

97. Ibid.

98. HL 48, 13 December 2001, 2001–02, at: http://www.publications.parliament.uk/pa/ld200102/ldselect/ldeucom/48/4802.htm#a1.

99. See, for example, HC Deb, 21 June 1999, cc. 267–268W; HC Deb, 5 November 2001, c. 15W.

100. The Home Office Review was published in May 2000 (Deposited paper, 00/820).

101. COM (2001) 428 final, 25 July 2001 at http://europa.eu.int/eur-lex/en/com/cnc/2001/com2001_0428en01.pdf.

102. Government EM, 24 October 2001.

103. ESC, Sixth Report, 14 November 2001. The ESC did not clear the document, requesting further information from the Government.

# 6

# Employment Law and the Social Chapter

*Julia Lourie*

## Introduction: what is the Social Chapter?

There has been a Social Chapter in the Treaty establishing the European Economic Community ever since it was signed in Rome by the Six in March 1957.[1] Although it is called a "social" chapter, it is principally concerned with employment and was inserted because Member States agreed "upon the need to promote improved working conditions and an improved standard of living for workers".[2] The Social Chapter from which John Major obtained an "opt out" at Maastricht in December 1991 was a revised version of this chapter which the Dutch Presidency had hoped would replace the existing chapter. In the face of John Major's refusal to agree the change, the existing chapter remained in the Treaty, but a Protocol containing an "Agreement on Social Policy concluded between the Member States of the European Community with the exception of the United Kingdom" was added to the Treaty. It was this Agreement from which the United Kingdom had an opt-out between 1 November 1993, when the Maastricht Treaty came into force and 1 May 1999 when the Amsterdam Treaty, agreed by Tony Blair in June 1997, came into force.

## Changes agreed at Maastricht, 1991

There were two major differences between the Social Chapter covering the Twelve and the Agreement on Social Policy covering the Eleven.[3] First, the Agreement allowed a wider range of subjects to be decided by Qualified Majority Vote (QMV). Previously the only directives which could be adopted by a qualified majority were those concerned with health and safety at work, brought forward under Article 118A of the pre-Maastricht Social Chapter. Ironically, it was Mrs Thatcher, who, as Prime Minister in 1985 had agreed the Single European Act which amended the Treaty of Rome to allow QMV in this area.[4] The *Working Time Directive*, which the Conservative Government always opposed, was effectively forced upon them because they could not veto a measure brought forward under the health and safety provisions of the Treaty. The Agreement on Social Policy allowed more topics, including "working conditions" and "the information and consultation of workers" to be adopted by QMV. The Conservative Government had been blocking proposals for directives in these areas – notably for European Works Councils, parental leave and equal treatment for part-time and temporary workers – for many years. Without a veto, they feared that these, too, could be forced upon them.

Second, the Agreement on Social Policy introduced a new procedure under which European trade unions and employers, organisations (the "social partners") could negotiate agreements on the areas it covered (health and safety, working conditions, information and consultation, etc.). In practice, the social partners are the European Trade Union Congress (ETUC), the Union of Industries of the European Community (UNICE) and the European Centre for Public Enterprises (CEEP). The Trades Union Congress (TUC) is a member of ETUC and the Confederation of British Industry (CBI) is a member of UNICE. Before introducing any draft legislation, the Commission was to consult the social partners to offer them the opportunity of negotiating a "framework agreement". These agreements could then be adopted as European legislation and made binding on the Member States.[5] If the social partners did not want to negotiate an agreement or if their negotiations were unsuccessful, the Commission could bring forward a draft directive in the traditional way.

### The UK opt-out: a "negotiating triumph"?

John Major held a Commons debate "to gain approval for [the UK's] negotiating stance" before the Maastricht summit.[6] He believed that if the Commons backed his position ("No commitment to a single currency ... No Social Chapter ..."), it would "add authority to [his] rejection of parts of the Treaty".[7] The Commons did back him, by a majority of 101, with only six Conservative MPs voting against.

The opt-out was hailed as a negotiating triumph by Conservative Ministers and MPs. In his statement to the House on his return from Maastricht, John Major argued that it would ensure the United Kingdom's competitive position by protecting it from burdensome labour market regulation.[8] Conservative backbenchers congratulated him on showing "the utmost skill and stamina in keeping us away from the dangerous path towards a centralised Europe",[9] on winning a settlement that "will be welcomed by the overwhelming majority of people in this country",[10] and on "an excellent result for Britain and Europe".[11]

In reply, Neil Kinnock, the Leader of the Opposition, laid down the battlelines which would characterise the Labour party's attack on the Social Chapter opt-out for the rest of the next Parliament: the United Kingdom would be excluded from important decisions on social policy and employment standards; British workers would be denied basic, minimum employment standards; and, contrary to what the Prime Minister said, this would detract from our competitive position.[12]

Despite party support for the opt-out, it became the issue on which the Eurosceptic group of Conservative backbenchers (led by Bill Cash and including Iain Duncan Smith) nearly brought down the Government in July 1993 by voting with the Labour party to defer ratification of the Maastricht Treaty until the United Kingdom agreed to opt back into the Social Chapter.[13] What, then, were the practical effects of the opt-out?

## 1992–97: out of the Social Chapter

### European Works Councils: should Parliament scrutinise Agreement measures?

Once the Maastricht Treaty came into force, the European Commission lost little time in transferring measures, stalled by UK opposition, to the Agreement. A Social Affairs Council on 12 October 1993 (a fortnight before the Treaty came into force) agreed to move consideration of proposals for a *European Works Council Directive* to the Agreement.[14] The social partners failed to reach agreement, so, in April 1994 the Commission issued a *Draft Directive on the establishment of European committees or procedures in Community-scale undertakings and Community-scale groups of undertakings for the purposes of informing and consulting employees.*[15] This applied to undertakings with at least 1000 employees in the Eleven and at least two establishments in different Member States with at least 100 employees each.[16] Such multinational companies would be required to establish machinery for consulting and informing their employees about the progress of the business.

This immediately raised the question of how – and, indeed, whether – the UK Parliament should deal with draft European Community (EC) legislation which did not apply to the United Kingdom. The Conservative Government took the view that such legislation had nothing to do with them, so there was no need for the normal scrutiny procedures to apply. The European Legislation Committee, perhaps more realistically, considered that the Government's attitude was crucial to determining whether proposed legislation was to apply in the United Kingdom or not, and, that, in any case, the Standing Orders required the Government to submit Explanatory Memoranda on proposals brought forward under the Agreement.

Standing Order No. 127 provided that the Committee should examine "European Community Documents" which included:

1. any proposal under the Community Treaties for legislation by the Council of Ministers; and
2. any document which is published for submission to the European Council or the Council of Ministers.

A battle of wills developed between the Committee and the Government.

The Government did deposit the text, but referred only briefly to it in a "Supplementary Explanatory Memorandum" on an earlier (pre opt-out) version of the draft directive. Eric Forth, Minister of State at the Department of Employment, said:

> The Government does not consider acts of the 11 to be Community acts for the purpose of Standing Order 127. The deposit of the text is without prejudice to the discussions on future arrangements on Directives brought forward under the Agreement of the 11 taking place between the Government and the House Authorities.

In its report, the European Legislation Committee disagreed. It had no doubt that the draft European Works Council directive fell within category (2). It was "clear from the face of the document" that it was submitted to the Council of Ministers, and the Protocol on Social Policy specifically authorised the Eleven "to have recourse to the institutions, procedures and mechanisms of the Treaty" for the purposes of taking action under the Agreement. While Explanatory Memoranda on Social Chapter proposals might need to take a different form, they were, nevertheless essential to proper accountability:

> The attitude of the British Government will be crucial in determining whether a proposal is to be taken forward by the 12 or by the 11. It is therefore important that the Scrutiny process should make Ministers directly accountable for their policies in this respect.[17]

The Committee recommended that the proposal should be debated in European Standing Committee B, together with two earlier documents – the Commission's Green Paper on *European Social Policy options for the Union*,[18] and its *Communication concerning the application of the Agreement on Social Policy*.[19] The Committee's reports on these two documents had already questioned the sustainability of the Government's dismissive line that "the operation of the Agreement on Social Policy is not a matter for the United Kingdom Government".[20] Social Chapter directives would be part of the *acquis communautaire*, accepted by any new Member States, making the United Kingdom's isolation yet more acute. There would be pressure from employers and employees in companies with branches in both the United Kingdom and other Member States for the same laws to apply. And there would be concern that the United Kingdom was excluded from drawing up legislation that, at least indirectly, affected its interests.[21]

The Government did not arrange a debate in European Standing Committee and eventually, the Committee recommended that the *European Works Council* proposal, the *Communication on the Agreement on Social Policy* and what had by now become the *White Paper on European Social Policy*, should all be debated on the Floor of the House.[22] The Government was "unfortunately" unable to find time for a debate to be held on the Floor, but it did, eventually, concede a debate in European Standing Committee B.[23] Given the wide scope of the debate, the Government was content to allow the *European*

*Works Council* proposal to be among the matters discussed, but this was still "without prejudice to any future decision about arrangements for scrutinising proposals put forward under the Agreement on Social Policy".[24] The Committee was not happy with the Government's refusal to allow a debate on the floor of the House, but there was little more they could do, and the debate in European Standing Committee B took place on 1 February 1995. This was after the final version of the directive had been adopted at the Social Affairs Council on 22 September 1994.[25]

### Parental leave: social partner framework agreements and democratic accountability

The next measure to be transferred to the Agreement was a proposal on parental leave and leave for urgent family reasons. The UK Government had been blocking draft directives on these topics since 1983. This time the European social partners decided that they would try to negotiate a framework agreement under the new procedure contained in Article 4 of the Agreement. This procedure raises a number of questions for the whole scrutiny process as European legislation is being decided by trade union and employer representatives, rather than elected Government Ministers who are accountable to their national parliaments. Despite the UK opt-out, the TUC and the CBI sent representatives to the negotiations but, as the European Legislation Committee pointed out in relation to the parental leave directive, "they had no vote, though they were given the opportunity to express opinions".[26]

In an Explanatory Memorandum on a European Commission *Communication concerning the development of the social dialogue at Community level*, issued in September 1996, John Taylor, then a Junior Minister at the Department of Trade and Industry (DTI), claimed that this was one of the reasons the Conservative Government had opposed the Agreement on Social Policy. The United Kingdom had:

> opposed the revised social dialogue provisions on the grounds that it is wrong for employers and employees throughout the Community to be bound by centralised agreements reached at a remote European level by bodies which are far from fully representative.[27]

In a debate on the Communication in European Standing Committee, he called the procedure "iniquitous", "undemocratic" and "dangerous". Policy- and law-making was passed "into the hands of European federations of employers and unions". The Council was "unable to amend what emerges from negotiations" and "the European Parliament has no chance to have a go at it at all".[28]

The House of Lords' European Union Select Committee investigated the role of the social partners in some detail in its report on the *EU Social Policy Agenda*, published in November 2000. It too was concerned at their unrepresentative and unaccountable nature. The Lords argued that the structured dialogue of management and labour harked back to the days of the European Coal and Steel Community, precursor of the European Economic Community, which was based on a few major industries – a small number of large employers, and heavily unionised workforces. It was inappropriate in modern Europe with a far greater preponderance of small- and medium-sized enterprises, and far lower rates of trade union membership. The social dialogue was a procedure "little known in the United Kingdom" which ran "counter to the UK's tradition of parliamentary sovereignty".[29]

The social partners were successful in negotiating a framework agreement on parental leave. It was signed by UNICE, ETUC and CEEP in December 1995 and provided that all employees (both men and women) should be entitled to a minimum of three months' unpaid parental leave to enable them to care for their child until a given age of up to eight years. It also required Member States to ensure that workers were entitled to time off work "on grounds of force majeure for urgent family reasons in cases of sickness or accident making the immediate presence of the worker indispensable". The Commission issued a draft directive giving legal force to the framework agreement on 31 January 1996.[30]

The Government did deposit this document with the European Legislation Committee, but, as it had done with the draft directive on European Works Councils, it produced only a brief Supplementary Explanatory Memorandum, claiming that the agreement followed on from earlier proposals discussed under the Social Chapter of the main Treaty covering all Member States. The Memorandum asserted that "employers in the UK will be under no obligation to grant parental leave or time off for family reasons" and that depositing the text was "without prejudice to any future arrangements for handling of proposals brought forward under the Social Agreement which may be agreed between the Government and the House authorities".[31]

The European Legislation Committee disputed this interpretation, arguing that the provisions of the framework agreement were very different from the earlier proposals, that the draft directive was a new document with a new number, and that they were certain of their right to scrutinise documents issued under the Agreement on Social Policy under Standing Order No 127.[32] They asked to be sent the final version of the directive with an accompanying explanatory memorandum when it was adopted.

The Conservative Government continued its policy of distancing itself from everything to do with the Agreement on Social Policy. Although the directive was adopted on 3 June 1996, it did not send the Committee a copy until six months later. This provoked the Committee to issue a stern rebuke, demanding an explanation for the delay and comments on the changes.[33] The Committee was sceptical of the Minister's explanation that:

> Since the UK was not involved in the adoption procedure for this directive there was no provision for us to be notified of publication in the OJ of the formal text and unfortunately due to an oversight in this instance, it only recently came to the attention of officials that the directive had already been published.[34]

But, as the directive had long been adopted and as the United Kingdom had no locus in its negotiation, there was very little point in pursuing the matter.

### Burden of proof and part-time work

Two other measures which had made little progress under the pre-Maastricht Social Chapter were moved to the Agreement on Social Policy while the Conservative party was in power in the United Kingdom. These were the proposals for a directive changing the burden of proof in sex discrimination cases and for a directive on part-time work. The former was published as a draft directive in July 1996 and considered by the European Legislation Committee in December 1996. As with the proposals on European Works Councils and parental leave, the Government submitted only a brief Memorandum, claiming that it was supplementary to earlier consideration of a similar pre-opt-out draft directive. Again, the Committee asserted its right to scrutinise the proposal and asked to be kept informed.[35] The social partners decided to negotiate a framework agreement on equal treatment for part-time workers. This was agreed and incorporated in a draft directive after Labour had won the May 1997 General Election. It was, therefore, the subject of friendlier and fuller, though rather rushed, Explanatory Memoranda.

## Working time directive: employment measures from which we had no opt-out

European Works Councils, parental leave, the burden of proof and part-time workers were not the only items of European "social" legislation confronting the Conservative administration of 1992–97. They were involved in an unsuccessful challenge to the *Working Time Directive* adopted on 23 November 1993 under Article 118A of the main Treaty Social Chapter. They implemented the *Pregnant Workers Directive*, adopted on 19 October 1992, also under Article 118A. And they started the process of implementing the *Young Workers Directive*, adopted on 22 June 1994, again under Article 118A. All these measures had started their passage through the European legislative waters before the Maastricht Treaty came into force, so use of the Agreement on Social Policy was not considered. In any case, they were all based on Article 118A as health and safety measures. The United Kingdom could not veto them as they were subject to QMV.

The *Working Time Directive* in particular had enormous implications for UK employment law. It required Member States to place a limit of 48 hours on the working week, to ensure that workers had at least one day's rest a week and 11 hours' rest a day, and to introduce a right to four weeks' paid holiday a year. While most other Member States already regulated working time, these were dramatic changes for the deregulated labour market of the United Kingdom. The Conservative Government challenged the directive in the European Court of Justice (ECJ), arguing that it was not a genuine health and safety measure and so should not have been brought forward under Article 118A, with its QMV procedure.

However, on 12 November 1996 the ECJ ruled that Article 118A was the correct Treaty base.[36] This was a mere 11 days before Member States were supposed to have implemented the Directive. The Court ruling dominated Prime Minister's Question Time that day and was the subject of an oral statement by Ian Lang, the Secretary of State for Trade and Industry. The Government considered the ruling a betrayal of the spirit of the Social Chapter opt-out: the Commission would be able to argue that almost any employment measures were "health and safety" measures, which could not be vetoed by one country. John Major announced that he would table Treaty amendments at the Intergovernmental Conference (IGC): if they were not accepted, there would be "no end" to the conference. Tony Blair noted that the conference would be "conveniently" after the election and predicted the Government would "talk tough" but "cave in".[37]

In the event, of course, it was Tony Blair, not John Major, who was Prime Minister when the IGC ended in June 1997. The Conservative Government had delayed implementation of the *Working Time Directive* for so long that it was, in any case, left to the Labour Government to implement it. To do so, they used the power conferred by section 2(2) of the *European Communities Act 1972* to implement EC directives by secondary rather than primary legislation. Secondary legislation is normally only debated for an hour and a half, usually in the delegated legislation committee, rather than on the floor of the House, and it cannot be amended. This generated many complaints from MPs who felt that there was insufficient opportunity for Parliamentary scrutiny – particularly as the *Working Time Regulations 1998* were laid before Parliament the day before it rose for the summer recess and came into operation before it returned.[38] When the regulations were eventually debated, Ian Bruce, a Conservative backbencher was "amazed" to discover there was so little time to debate "43 clauses and two schedules of what would constitute a major Bill" and asked whether there was no way in which the House could be protected against this.[39] Unfortunately, the House's main opportunity to influence the content of the Regulations had passed more than seven years earlier when the draft directive was debated – along with three other documents – in European Standing Committee B.[40]

## 1997–2001: back in the Social Chapter

The Labour party had made it clear in Opposition that it would sign the Social Chapter and accept any measures already adopted under its auspices, if returned to power. Their manifesto for the May 1997 General Election promised:

Britain to sign the Social Chapter. An 'empty chair' at the negotiating table is disastrous for Britain. ... We will use our participation to promote employability and flexibility, not high social costs.[41]

The Conservative manifesto promised to preserve – and even extend – the opt-out:

We will insist that any new Treaty recognises that our opt-out from the Social Chapter enables Britain to be exempt from the Working Time Directive, and prevents any abuse of our opt-out.[42]

Labour won the election on 1 May 1997 and returned to power with a majority so large that there was no doubt about their ability to push through any legislation needed to overturn the UK opt-out. One of Tony Blair's first actions as Prime Minister was to appoint Doug Henderson as Minister for Europe and send him to the IGC to announce that the United Kingdom wished to end the opt-out.[43] The other Member States were delighted and did all they could to facilitate the change.

However, even at this early stage of the New Labour Government, there was a noticeable cooling of enthusiasm for the Social Chapter and its potentially burdensome labour legislation. In his statement to the House on the Amsterdam summit, Tony Blair referred only obliquely to the opt-in:

We have prevented the extension of qualified majority voting in areas where it might cause damage. Others wanted to extend QMV in the social chapter, which would have affected our companies even if we had not been party to the chapter. Because we were in it, we were able to stop that.[44]

Mr Blair preferred to concentrate on the new Employment Chapter which "recognises the importance of job creation and sets member states and the Community the task of promoting flexible labour markets, and education and skills".[45]

Although the Conservatives continued to castigate the Government for signing the Social Chapter, most accepted it as a *fait accompli*. They did put down an amendment on the Social Chapter to the *European Communities (Amendment) Bill 1997–98* (which was required to ratify the Treaty of Amsterdam), but it only called for a half-yearly report from the Government on the legislative and employment implications of the chapter for the United Kingdom.[46] The amendment was resoundingly defeated by 332 votes to 126. During the debate, a Labour backbencher, Bill Rammell, argued that "the key issue of the social chapter was fundamentally and conclusively resolved in the general election".[47] And the Conservative who followed him, Desmond Swayne, accepted that "the British people were warned and . . . gave the Government a mandate".[48]

In practice, the way in which the United Kingdom opted back into the Social Chapter was that the Amsterdam Treaty replaced the old "Social Chapter" with a new version which replicated the Agreement on Social Policy, with one or two minor changes. The Social Chapter was "repatriated" to the main Treaty establishing the European Community (TEC) and so covered all Member States, including the United Kingdom. The Social Chapter can now be found in Articles 136–145 of the TEC. However, as it would be nearly two years before the Treaty of Amsterdam came into force, the Member States agreed at Amsterdam that the United Kingdom could participate fully in the Agreement on Social Policy before then.[49]

It was also agreed at the Budget Council on 24 July 1997 that the measures already adopted under the Agreement on Social Policy, and any more which might be adopted before the Amsterdam Treaty came into force, would be extended to the United Kingdom by an Article 100 Directive. Article 100 directives need the unanimous support of all Member States and concern provisions which "directly affect the establishment or functioning of the common market".

### Burden of proof: contrasting approaches of Labour and Conservative administrations

The first time the "empty chair" was filled was for discussion of the *Draft Directive on the burden of proof in cases of discrimination based on sex* which had already made considerable progress under the Agreement on Social Policy. The General Election, the change of Government, the change of policy and the establishment of new Select Committees made it difficult for the House's scrutiny procedures to keep up with what was happening in Brussels. Andrew Smith, the Labour Minister for Employment, submitted an Explanatory Memorandum on this *Draft Directive* to the European Legislation Committee on 23 June

1997 and wrote to them on 8 July 1997 explaining that the Secretary of State had felt it necessary to support political agreement on a common position on the text at the Social Affairs Council on 27 June 1997, even though the document had not cleared scrutiny. This was because the Council had accepted two amendments proposed by the United Kingdom which ensured that the directive would fully reflect existing UK practice. Had he sought a postponement, there was "a serious risk that our negotiating objectives would [have been] lost".[50]

The Committee seemed to accept the Minister's explanation. It did, however, point out that although the draft directive was not very different from the pre-Agreement on Social Policy version opposed by the Conservatives, the assessment of its impact on the United Kingdom made by the Labour Minister was very different from that of his Conservative predecessor. Eric Forth, the Conservative Minister, had said that the Government was opposed to a reversal of the burden of proof where a presumption of discrimination is established "as a matter of principle" and that the proposal was "contrary to the basic rule in civil cases that 'the asserter must prove' ". He had also said that the "Directive could be expected to lead to an increase in United Kingdom employers' costs in the range of £4.95 million to £5.53 million."[51] (The Conservative Government had even decided to grant a debate on the Floor of the House on the proposal,[52] although the European Legislation Committee had only recommended it for debate in European Standing Committee.)[53] Andrew Smith, however, assured the Committee that "informed legal opinion is that the Directive would make very little difference to the way in which sex discrimination cases are decided in the UK in practice" and that the financial implications would be "very few".[54] The Committee eventually cleared this directive without debate because it felt that the issues had already been fully aired in the debates on the earlier versions.[55]

### Part-time work, European Works Councils and parental leave: making up for lost time?

On 6 June 1997, the social partners had signed a framework agreement on part-time work and this was incorporated into a draft directive applying to the Fourteen published on 23 July 1997.[56] Shortly after this, the first two Article 100 directives extending the European Works Council and parental leave directives to the United Kingdom were published in draft in October 1997.[57] The European

Legislation Committee reported on all three of these draft directives on 12 November 1997.

Not surprisingly, the Explanatory Memoranda submitted by the Labour Minister, Ian McCartney, were much more positive than those of his Conservative predecessors. They carried on the theme of support for minimum standards, while retaining flexibility. The part-time workers proposal contributed to "labour market flexibility". The parental leave proposal supported the key Government aim of helping "people to balance the demands of work and family life". And the European Works Council proposal accorded with the Government's view that "informing and consulting employees is an essential element of the good management of companies which can help to improve their economic performance".[58]

The Committee recommended all three draft directives for debate in European Standing Committee B before the December Social Affairs Council at which they were likely to be adopted. The debate took place on 3 December 1997 and bore all the hallmarks of a rushed job. David MacLean, a Conservative MP, complained that by debating all three proposals together there would be insufficient time to consider any properly. He queried the need for the Standing Committee or the Government to be "slavishly bound" by the Select Committee's recommendation.[59] Certainly, in the question and answer session it was often not clear which measure was under discussion. At one stage, the Minister appeared to be discussing an entirely separate proposal to extend the *Working Time Directive* to sectors excluded from it and the Conservative spokeswoman seemed to be discussing proposals which had not yet even been published for national works councils.

To a certain extent the debate was academic as the directives had already been agreed under the Agreement on Social Policy without any formal input from the UK Government or Parliament. There might have been some sympathy with the views expressed by John Wilkinson, an arch Eurosceptic Conservative, about the impotence of the UK Parliament in the face of European legislation in general:

Hon Members are sent to the House of Commons...to pass appropriate legislation that will stand the test of time. That is why I was foolhardy enough to suggest that these three important social employment directives merited rather more than two and a half hours cursory – indeed illusory – scrutiny in this European Standing Committee. . . .

[There is no point in suggesting an amendment as . . .] the chances of Her Majesty's Government implementing it at the Social Affairs council would be relatively small, and they could be outvoted. To put forward amendments would be like whistling in the wind and I am not prepared to indulge myself with such illusions.[60]

## Social partner framework agreements: the Labour view

However, the debate did give the Minister, Ian McCartney, an opportunity to set out the Labour Government's approach to the new Social Chapter and to endorse the negotiation of framework agreements as an example of "partnership in action". In his view, the "legislative technicalities" in the draft directive agreed in the Council of Ministers were unimportant compared with the attached "practical agreements" reached through partnership. Because employers and employees had drafted the provisions, they would be "signed up" to them. The agreements still left room for manoeuvre to suit national conditions:

In implementing them, we have the opportunity to decide many details: up to what age of child should parental leave be taken; should conditions apply to taking urgent family leave; and how can a business find an equivalent full timer with whom to compare the part-time worker.[61]

It is true that the framework agreements do allow considerable latitude for Member States to make their own decisions. The United Kingdom, for example, decided to limit parental leave to parents of children under five and to those with a minimum of one year's service. It could not, though, have limited the right to people with a minimum of two years' service. And its restriction to children born on or after 15 December 1999 was later overturned after the TUC challenged its compatibility with the EC Directive.[62]

## Informing and consulting workers: the consequences of opting back in

During the Labour administration of 1997–2001, several more legislative proposals were brought forward under or transferred to the new Social Chapter:

- the "horizontal directive" extending the *Working Time Directive* to the excluded sectors, and associated directives on the working time of mobile workers in road transport, seafarers and mobile workers in civil aviation;
- a directive amending the 1976 directive on equal treatment for men and women in employment;
- a directive amending the 1980 directive on protection of employees in the event of the insolvency of their employer;
- a fixed-term work directive; and
- a directive on a general framework for informing and consulting employees.

The first three were designed to update and improve existing EU legislation covering all Member States. The last two, though, were introducing legislation in new areas, and are precisely the sort of measures which would not have applied to the United Kingdom had the Conservative Government been returned at the May 1997 election, and had it successfully maintained its "social chapter opt-out".

Shortly after Labour's election victory, the European Commission started consulting the social partners about proposals for national works councils. Although the Labour Government had embraced the directive on European Works Councils, it had made it clear from the beginning that it was opposed to European legislation requiring companies with employees in only one Member State to establish machinery for informing and consulting their employees at national level.[63] William Hague challenged Tony Blair about his power to stop this at Prime Minister's Question Time on 5 November 1997:

*Mr Hague*: . . . Now that he has signed away our veto by signing up to the social chapter, can he . . . confirm that there may be nothing that he can do to stop that?

*The Prime Minister*: No. We have already made our position clear; we do not believe that such extensions are sensible. It is simply a Commission proposal at present. . . .[64]

The social partners – and in particular UNICE, the employers' organisation – decided against negotiating a framework agreement on this issue and, in November 1998, the European Commission issued a *Draft Directive establishing a general framework for informing and consulting employees in the European Community*.[65] Under this, undertakings with

50 or more employees in just one Member State would be required to set up arrangements for informing and consulting employees on recent and reasonably foreseeable developments (including possible job losses or transfers to other companies). The European Scrutiny Committee held an evidence session on this proposal on 7 July 1999 and went on to clear it.[66] However, when the French Presidency produced a revised version in October 2000, the Committee recommended it for debate in European Standing Committee C.[67]

This debate, held on 28 February 2001, was remarkable for the fact that the Labour Government got more support from the Opposition for its policy regarding the draft directive than it did from its own backbenchers. Alan Johnson, the Minister for Competitiveness, said the Government thought it "desirable to inform and consult employees", but was "not convinced that a constructive dialogue between management and employees is best achieved through statutory requirements and the sanctions and penalties that would flow from a directive".

Nick Gibb, speaking for the Conservatives, was "delighted to hear the Minister's statement" and assured him that "the Opposition fully agree with the Government's approach". Dr Stephen Ladyman, elected as Labour MP for South Thanet in May 1997, countered that, while the Opposition might be satisfied with the Government's position, he was not so sure that Labour Members would be:

> if no one sets down in statute the minimum requirements for information to be given to employees, what are the chances of building partnerships in companies where employers have little respect for their employees?

The debate also suggested that some of the new Members had not fully grasped the significance of the Social Chapter opt-out. Neither Nick Gibb nor Dr Ladyman appeared to appreciate that although QMV was applied to information and consultation at Maastricht, it was only applied in the case of measures brought forward under the Agreement on Social Policy. A Conservative Government would not have been bound by the directive because it would have maintained the opt-out.[68]

Labour backbench uneasiness about the Government's hostility to the measure surfaced outside the formal scrutiny process as well – for example, in a Westminster Hall debate initiated by Tony Lloyd on 31 January 2001 and in Kelvin Hopkins' *Employee Consultation Rights Bill* introduced on 6 April 2001. In the event, William Hague's predictions proved correct and the directive was more or less forced upon the United Kingdom after the 2001 General Election. The Government was able to extract a few concessions, notably phased implementation for those countries (the UK and Ireland) which did not already have a "general, permanent and statutory system of information and consultation of employees", but such a system would not being introduced in the United Kingdom from 2005 if the Labour Government had not signed the Social Chapter.

The history of the information and consultation directive also illustrates the point that the European Parliament is in a stronger position to influence European directives than national parliaments – particularly since the co-decision procedure was introduced in the Maastricht Treaty. Co-decision was extended to Social Chapter measures by the Treaty of Amsterdam. At every opportunity, the European Parliament put forward amendments designed to strengthen the position of workers. Eventually, the draft directive went to a Conciliation Committee, which, amongst other things, accepted the European Parliament's proposals for reducing the transitional period for the United Kingdom and Ireland agreed by the Council.[69]

### Fixed-term work: framework agreements revisited

In March 1999, the social partners, UNICE, ETUC and CEEP, concluded a *Framework Agreement on Fixed Term Work*. This provided that workers on fixed-term contracts should receive no less favourable treatment than comparable workers on indefinite contracts and required Member States to take specified measures to prevent the abuse arising from the use of successive fixed-term contracts. The European Commission issued a draft directive giving legal force to the agreement on 28 April 1999.[70] The European Scrutiny Committee considered the draft directive in a report published on 16 June 1999 and in a brief follow-up report on 7 July 1999.[71]

Scrutiny of draft directives implementing framework agreements is necessarily rather limited as Ministers are not in a position to influence the text agreed by the social partners. Ian McCartney, the Minister responsible, was at pains to stress in his Explanatory Memorandum, that Member States had sought "clarification of the social partners' intentions and some of the content of the framework agreement". The United Kingdom had "secured an important point when the social partners confirmed that they did not intend the agreement to apply to combatant personnel in the armed forces, as these are not represented by the social partners". This rather begs the question of precisely who is represented by the social partners. Although the Committee considered the draft directive politically important, it did not recommend it for debate. The first substantial Parliamentary discussion of the directive's provisions came during the debates on the *Employment Bill 2001–02*[72] – an example of the use of primary legislation to implement an EC Directive.

The role of the European Parliament in relation to social partner framework agreements is equally limited. It only considers the draft directive implementing the agreement, not the agreement itself, and the co-decision procedures do not apply to them.[73]

### Article 13 directives on discrimination in employment: the impact of lobbies

Despite the importance of the Social Chapter directives for UK employment law, it is quite possible that, of all the directives adopted between 1997 and 2001, the most significant will be the one adopted under a completely different part of the Treaty – Article 13. This Article was inserted by the Treaty of Amsterdam and allows the Council, acting unanimously, to "take appropriate action to combat discrimination based on sex, racial or ethnic origin, religion or belief, disability, age or sexual orientation".

In November 1999, only seven months after the Treaty of Amsterdam came into force, the European Commission introduced a package of measures designed to combat discrimination. The package included a *Draft Directive establishing a general framework for equal treatment in employment and occupation*,[74] and a *Draft Directive implementing the principle of equal treatment between persons irrespective of racial or ethnic origin*.[75] The package was, in part, a response to the success of Jorg Haider's far-right Freedom Party in Austria's General Election in October 1999, and related fears about the growth of xenophobia and racism in Europe. Perhaps because of the sense of urgency this generated, the package completed its European stages remarkably quickly – even though unanimity was required. The race directive was adopted on 29 June 2000,[76] and the employment directive on 27 November 2000.[77]

The employment directive outlaws discrimination in employment on the grounds of religion or belief, disability, age and sexual orientation. As the United Kingdom currently has no laws on discrimination in any of these areas except disability, its potential impact in this country is huge. The provisions on age discrimination, for example, are likely to mean that compulsory retirement ages are outlawed.

Although the timescale was short, there were substantial reports from the Scrutiny Committee,[78] and the House of Lords European Union Select Committee,[79] and debates in both Houses.[80] The reports provided a thorough discussion of the implications of the directives. The debates were somewhat skewed towards discussing the implications of the ban on religious discrimination in employment for Church organisations. This was the result of a well-organised lobby by the Church and linked organisations with a religious ethos, concerned that they would lose their right to employ only staff who shared their beliefs.

Members of Parliament in particular, were deluged with constituency correspondence on this aspect. Tessa Jowell, Minister for Equal Opportunities, was pressed to make representations to the EU on the issue when she appeared before European Standing Committee C. She replied that the "enormous amount of correspondence I have passed on to the Commission shows that the matter is of great public concern". Although the Government intended to ensure that the existing provisions of the *School Standards and Framework Act 1998*, under which religious schools were able to advertise for teachers of a particular faith, could be retained, Mrs Jowell made it clear they had no intention of providing a "cover for bigotry".

It is possible that this lobby, and its reflection in Parliament, did have an impact on the final form of the directive as the draft was amended to allow Member States to maintain laws already in place that permitted religious organisations to discriminate on religious grounds where the ethos of the organisation meant that a person's religion becomes a genuine, legitimate and justified occupational requirement. However, other changes to the draft, made at a six-hour negotiating session in the Council of Ministers on 17 October 2000, were clearly not influenced by Parliament as Parliament did not even know they were on the Government's negotiating agenda. These last minute changes included the exemption of the armed forces from the provisions on age and disability and an exemption for police and teachers in Northern Ireland from the religious discrimination provisions.

The House of Lords was particularly critical of the Government's failure to keep Parliament informed and devoted a significant part of its post-adoption report on the *EU Framework Directive on Discrimination* to the failings of the scrutiny process leading up to its adoption. Mrs Jowell argued that the French presidency's desire to reach political agreement on 17 October 2000 had offered the Government a unique opportunity to secure their "bottom lines". Had they delayed to submit revised proposals to Parliament, the moment would have passed. She considered that the scrutiny process should contain "sufficient freedom…to combine proper accountability to Parliament with negotiating the best deal available".[81] The Lords, though, felt that any conflict between "proper accountability to Parliament" and "negotiating the best deal available" should be resolved in favour of the former.[82]

## Conclusion

European employment legislation in the period 1992–2001 presented some new challenges to the scrutiny process. First, there was the question of whether the normal scrutiny procedures should be applied to Social Chapter measures proposed during the period of the UK's opt-out. The European Legislation Committee's persistence maintained a minimal degree of scrutiny, but the question was only really resolved by the UK opting back in. The hasty scrutiny necessitated by the application of directives adopted before 1997 to the United Kingdom after 1997 meant that Parliament's scrutiny of the European Works Council, parental leave, part-time work and burden of proof directives was less thorough than it might have been and exposed a degree of ignorance which might have been avoided had the UK never opted out.

Second, the negotiation of framework agreements by the social partners which were adopted as they stood as binding European legislation, raised questions of democratic accountability both at national and European level. Ministers had no formal role in determining the content of the parental leave, part-time work and fixed-term work directives, and such scrutiny as there was took place at a time when the content had been decided. Even if Parliamentary scrutiny had persuaded Ministers of desirable changes, they were not in a position to argue for them. These questions are still outstanding.

Finally – a not so new challenge – the experience of the Conservative Government with the *Working Time Directive* and the Labour Government with the information and consultation directive illustrates the relative impotence of national governments in the face of a determined Europe. Where QMV is involved, national governments might be able to delay and tinker with legislation they oppose, but they rarely succeed in blocking it altogether. The influence of Parliament is even more remote.

## Notes

1. Chapter 1 ("Social Provisions") of Title III ("Social Policy").
2. Article 117, Treaty of Rome.
3. When Austria, Sweden and Finland joined the European Union in January 1995, the Twelve became the Fifteen and the Eleven, the Fourteen.
4. It introduced Article 118A.
5. Articles 3 and 4 of the Agreement on Social Policy.
6. HC Deb, 20 November 1991, cc. 279–280.
7. John Major, *The Autobiography*, 1999, p. 274.
8. HC Deb, 11 December 1991, c. 861.
9. David Howell, c. 865.
10. Sir Norman Fowler, c. 867.
11. Cranley Onslow, c. 867.
12. Ibid., c. 863.
13. See Richard Ware, *Westminster and Europe*, Chapter 11.
14. European Legislation Committee, HC 79-xxxviii, 1992–93, 27 October 1993, para. 9.3.
15. COM (94)134.
16. Later increased to 150.
17. HC 48-xx, 1993–94, 25 May 1994.
18. COM (93)551.
19. COM (93)600.
20. Eric Forth, quoted in the European Legislation Committee's report on the *Agreement on Social Policy*, HC 48-vii, 1993–94, 9 February 1994.
21. Ibid. The Report lists eight principal issues raised by the opt-out.
22. HC 48-xxvi, 1993–94, 19 October 1994.
23. Letter from the Leader of the House to the Chairman of the Committee, dated 17 January 1995, and reproduced in HC 70-iv, 1994–95, 18 January 1995.
24. Ibid.
25. Dir 94/45/EC.
26. HC 155-vi, 1997–98, 12 November 1997.

27. European Legislation Committee, HC 36-ii, 1996/97, 6 November 1996, para. 6.7.
28. European Standing Committee B, 18 December 1996, cc. 3, 5.
29. Twentieth Report, 1999–2000, HL 128, para. 71.
30. COM (1996) 0026.
31. HC 51-xix, 1995–96, 15 May 1996.
32. Ibid.
33. HC 36-xii, 1996–97, 5 February 1997.
34. HC 36-xvi, 1996–97, 5 March 1997.
35. HC 36-v, 1996–97, 4 December 1996.
36. Case C-84/94, *United Kingdom of Great Britain and Northern Ireland* v. *Council of the European Union*, 12 November 1996.
37. HC Deb, 12 November 1996, c. 152.
38. SI 1998/1833. The regulations were laid on 30 July 1998, came into force on 1 October 1998 and were debated on 27 October 1998.
39. HC Deb, 27 October 1998, c. 213.
40. 20 March 1991.
41. *New Labour because Britain deserves better*, p. 37.
42. *You can only be sure with the Conservatives*, p. 46.
43. *Western Europe Reuter Textline*, 5 May 1997, "EC lawyers study British Government's Social Chapter move"; "First steps taken towards social chapter", *Financial Times*, 6 May 1997.
44. HC Deb, 18 June 1997, c. 313.
45. Ibid., c. 314.
46. HC Deb, 2 and 3 December 1997, cc. 248–256, 396–443.
47. HC Deb, 3 December 1997, c. 425.
48. Ibid., cc. 425–426.
49. Presidency Conclusions following the Amsterdam Summit, 16 and 17 June 1997.
50. HC 155-ii, 1997–98, 22 July 1997.
51. HC 48-v, 1993–94, 26 January 1994.
52. HC Deb, 9 May 1994, cc. 100–126.
53. HC 48-v, 1993–94, 26 January 1994.
54. HC 155-ii, 1997–98, 22 July 1997.
55. HC 155-ix, 1997–98, 3 December 1997.
56. COM (1997) 0392.
57. COM (97) 457 Parts A and B.
58. HC 155-vi, 1997–98, 12 November 1997.
59. European Standing Committee B, 3 December 1997, c. 2.
60. Ibid., c. 30.
61. Ibid., c. 41.
62. TUC press notice, 30 April 2001, *Government in "total climbdown" over parental leave*; and *Maternity and Parental Leave (Amendment) Regulations 2001* SI 2001/4010.
63. See, for example, "Blair on EU collision course", *Financial Times*, 5 June 1997.
64. HC Deb, 5 November 1997, cc. 306–307.

65. COM (98) 612.
66. HC 34-xxvii, 1998–99, 21 July 1999.
67. HC 23-xxx, 1999–2000, 22 November 2000.
68. See, for example, Debate in European Standing Committee C, 28 February 2001, cc. 8, 14.
69. The Conciliation Committee was held on 17 December 2001.
70. COM (99) 203.
71. HC 34-xxii, xxv, 1998/99.
72. SC Deb (F), 22 January 2002, cc. 531–558.
73. Framework agreements are now covered by Article 139 of the Treaty, as amended at Amsterdam.
74. COM (99) 565.
75. COM (99) 566.
76. Dir 2000/43/EC.
77. Dir 2000/78/EC.
78. HC 23-vii, xix, xxiv, xxix, 1999–2000; HC 581, 1999–2000, HC 28-v, 2000–01.
79. Ninth Report, 1999–2000, HL 68; Fourth Report 2000–01, HL 13.
80. European Standing Committee C, 24 July 2000; HL Deb, 30 June 2000, cc. 1177–1241.
81. HL 13, 2000–01, 19 December 2000, para. 25.
82. Ibid., para. 29.

# 7
# Westminster, EMU, and the Euro

*Philip Giddings*

> Our debates on ... the European Union are like intermittent
> meetings of the Sealed Knot society, fighting the battles of
> 1972, 1975, enlargement, the euro, the Maastricht treaty
> and so on. Sometimes we swap uniforms. Sometimes each
> side stands on its head and fights on the opposite side to the
> one on which it was fighting just a few years ago.
>
> Austin Mitchell, MP, HC Deb, 23 November 2000, c. 501

## Setting the scene

Economic and Monetary Union (EMU) has long been a highly controversial issue in British politics. Although complex and technical, it
is also profoundly political and, by common consent, of major constitutional significance. It led to the resignations of two of the most
senior ministers of the 1987–90 Government (Nigel Lawson and
Geoffrey Howe) which contributed significantly to the fall from
office of Prime Minister Margaret Thatcher. It plagued the Government of John Major, creating divisions which contributed substantially to its overwhelming defeat in the 1997 General Election. And
since then it has frequently been reported as a source of tension
between Prime Minister, Tony Blair, his Chancellor, Gordon Brown,
and other leading members of his Cabinet.

For all its complexities, EMU has been high politics, on which the
fate of governments can depend. That combination of complexity
and high politics is the context in which the work of Parliament
has to be assessed. In this chapter we shall therefore first recount the

evolution of policy with regard to EMU and then, in the section 'The Westminster Parliament and the Euro, 1993–2001', examine the way in which the UK Parliament has dealt with EMU and related issues in the period between 1993 and the General Election of 2001.

## The evolution of policy

### From Rome to Maastricht

Economic and Monetary Union is part of a long-running saga, the evolution of the European Community/Union itself. The Treaty of Rome makes no direct reference to monetary union or a single currency, but by the end of the 1960s the Six could see the advantages which might be obtained from currency co-ordination. When the Werner Group's recommendations were adopted in 1971 – before the United Kingdom joined the Community but endorsed by it – commitment to EMU, the concept of three stages, and the language of 'total . . . irreversible . . . irrevocable' became established European Community objectives. From 1971 onwards the question was not *whether* there should be a European single currency but *how*.

First voluntary co-ordination and then a system of limited currency variations (the Snake) failed to yield the desired stability. Dissatisfaction with the Snake's successor, the exchange rate mechanism (ERM), led to the setting up of the Delors Committee whose Report proposing EMU with a single currency formed the basis of the Commission's proposals for the Maastricht Inter-governmental Conference (IGC). The Delors Report was, however, opposed 'root and branch' by the then British Prime Minister, Margaret Thatcher, who issued her own 'unilateral declaration' that there was 'no automaticity about the move to nor the timing or content of Stage 2'.[1] Here lay the battle lines of British politics not only with respect to the Maastricht Treaty but also for the next decade and more.

The so-called 'opt-out' protocol to the Maastricht Treaty (Box 7.1) is fundamental to understanding the political and parliamentary debates which have raged around the single currency and the issue of the United Kingdom's adoption of it. It is important to underline that the protocol provides for the United Kingdom to opt-in as well as to opt-out: it is concerned with how the United Kingdom might come to participate in Stage 3 of EMU should it decide to do so. The

---

*Box 7.1    The Treaty on European Union – provisions of the British protocol*

- The United Kingdom may notify its intention whether to participate in a collective move to Stage 3.
- If the United Kingdom decides not to participate in the move to Stage 3, then it 'shall retain its powers in the field of monetary policy according to national law' and not be subject to the disciplines imposed by the treaty on the participating Member States. Correspondingly, the United Kingdom is excluded from the processes of decision-making in regard to monetary policy, including specifically the appointment of the President, Vice-President and other members of the European Central Bank (ECB).
- The United Kingdom may change its notification (i.e. signify its desire to participate in Stage 3) at any time after the beginning of that stage. In that case, the United Kingdam has the right to move to that stage provided only that it satisfies the convergence criteria set out in the treaty for the collective move to Stage 3.

---

protocol recognises that the United Kingdom 'shall not be obliged or committed to move to the third stage of EMU without a separate decision to do so by its government and Parliament'. That provision in itself has created the fulcrum for the role of the Westminster Parliament in subsequent debate and decision-making in the United Kingdom. In the event, the United Kingdom has continued to exercise its right not to participate in Stage 3 of EMU. But neither the current Labour Government nor its predecessor ruled out the possibility that it might decide to participate at some time in the future. When, and how, such a decision might be taken, have provided the fuel for the continuing UK domestic debate on EMU in general and the single currency in particular since the Treaty of European Union (TEU) was ratified in 1993.

### The Major Government and the coming Euro

Between the successful conclusion of the European Council at Maastricht in December 1991 and the completion of the treaty ratification process, the ERM in general, and the United Kingdom's relationship with it in particular, ran into very heavy water. At the height of the storm in September 1992 the United Kingdom was forced out of the ERM by intense currency speculation, notwithstanding several unprecedented hikes in interest rates on the same day. The Conservative Party's reputation with the electorate for economic competence has still not recovered from that disaster.[2] The fact that the United Kingdom was not able to maintain its position within ERM has strongly coloured British perceptions of the EMU ever since.

Neither the difficulties with the ERM nor the problems encountered in several states obtaining ratification of the Maastricht Treaty deterred the EU from continuing the progress towards monetary union. Stage 2 began as scheduled on 1 January 1994 and from that point on preparation for Stage 3, and the introduction of the single currency on 1 January 1999, marched steadily forward.

In the immediate post-Maastricht period it looked as if only a few of the Member States would meet all four of the convergence tests required by the TEU (Box 7.2). But notwithstanding the concerns about convergence and the uncertainties about how many Member States would actually choose and be able to proceed to Stage 3 on the

---

*Box 7.2   The Treaty on European Union – convergence criteria*

Four criteria are specified for movement to Stage 3:

1.  price stability, i.e. a rate of inflation which is close to that of the three best performing Member States;
2.  a sustainable government financial position, i.e. no excessive budget deficit as defined by the Treaty;
3.  exchange rate stability, i.e. observing the normal fluctuation margins of the ERM for at least two years, without devaluing against any other Member State currency; and
4.  durability of convergence achieved by the Member State and of its participation in the ERM, as reflected in long-term interest rate level.

*Source*: TEU, Article 109j.

appointed date, preparations for that stage and the introduction of the single currency continued apace.

If in Brussels Stage 2 was a 'waiting room'[3] with mounting anticipation of a momentous journey about to begin, in the UK deepening hostility to the whole concept within sections of the Conservative Party played havoc with the already gloomy political prospects of John Major's Government. In November and December 1996 there were a series of rows within the Cabinet and the Parliamentary Party as the Prime Minister sought to maintain a balance between his (more) pro-European Chancellor and Deputy Prime Minister and the Euro-sceptics.[4] On 19 December the Cabinet was almost equally divided on whether to adopt a 'wait and see' position on the single currency or reject it outright. The outcome was an uneasy compromise around a 'when the time is right' formula. Nevertheless, an increasing number of leading Conservatives made public their opposition to entry in principle, some linking this with the need for a referendum – an issue that was given added salience by the Referendum Party's General Election campaign.

Although the United Kingdom had left the ERM, and the Government had made clear that it was likely to exercise the opt-out negotiated at Maastricht, the United Kingdom was as fully involved as other Member States in the debates and decisions about the procedural and institutional arrangements for EMU. And UK participation in this work provided the opportunity for a newly elected Parliament and a new Government with a substantial majority to exercise such influence as it thought it had.

### New Labour and the coming Euro: 1997–2001

The May 1997 General Election brought to power a Labour Government with a very large majority and an apparently more positive and united stance on the Euro. One of its first actions, at the Amsterdam Summit, was to reverse the Major Government's 'opt-out' from the Social Chapter (see Chapter 6) and agree to the 'Stability and Growth Pact'. However, on the single currency itself, the new Government's position was more circumspect and not set out in full until Chancellor Gordon Brown made a statement to the House of Commons on 27 October.[5]

Widely perceived to be a pragmatic compromise between Tony Blair and Gordon Brown, the new Government's position was that in principle the single currency would be of benefit to Europe and to Britain. The major pooling of economic sovereignty it involved should not prevent British participation provided that it could be shown to be in the best economic interests of the country – and that should be judged by the Chancellor's five economic tests (Box 7.3). Nevertheless, recognising the magnitude of the decision – 'probably the most important this country is likely to face in our generation'[6] – the Government intended that 'whenever the decision to enter is taken by government, it should be put to a referendum of the British people. Government, Parliament and the people must all agree'.[7]

The Chancellor also announced that the Government would not join the single currency at its inception, since there was as yet no proper convergence between the British and the other European economies. Moreover, as there was no realistic prospect that sustainable convergence would be achieved before the end of the current Parliament, making a decision to join during its life was not realistic.[8]

The findings of the Treasury studies of the Chancellor's five tests were published in June 2003. After much discussion with the Prime Minister and Cabinet colleagues Gordon Brown made a detailed statement to the House of Commons on the Government's conclusions. In essence, it remains 'yes, but not yet'. The Chancellor confirmed 'the principled case: our view that membership in a successful single currency would be of benefit to the British people as well as to Europe is strengthened by the results of our assessment'. The financial services test had been met, but the sustainable convergence and flexibility tests were not yet met, and those for investment and employment depended upon them. The Government therefore intended to make a

---

*Box 7.3    Labour's five economic tests*

1. Whether there can be sustainable convergence between Britain and the economies of the single currency.
2. Whether there is sufficient flexibility to cope with economic change.
3. The effect on investment.
4. The impact on our financial services industry.
5. Whether it is good for employment.

further assessment at the time of the 2004 budget report. In the mean-time a draft referendum Bill would be published in the autumn and further measures taken in preparation for entry.[9]

In the 1997–2001 Parliament the Conservative Opposition's stance was to rule out UK participation in the single currency before the end of the next parliament. After the 2001 General Election when Ian Duncan-Smith was chosen as leader the party moved to a position of outright opposition to British participation. Thus whilst most of the Member States of the EU were preparing for the launching of the single currency in January 2002, the United Kingdom remained outside the EMU but with the right under the Maastricht Treaty to opt in. That is the essential context against which to view the UK Parliament's work in relation to EMU between the adoption of the TEU and the launch of the Euro in January 2002. To that work we now turn.

## The Westminster Parliament and the Euro, 1993–2001

What was 'Parliament's work in relation to the Euro' in this period? With the Government's position under both prime ministers' different forms of 'wait and see', there were no great decisions to be taken or endorsed and little in the way of legislation to be processed. Apart from the few legislative measures Parliament's task has been the classi-cal one of providing a forum of debate and accountability, informing and shaping the debate and reflecting the conflicting currents of opinion in the nation. We shall therefore examine Parliament's work under four heads: legislation; accountability; forum of debate; and shaping opinion and policy.

### Legislation

As indicated above, the TEU and its protocols set the framework for parliamentary consideration of the single currency. The main legislative implications of the Treaty were exhaustively dealt with in the passage of the European Communities (Amendment) Act 1993[10] since when legislative debate has been minimal. However, one provision of that Act gives a regular opportunity for re-visiting the issues, as the then Labour Opposition intended in proposing it.[11] Section 5 requires the Government to report to Parliament for its approval of an assessment of the medium-term economic and budgetary position in relation to public investment expenditure and to the social, economic and environmental goals set out in Article 2 of the Treaty of Rome as amended by the TEU. The first such debate took place in the House of Commons on 9 February 1994. As Labour had intended, it gave some Conservative Euro-sceptics a further opportunity to express their anxieties about the likely influence of the European Commission on national economic policy-making. In spite of the Financial Secretary's insistence that little debate was needed because the House had already approved the content of the statement several times when carrying the terms of the Budget, the debate provided an occasion both for the Official Opposition and for Conservative dissidents to embarrass the Government.[12]

This scenario was repeated in each of the next two years. In 1996 the Euro-sceptics – Peter Shore, Nigel Spearing, Barry Legg, Bill Cash, Nicholas Budgen, Tony Marlow and Teddy Taylor – in a succession of speeches and interventions attacked the EMU and the convergence criteria.[13] In February 1997, the Lords debate was much influenced by a reported row between the Foreign Secretary and the Chancellor about the former's remark in a radio interview that 'we are all hostile to the single currency'. So yet again the Section 5 debate was doing its intended work of providing a parliamentary occasion for embarrassing the Conservative Government.[14]

From May 1997 onwards it was Labour Ministers who were on the receiving end of the Euro-sceptics' criticisms. In 1998 in a pointed intervention Tony Benn drew attention to the restrictions on democracy and Parliament which in his view EMU and the ECB implied.[15] In July of that year the Earl of Dartmouth attacked this 'seemingly innocuous proposal' and complained that 'the Maastricht criteria have been comprehensively fudged.... [T]his submission to the European Communities has an almost Salvador Dali surrealist quality'.[16] By the following year, when the Lords debate did not take place until December, interest had significantly declined, with Lord Newby describing the debate as 'a futile exercise'.[17]

The Section 5 debates are opportunities for parliamentary oversight rather than legislative debates strictly understood. By contrast the need to amend the European Communities Act to accommodate Treaty amendments are legislation in its fullest sense. The Treaties of Amsterdam and Nice both required the passage of a European Communities (Amendment) Act. Although neither was directly concerned with EMU and the single currency they nevertheless provided an opportunity for parliamentarians to raise those issues. In the Commons Committee stage on the Amsterdam Bill, EMU was raised occasionally, in particular by Dr Julian Lewis attempting to defend the new Conservative line of not joining before the end of the next parliament.[18]

There was a more vigorous debate in the Lords, where Peter Shore moved amendments relating to EMU and the single currency.[19] At Committee stage Lord Stoddart moved an amendment calling for a report on EMU to take into account the constitutional, monetary and financial impacts as well as its impact on economic and social progress. Such a wide-ranging proposition enabled a debate on all aspects of EMU, which was repeated at Report Stage when the Opposition moved a similar amendment. That provided an opportunity for further Euro-sceptic attacks on the convergence criteria and the Chancellor's five economic tests, with liberal use made of material from a recently published Commons Treasury Committee report and press reports of the difficulties Heads of Government had experienced in agreeing the appointment of a President for the ECB.[20]

To sum up on legislation, opportunities were taken by critics of the Government in both Parliaments to raise the issue of the single currency and to launch political attacks on the Government's policy. The resulting debates required ministers to explain and defend that policy and on occasion to resist – successfully – attempts to amend their legislative proposals. In this respect the effect of these legislative opportunities was strikingly similar to the accountability procedures to which we now turn.

## Accountability

Most parliamentary activity contributes towards accountability to some extent, but in this section we shall concentrate upon three procedural opportunities: Questions, Ministerial Statements, and pre-Council debates.

Oral Questions, particularly in a televised parliament, are more an opportunity for embarrassing Ministers than for obtaining information or explanation. With both major parties perceived to be divided on the issue, it is not surprising that question-time saw many attempts to draw Ministers into statements in conflict with the official Government line. Oral questions about EMU or the single currency were asked in the House of Commons much more frequently in the 1997–2001

Parliament than in its predecessor. Over the whole period about half were put to Treasury Ministers, with the other half being evenly divided between the Foreign Office, Department of Trade, the Leader of the House, and the Prime Minister. A typical example would be the exchange at Commons Treasury Questions on 2 March 1995 when Opposition members sought to differentiate the position of Chancellor Kenneth Clarke on the implications of monetary union from that of Prime Minister John Major by means of what Mr Clarke called 'absurd nit-picking textual analysis'.[21] The equivalent in the 1997–2001 Parliament were attempts to draw Labour Ministers into elaboration of the five economic tests announced by Gordon Brown in October 1997[22] or the date or format of a referendum on the Euro.[23] Another frequent Opposition 'line of attack' in this Parliament was that the convergence criteria were being 'fudged' by ECOFIN or the European Council, a charge pressed strongly during the UK Presidency in 1998.[24]

Although the culture of the House of Lords is less adversarial than the Commons, and the nature of Questions somewhat different,[25] the starred Question leading to a mini-debate is often more searching. Their Lordships were as active as Members of the Lower House in asking about Government policy on the single currency, with Lord Barnett raising the matter on a number of occasions through the two Parliaments we are considering.[26]

No one expects that asking Questions will lead to a change in Government policy, still less by the EU's Council of Ministers. Rather its purpose is to test ministerial, and to a lesser extent Opposition, policy positions through repeated scrutiny. It is a political exercise, aimed at building or undermining support for party positions. The Questions asked and answered through these two Parliaments confirmed two things: first, the increasing difficulty Mr Major's Government and party had in maintaining a common line on EMU and the single currency; and, second, that although the Blair Government was more cohesive on the issue, the practical effect of its policy was not noticeably different – a more fully articulated version of 'wait and see'.

Prime Ministerial statements after meetings of the European Council provide a more extended opportunity for interrogation. An hour is normally allotted, enabling between 20 and 25 MPs to ask questions. The statement is repeated in the House of Lords and a similar period of questioning follows there also. European Council agendas vary but the single currency featured frequently through the 1992–2001 period. A good example of the resulting parliamentary scrutiny was provided by John Major's statement after the Cannes Summit of June 1995. Mr Major emphasised the many issues about the move to a single currency which still had to be addressed and would be examined by Finance Ministers. It was essential in his view for the United Kingdom to participate fully in and influence that debate, which would not be possible if it exercised its opt-out now.[27]

The Leader of the Opposition seized upon the apparent differences within the Cabinet over both the single currency itself and the desirability of a referendum.[28] The Liberal Democrats' leader also attacked the Prime Minister's indecision.[29] In the exchanges which followed, twelve of the interventions were about the single currency. The political context was extraordinary: Mr Major, frustrated by continual sniping from the Euro-sceptics, had resigned the Conservative Party leadership and offered himself for re-election. The divisions within the parliamentary party were well illustrated by the stances taken by the six Conservative contributors (David Howell, William Cash, Hugh Dykes, Iain Duncan Smith, Tim Renton, and Ray Whitney).[30]

A re-run occurred in December 1995 with the Prime Minister's statement on the Madrid Summit, which agreed to call the single currency the 'Euro' and formally commissioned a study into the implications of some Member States adopting the currency and some not. Mr Blair made an even longer denunciation of Cabinet divisions and the Prime Minister's indecisiveness, provoking Mr Major to quote in terms the contrasting views of members of the Shadow Cabinet. Again Mr Ashdown echoed the charge that the Prime Minister was 'ducking difficult decisions...to cover divisions in the Conservative party'.[31] Of the 24 backbenchers who followed, all but five referred explicitly to the single currency and on this occasion the spread of the opinion in Labour ranks (Peter Shore, Nigel Spearing, Dennis Skinner, Giles Radice, Jeremy Bray, and Tony Banks) was as evident as among the eleven Conservatives, amongst whom the pro-Europeans were on this occasion more vociferous.[32]

In his statement on the Dublin Council in December 1996 Mr Major confirmed that the ECOFIN report on EMU, a stability pact and a new ERM had been agreed, subject to the United Kingdom's parliamentary reserve.[33] The ECOFIN report had already been the subject of a full statement from Chancellor Kenneth Clarke on 3 December

1996,[34] and there had been a two-day debate on 11–12 December on the proposed stability pact prior to the Dublin Council.[35] But in the background were press reports that as many as 147 Conservative candidates would not sign up to the Government's position on the single currency in their personal election manifestos. It was not surprising, therefore, that the Prime Minister's statement after the Dublin Council was subject to searching questioning, both from the Leader of the Opposition seeking to draw further attention to the divided and indecisive position of the Government, and also from opponents of the single currency from both sides of the Chamber. They were concerned to establish that the United Kingdom's 'opt-out' was secure, that the convergence criteria would not be fudged. The same was also true in the House of Lords.[36]

It is clear from that episode, and the earlier Prime Ministerial statements we have cited, that much of the parliamentary interest in the single currency was a function of the divisions within the Conservative Cabinet and Parliamentary Party. But that in itself is not a sufficient explanation as there was close and critical questioning from Labour Euro-sceptics in both chambers after the change of government in May 1997.

Thus, although Tony Blair made little reference to the single currency in his statement on the Amsterdam Council, he was pressed by questions from his own side as well as Conservative critics.[37] By the time of Luxembourg Council in December 1997 the Chancellor had announced that the United Kingdom would not seek membership of the single currency in the current Parliament and William Hague was Leader of the Opposition. He challenged the Prime Minister strongly on whether the United Kingdom would be a full member of the 'Euro X Committee' which would manage the single currency and also raised the issue of tax harmonisation which was to be a continuing theme through the exchanges between the Opposition and the Government.[38]

The familiar battle lines were joined in May 1998 when the Prime Minister reported on the special Brussels Summit on the single currency, held under the United Kingdom's presidency. The Summit had agreed that 11 of the EU's 15 Member States[39] should join the single currency and endorsed a declaration on fiscal discipline and economic reform. But the appointment of the ECB President, and the length of his term, proved the source of much controversy. Mr Hague described it as 'a fiasco...political horse-trading' which demonstrated that 'politics, not economics [] is the driving force behind the single currency'. Reflecting the disbelief that so many states had been found to have met the Maastricht criteria, he also accused Mr Blair of 'colluding in the launch of a fudged and flawed single currency'.[40] The 21 speakers who followed again reflected the spread of opinion in the House, albeit that a large Labour majority had replaced the previous narrow Conservative one. Tony Benn, William Cash, Teddy Taylor, and Dennis Skinner were balanced by Giles Radice, Tam Dalyell, and David Currie.[41]

Although the single currency was not the principal focus of European Council meetings in the period to June 2001, Mr Blair's statements to the House of Commons on those meetings evoked similar lines of questions – tax harmonisation, including a possible withholding tax, the timing and form of a referendum, as well as the investment, employment, and constitutional implications of the single currency itself – interspersed amongst currently more topical issues such as Kosovo (Cologne), enlargement (Helsinki); the IGC (Nice), or Foot and Mouth Disease (Stockholm).[42] In the background, and sometimes in the foreground, were contemporary political events such as elections – the European Parliamentary elections in June 1999 and the forthcoming British General Election in March 2001. Thus throughout the 1997–2001 Parliament Mr Blair in his regular statements on meetings of the European Council was confronted with the need to explain and justify the policy of his Government with regard to EMU and the single currency.

In addition to the statements on the outcome of European Council meetings, there have been two other major statements on the single currency in the life of the Blair Government. The first, and most important, was that made by Chancellor Gordon Brown in October 1997 (see pp. 149–150) on which he was questioned for an hour. The second was made by the Prime Minister in February 1999 when he announced publication of a 'national changeover plan' for consultation. Pointing out that the Euro was already a reality, the Prime Minister re-iterated the Government's view that British membership of the single currency was 'conditional, not inevitable'. Mr Blair did not dismiss the real constitutional or political issues but insisted it would be right to overcome those obstacles 'if joining a single currency is good for British jobs and British industry, and if it enhances British power and

British influence'.[43] Although dismissed by the Opposition Leader William Hague as 'a long list of cliches and verbiage accompanied by...little information'[44] the statement did commit the Government to seeking explicit parliamentary approval for the expenditure which would be incurred by Government Departments in their advance preparations. It also revealed that the Government envisaged a time-table of four months from a Government decision to a referendumn and a further 24 to 30 months from a positive referendum decision to the introduction of notes and coins.[45]

The third strand in accountability has been the regular pre-summit debates, normally held in the week prior to the meeting of the European Council. These are based upon – *inter alia* – a Government White Paper *Developments in the European Union* covering the previous six months and any immediately relevant EU documents. Thus the May 1994 debate considered the Government's White Paper and the Commission's Paper on Employment.[46] For the December 1996 debate fourteen Relevant Documents were cited: the Government's White Paper; the Presidency's General Outline for a draft revision of the Treaties; two Work Programmes from the Commission, covering New Legislative Proposals and Political Priorities respectively; three major EC documents – one on the introduction of the Euro, one on convergence procedures and a new ERM, and one on the stability pact for ensuring budgetary discipline in Stage 3; three Reports from the Select Committee on European Legislation; and a set of Minutes of Evidence from that Committee; a Report from the Treasury Committee on Stage 3 of EMU, and two sets of Minutes of Evidence from the Foreign Affairs Committee.[47] It was not surprising that two days were set aside for debate.

March 1996 brought a major debate on the approaching IGC which laid bare the hesitations, divisions, and anxieties on both sides of the House about the future direction of the EU.[48] Foreign Secretary Malcolm Rifkind's opening speech was remarkable for the number of occasions on which he took interventions from his own backbenchers. Shadow Foreign Secretary Robin Cook also faced interventions from Euro-sceptics, including Peter Shore[49] and Tony Benn.[50] Pro-European voices were not entirely absent: Sir Edward Heath attacked the White Paper and the Foreign Secretary's speech for being 'riddled with schizophrenia...He says something good in one paragraph and then cancels it out in the next paragraph'. Echoing Sir Edward, Giles Radice,

Chairman of the European Movement, criticised the White Paper for being too inflexible, designed mainly for internal party reasons.[51]

The pre-Dublin Council debate seven months later followed similar lines.[52] But in a key speech the Chairman of the European Legislation Committee, Jimmy Hood, criticised Ministers' resistance to allowing time for it which had meant that 'the integrity of Parliament was in danger of being held up to ridicule'. He regretted that the debate was not on a substantive and amendable motion as the Committee would have preferred.[53] As Austin Mitchell points out in the quotation in the beginning of this chapter[54] these six-monthly debates contained a significant element of repetition, both of participants and content. Again and again[55] each major party sought, with some success, to show that opinion in the other was divided, yet Chancellor and Shadow Chancellor were in fact in broad agreement on the substance of the issue – it was important to 'wait and see'.

In that respect the change of government in 1997 did not make much difference. The motion[56] for the first debate under the Labour Administration in July of that year again showed how a number of different strands in the House's work are brought together – draft texts, recommendations, and policy guidelines from the EU and explanatory memoranda from the Government. For the debate in June 2000, three Commission documents (on enlargement and insti-tutional reform) were tagged, as were a report from the Scrutiny Committee, the Government's *Developments in the European Union* White Paper, a report from the Defence Committee, and Minutes of Evidence from the Foreign Affairs Committee.[57] Much as Foreign Secretary Robin Cook wanted to speak about defence and security, Members repeatedly returned to the single currency. Vainly though Mr Cook insisted that the argument on a withholding tax had been won,[58] Euro-sceptics on both sides repeatedly returned to the con-nection between EMU, taxation, and the nature of the EU itself.

### The Westminster Forum

In traditional accounts of the British political system Parliament – 'the grand inquest of the nation' – is the principal political forum of the nation. Its representative nature (in the Commons), and its proceedings and debates articulate the interests and aspirations of the nation. Such an account nowadays faces a stern challenge from the mass media which have reduced the perceived need for intermediaries between government and citizens. However, the explosion in interest group activity and the volume of MPs' constituency correspondence indicate that the Westminster Parliament remains a very significant forum for the expression and exchange of political views. That exchange takes place in all parliamentary proceedings but we focus here on the mechanisms by which non-governmental members can bring matters to the parliamentary agenda – Opposition Days; Adjournment debates; debates in Westminster Hall; Private Member's Bills and Motions; and Early Day Motions (EDMs).

As we have seen, there has been no lack of opportunities for Opposition members to raise European issues in the Commons, so recourse to supply days was something of an exception. Nevertheless, in the unusual circumstances of the early months of 1995, when Mr Major's Government temporarily lost its overall majority, first the Liberal Party[59] and then the Official Opposition used this device to highlight the Government's embarrassment on the European issue. The Labour Opposition's motion on 1 March[60] produced a substantial debate. Interventions from both sides were designed to point up the divisions which each saw amongst their opponents – a situation to be repeated many times in the next six years. It was, for example, echoed in a short debate initiated by the Liberal Democrats in July 1998, in which the arguments mainly focused on whether the Conservatives' new policy of ruling out joining the single currency for two parliaments meant ruling it out for ten years.[61] The only other Opposition debate related to the Euro in the 1997–2001 Parliament was called in the run-up to the 2001 election and concerned with the implications for manufacturing industry.[62]

Opposition Day debates are initiated by the frontbenchers. For backbenchers there are similar opportunities in balloted private member's motions and adjournment debates and, in the 1997–2001 Parliament, debates in Westminster Hall. These procedural opportunities were used by 'Euro-sceptics'[63] to initiate discussion of the single currency and put further pressure upon the Major Government. There were three adjournment debates initiated by Euro-sceptics (two Conservative, one Labour) and two 'balloted' motions.[64] On the same day in February 1995 two of the 'whipless' Conservatives introduced private member's bills to draw attention to the single currency issue.[65]

By contrast, in the 1997–2001 Parliament the focus in the Commons moved away from the Conservatives' internal debate. These procedures were used in less 'high profile' ways, though the extent of their use was about the same: one adjournment debate, on convergence criteria, initiated by the Liberal Democrat Dr Vincent Cable,[66] and four Westminster Hall debates, in which the implications of the Euro for the future of the Rover car company (again Dr Cable),[67] and the steel industry (twice)[68] as well as the cost of the national changeover plan[69] were raised.

In this second Parliament, peers were more active on this front. Lord Taverne, introducing a motion on the single currency in January 1999, criticised the Government's cautious policy.[70] His pro-European views were not entirely shared by the distinguished cast which followed him – Lords Lamont, Skidelsky, Barnett, Roll, Grenfell, Cobbold, Shore and Howe, and Baroness Williams.[71] Lord Waddington, no doubt with his eye on the European Elections which had just taken place, struck a very different note with his Tax Harmonisation (Veto) Bill in June 1999.[72] In March 2000 Lord Pearson of Rannoch introduced a bill to require the Treasury 'to set up an independent committee of inquiry into what life would be like outside the EU for our economy, defence and constitution'.[73] Although the theme of the motion was much wider, a number of contributors focused specifically on the single currency and the ECB.[74]

Another procedural opportunity for ventilating backbench opinion is provided by EDMs but these have not been a major vehicle in the ongoing controversy about EMU. In the 1997–2001 Parliament there were just nine EDMs relating to the EMU (one of which was concerned with the IT implications of its introduction coinciding with the Millennium) and of those only two attracted a significant number of signatures. Five of the nine were from anti-EU campaigners (Tony Benn (2), Bill Cash, Teddy Taylor, and Austin Mitchell). The one positively pro-Euro motion, from Ken Livingston, attracted only 8 signatures.[75]

We can thus see that these procedural opportunities for both front- and back-benchers have been used to a limited extent to continue the campaigning within and across the parliamentary parties which has so marked the debate about the Euro at Westminster.

### Shaping opinion and policy

Although in principle any parliamentary activity can have an effect upon the shaping of opinion and policy, select committees provide an important instrument for parliamentary input into governmental policy-making and it is upon them that we shall concentrate in this section.

In July 1996 the Lords' ECC issued a report assessing the consequences of EMU for the United Kingdom.[76] The Committee (like most parliamentary committees which have ventured onto this territory) deliberately avoided the issue of whether the United Kingdom should join, which enabled it to achieve unanimity despite the strongly held opposing views.[77] Nevertheless, it agreed that 'it is in the UK's interests that a decision to "wait and see" should be seen as a genuine postponement and not a disguised final rejection of economic and monetary union'.[78] For that reason the Committee were anxious about the lack of technical preparations, which would be necessary whether or not the United Kingdom joined at the outset, and so produced a further report, *Preparations for EMU*, in November 1996, and debated the following month.[79] When that report was debated, Lord Barnett highlighted three main issues: the stability pact – the Committee strongly supported measures to maintain fiscal discipline; fines and sanctions, which raised questions of feasibility and political acceptability; and, as in their July report, ERM2.

In his response on behalf of the Government, Lord Mackay of Ardbrecknish acknowledged that the reports were a valuable contribution to the debate about EMU and accepted the Committee's analyses of the issues.[80] This format was seen again in 1998 when the ECC produced a report on the newly established ECB shortly after the controversial decision of the European Council on the appointment of its first President.[81] The Committee's sole recommendation was 'that the operation of the ECB raises important questions to which the attention of the House should be drawn and makes this Report to the House for debate'.[82] That may seem bland, but the topics covered show that the Committee got to the heart of the matter: the key connection between the bank's independence, transparency and accountability, and its credibility; the EP's role in achieving accountability; the definition of price stability; the bank's monetary policy strategy; the effectiveness of the stability pact; and exchange rate policy.

The Committee, which took evidence in Bonn, Brussels, and Frankfurt as well as Westminster, heard from an impressive list of witnesses[83] – testimony to the seriousness of the investigation and the respect with which the ECC's work is viewed.[84] Introducing the debate on the report in October, Lord Barnett emphasised that the ECB's role was crucial: 'if the European Central Bank fails, so does economic and monetary union'. The Committee had drawn attention to the risk of fiscal profligacy which the stability pact was designed to avoid. He also pointed to the particular importance of accountability, and transparency was therefore particularly important. The debate, like the report, exposed the issues but led to no change in the way the policy of the Government was articulated.

Debates on committee reports are more frequent in the Lords than in the Commons. Thus the Commons Treasury Committee report of April 1998[85] was followed not by a debate but by a letter to the Chairman of the Committee from the Chancellor of the Exchequer. This was not the Committee's liking[86] particularly as its substance was a re-iteration of the Government's line on the five economic tests. The Committee's request for a Government report before a recommendation to join was evaded but the Chancellor welcomed the Committee's support, as he interpreted it, for the programme of practical preparations being put in place.[87]

An important dimension of the debate about both the single market and EMU has been the implications for taxation policy. The Lords' ECC's 1999 report looked both at the fundamental issues underlying taxation questions in the EU and at the detailed proposals which had been bought forward, both for direct and indirect taxation.[88] In an impressive analysis of the issues, the Committee drew out the conflicting views on the impact of EMU on pressure for more tax co-ordination: either it would *increase* that pressure since the successful management of monetary and tax policies could be achieved only if both were under the same political control; or, since national governments could no longer have recourse to monetary policy, they would have an even greater need to use tax policy to manage their economies in pursuit of their own national objectives, which would *reduce* pressure for greater tax co-ordination.[89]

The Committee expressed some concerns about the way the Group on the Code of Conduct for business taxation was going about its work. The lack of transparency showed both the Council of Ministers and the Government in a very poor light and 'leaves the Code of Conduct open to being described as an obnoxious method of inflicting secret taxation, when in fact it may be little more than an innocuous discussion group'. The fact that the Government may have had some contact with industry about the discussions 'does nothing to remedy the deplorable lack of accountability to Parliament'. The Committee called upon the Government to 'seek agreement from other Member States that the progress reports which the Code of Conduct Group makes to ECOFIN should be published, and subject to Parliamentary scrutiny in the normal way'.[90]

In the light of the strength of opposition to the Commission's 'withholding tax' proposal, the ECC took extensive evidence[91] in order to discover why the Commission's proposals had proved so controversial. Much of the controversy had focused on its likely impact on the City, but, despite many claims and counter-claims, the Committee were 'left with no firm evidence about the likely scale of the effect of a withholding tax on the City of London' and were unable to reach a conclusion on that point.[92]

The Committee were persuaded that 'scare headlines about an EU tax takeover were unjustified' and concluded that, within certain parameters, 'pragmatic tax co-ordination and fair competition can not only co-exist but complement each other, to the greater benefit of taxpayers within the European Union'.[93] Nevertheless, the ECC had serious doubts about the feasibility of the Commission's alternative, 'co-existence model' but agreed with the Government that adopting a reporting option on an EU-wide basis would be preferable to imposing a withholding tax.[94]

Following the Government's written response, in which Ministers declined to comment on the Committee's lengthy discussion of informal ideas for further tax co-ordination, the Committee's report was debated in the House on 3 November 1999. In his reply for the Government, Lord McIntosh of Haringey cited Commissioner Monti's tribute to the outstanding quality of the report – but then went on to decline to comment on the part of the report dealing with ideas on the future of EU taxation.[95] The Government agreed with the Committee's overall conclusion and re-affirmed their view that 'tax policy is ultimately a matter for member states to decide. The Government have no intention of abandoning the veto on tax matters'.[96] As regards the draft directive, Lord McIntosh repeated that it had been 'made clear time and again, both to our European partners and to Parliament, that the Government would not accept [it] in its present form'.[97]

In this way, through its collecting of evidence, its reports and the debate, the ECC was fulfilling its design function: gathering evidence and opinion, drawing out the important questions of policy and principle, and highlighting those which it considered merited the special attention of the House – and the public. As a consequence the Government had further opportunity to place its position on the public record – and was able to use what was clearly acknowledged, outside the United Kingdom as well as within, as an expert and authoritative source in its negotiations with the Commission and Member States.

The beginning of Stage 3 of EMU on 1 January 1999 gave a clear opportunity for the key select committees in both Houses to monitor how it was working. The Commons Treasury Committee announced an inquiry in March 2000. The Committee had two major difficulties: first, its members had differing views on the intrinsic merits of EMU; and, second, 'save the pound' was emerging as the likely central plank of the Conservative Party's programme for the next election. This led the Committee, as in its previous enquiry in 1998, to decide that it would be 'unproductive' to try to reach an agreed view on the major question of principle, whether or not the United Kingdom should participate in Stage 3[98] with a very wide agenda. Instead it agreed a range of more specific issues, such as the ECB's performance; progress towards convergence within the Euro-area; the implications of enlargement for the Euro; the United Kingdom's progress towards meeting the convergence criteria and the Chancellor's five economic tests; and the national changeover plan. On these the Committee heard oral evidence from expert witnesses from the commercial, financial, and academic worlds, from Commissioner Sobles and his officials, from several major industrialists, from the CBI, TUC and the Institute of Directors, as well as from Government ministers (the Paymaster-General, the Economic Secretary, and the Chancellor himself).[99]

The considerable differences of opinion within the Committee resulted in a report which discussed the key issues in the debate about the Euro but produced findings were little more than balanced summaries of the evidence. And in spite of the deliberate avoidance of the central issue of whether the United Kingdom should join the Euro, the Committee was deeply split. When the Chairman's draft report was brought up for consideration, Conservative members introduced an alternative draft and the Committee also divided on the question whether the report should made to the House. In total there were 35 divisions on the report, of which just over a third (13) were straight party divisions; just over a half (18) involved some cross-party voting, and three resulted in ties, requiring the Chairman to use his casting vote.[100] This was far from the consensual mode which Commons' Committees normally strive to adopt. The effect was that in the end the Committee had little useful to add to the debate – and this was reflected in the complacent tone of the Government's response issued in October 2000.[101]

The Lords' European Union Committee (EUC) report, *How is the Euro working?* was published in December 2000.[102] This Committee too chose to sidestep the two most controversial issues – whether the United Kingdom should participate in Stage 3 of EMU and what the effects of the single currency might be. Instead the EUC focused on whether, to use the Government's word, the single currency had so far been 'successful'.[103] In this task the EUC took evidence from the Governments of nine Member States, four of them giving oral as well as written evidence, the central banks of France, Germany and Ireland, the Governor and Deputy Governor of the Bank of England, and HM Treasury.[104]

From that evidence the EUC derived ten criteria[105] by which the Euro's 'success' might be judged and went on to summarise both the 'many economic advantages' which that evidence suggested came with the single currency[106] and the potential disadvantages of a 'one size fits all' monetary policy.[107] On the ECB, the EUC stated clearly that the evidence was that the Bank had, to quote the Governor of the Bank of England, 'done pretty well so far', seemingly a banker's equivalent of high praise.

The EUC declared its intention to return to these themes in future inquiries.[108] But for future inquiries to be productive, the Committee would expect a more substantial response from HM Treasury than the two-page reply[109] given to its November 2000 report. That reply was described by senior members of the Committee as 'insulting', 'disgraceful', and 'during the six years I have had the job (Chairman of the Committee) the first time we have not had a proper response from a government department'.[110] The Minister's somewhat lame explanation for the Government's short reply was that the Treasury had provided a very substantial written memorandum of evidence as well as oral evidence and supplementary memoranda and given the general nature of the Committee's conclusions, there was not a great deal to add.[111]

At the same time as the EUC's Report was published, the Commons' Trade and Industry Committee was making a rare sally into this controversial territory in its report *What would the Euro cost UK business?*[112] The Committee was critical that neither edition of the National Changeover Plan adequately addressed the issue of the cost of a changeover to the single currency and were alarmed at the prospect of large costs arising from variation in coin manufacture, and of fraud.[113] The Committee noted that the Government was 'unwilling even to discuss the costs to business of UK membership of the Euro, let alone to estimate them. There may be good political reasons for this: but we fear that this policy is deterring companies from preparing estimates for a changeover and may eventually increase these costs. Unless and until the Government takes steps to identify the nature and scale of the possible costs, including in particular the implications for IT expenditure, its awareness campaigns will prove ineffective'.[114]

The Government's reply to the Committee, issued at the end of January 2001, largely re-stated existing Treasury positions, particularly that it was not possible to produce credible estimates of the cost of a changeover to the Euro for UK business. With only a few months to go to an expected general election in which entry to the Euro was likely to be a major issue, not much more could be expected.[115]

The Lords' and Commons' select committees have therefore done a great deal of solid work in examining and reporting upon the implications of Stage 3 of EMU and the launch of the single currency. Wisely given the divisions of opinions between and within the major parties, the Committees have eschewed considering the main policy issue – whether the United Kingdom should join the Euro – but have instead followed the classical select committee route of seeking to inform and guide Parliament and other opinion-formers. This was not an easy task as both the Major and Blair Governments had effectively adopted a 'wait and see' policy. Although there was considerable movement in the development of policy within the EU up to and including the launch of the Euro in January 2002, British Government policy hardly developed at all, apart from the announcement of the Labour Government's economic tests in October 1997. Select Committees were not able to force any development or elaboration in the Government's policy nor did they attempt to do so. But they did bring into the parliamentary and public domain a substantial body of expert evidence and informed opinion relating the key issues. The Lords' Committee's report on taxation is perhaps the best example of this. What is not clear, however, is the degree to which what has been brought into the public domain has been used – a much wider question, beyond the scope of this book.

## Conclusion

Economic and monetary union, and especially joining the single currency, have been and are matters of high public and parliamentary controversy. Notwithstanding its troubled history and Euro-sceptic doubts about the feasibility of the project, the strength of purpose and political will of the majority of the EU's Member States meant that progress to completion of Stage 3 was assured. Yet at the same time the genuine difficulty of the issue of convergence and the problem of managing party and public opinion meant that the British Government's position under both political parties has remained one of ambiguity – 'wait and see'.

As we have seen, the opinions of British parliamentarians on the issues of EMU and the single currency were strongly held and deeply divided, so much so that unusually in British political culture, party lines were crossed. Nor were these issues a simple reflection of views on membership of the EU itself. Some who were strongly in favour of British membership of the EEC were nevertheless opposed to United Kingdom participation in the Euro.[116] On European issues, notwithstanding the (in)famous cohesiveness of British political parties, a significant number of individual parliamentarians have been willing to defy their party whips and vote with 'the other side'. That unusual phenomenon has posed deep challenges for both Conservative and Labour party managers, particularly as parliamentary procedures gave plenty of opportunities for dissidents to raise the issue.

British membership of the European Community/Union has meant that over an increasing number of public policy areas, particularly but not only in the economic sphere, the Westminster Parliament has had to accept restrictions on its legislative competence and its ability to exert political control over policy-makers. In these areas the effective legislature and policy-maker is the Council of Ministers. With EMU and the single currency that has not been the case as the

British Government has exercised its rights under the Maastricht Protocol to decide not to join at launch but to be able to do so later – providing the United Kingdom meets the convergence criteria. Other than endorsing the negative decisions the Westminster Parliament has not had primary legislative or political decisions to take. Rather, its role has been to hold Ministers to account, to require them – again and again – to explain and justify their position. This was not *control* of policy in the sense of 'command and control'. But the state of parliamentary (and public) opinion has been a powerful limiting influence on the Government – especially in the period of the Major Government as the Conservative Party's majority ebbed away and the leverage available to the Euro-sceptics correspondingly increased. Moreover, since in both Parliaments there were divisions amongst Ministers on the issue, the task of crafting and then defending the united position of Her Majesty's Government which the doctrine of collective responsibility requires was not an easy one.

That the strictly legislative opportunities were few and the issue of parliamentary sovereignty rarely surfaced is not too surprising since the Westminster Parliament is accustomed to its more marginalised and reactive role on domestic budgetary and monetary questions. But the opportunities offered by questions and even more by regular Statements, particularly by the Prime Minister after meetings of the European Council, were frequently exploited in both Houses by pro-Europeans and Euro-sceptics alike. It was often the same cast making the same interventions or speeches, as Austin Mitchell has pointed out. But in this way on a highly controversial issue Parliament has been performing its accountability role and providing a public forum for debate. Moreover, the often unsung work of select committees in gathering, assembling, and analysing evidence on the key issues has also been noteworthy, not least for the quality and expertise of the witnesses who were heard. In the House of Lords that work fed through into some excellent debates on the floor in which the expertise of the speakers was also evident.

There were significant continuities and discontinuities between the 1992–97 and 1997–2001 Parliaments. The most obvious continuities were the 'wait and see' position of the two Governments as EMU Stage 3 progressed and the deep divisions of opinion between and within the two major parties. The 1997 General Election brought a new government with a more than comfortable majority. That discontinuity significantly reduced the Euro-sceptics' leverage and from October 1997 onwards focused the policy debate on the Chancellor's economic tests. But the mode in which the issue(s) surfaced remained the same – Questions, Statements and Committee Reports – as did the outcome: re-statement of the Government's position. So while momentous changes were occurring in the Euro-zone, in Westminster the position remained the same – both in the sense of the Government's stance and in the depth of controversy which the EMU and the single currency evoked.

## Notes

1. Margaret Thatcher, *The Downing Street Years*, pp. 708, 753.
2. A. Seldon, *Major: A Poitical Life*, Weidenfeld and Nicolson, 1997, pp. 309–324. Compare J. Major, *The Autobiography*, HarperCollins, 1999, pp. 312–341 and N. Lamont, *In Office*, LittleBrown, 1999, pp. 208–266.
3. D. Gros and N. Thygesen, *European Monetary Integration*, Longman, 1998, p. 425.
4. A. Seldon, op. cit., p. 681 et seq.
5. HC Deb, 27 October 1997, cc. 583–588.
6. loc. cit., c. 583.
7. loc. cit., c. 584.
8. loc. cit., c. 586.
9. HC Deb, 9 June 2003, cc. 408–415.
10. *Westminster and Europe*, Chapters 10 and 11.
11. In the 1994 debate, Hilary Armstrong, from the Opposition front-bench, referred to the section as 'a ticking time-bomb'.
12. HC Deb, 9 February 1994, c. 397ff.
13. HC Deb, 12 February 1996, c. 754ff.
14. HL Deb, 19 February 1997, cc. 757–771, especially 761, 763 and 769.
15. HC Deb, 21 April 1998, cc. 707–709.
16. HL Deb, 28 July 1996, cc. 1411–1412.
17. HL Deb, 9 December 1999, c. 1462.
18. HC Deb, 2 December 1997, c. 208.
19. HL Deb, 2 March 1998, c. 318ff.
20. HL Deb, 12 May 1998, c. 969ff.
21. HC Deb, 2 March 1995, cc. 1172–1173.
22. For example, HC Deb, 8 February 2001, c. 1078.
23. For example, HC Deb, 7 February 2001, cc. 918–919.
24. For example, HC Deb, 12 February 1998, cc. 543–544 and 25 March 1998, cc. 491–492.
25. See Mark Franklin and Philip Norton (eds), *Parliamentary Questions*, Clarendon Press, 1993, Chapter 6.
26. See HL Debates for 13 December 1994, 11 July 1996, 18 February 1998, 8 April 1998, 30 June 1998, 16 June 2001.

27. HC Deb, 28 June 1995, cc. 871–872.

28. loc. cit., c. 896.

29. Ibid., c. 899.

30. Ibid., cc. 898–906.

31. HC Deb, 18 December 1995, cc. 1221–1228.

32. Ibid., cc. 1227–1237.

33. HC Deb, 16 December 1996, c. 616.

34. HC Deb, 3 December 1996, c. 797ff.

35. HC Deb, 11–12 December 1996, c. 287ff.

36. HC Deb, 16 December 1996, c. 615ff.; HL Deb, 16 December 1996, c. 1302ff.

37. HC Deb, 18 June 1997, c. 313ff., especially cc. 326–327.

38. HC Deb, 15 December 1997, cc. 21–22.

39. Those remaining outside were Denmark, Greece, Sweden and the United Kingdom.

40. HC Deb, 5 May 1998, c. 565ff.

41. Ibid., c. 570ff.

42. HC Deb, 14 December 1998, c. 605ff. (Vienna Summit); 8 June 1999, c. 463ff. (Cologne); 13 December 1999, c. 21ff. (Helsinki); 21 June 2000, c. 339ff. (Feira); 11 December 2000, c. 349 (Nice); 26 March 2001, c. 579 (Stockholm).

43. HC Deb, 23 February 1999, cc. 179–184.

44. Ibid., c. 184.

45. Ibid., c. 181.

46. HC Deb, 16 May 1994, cc. 556–647.

47. HC Deb, 11 December 1996, c. 287.

48. HC Deb, 21 March 1996, c. 534ff.

49. Ibid., c. 534.

50. Ibid., c. 536.

51. Ibid., cc. 552–553.

52. HC Deb, 11 December 1996, c. 287ff.

53. Ibid., c. 459.

54. HC Deb, 23 November 2000, c. 501.

55. In the 1997–2001 Parliament pre-European Council debates were held in the Commons on 9 June 1997 (Amsterdam), 4 December 1997 (Luxembourg), 11 June 1998 (Cardiff), 3 December 1998 (Vienna), 1 December 1999 (Helsinki), 15 June 2000 (Feira), and 23 November 2000 (Nice). Similar debates were held in the House of Lords.

56. For full text, see HC Deb, 9 June 1997, c. 800.

57. HC Deb, 15 June 2000, c. 1122.

58. Ibid., c. 1125.

59. HC Deb, 13 February 1995, cc. 668–674.

60. HC Deb, 1 March 1995, c. 1052ff.

61. HC Deb, 21 July 1998, cc. 978–1019.

62. HC Deb, 24 January 2001, c. 927ff.

63. Care is needed with this term which implies a cohesive and continuing grouping. Not all who oppose or who have doubts about the single

currency are 'Euro-sceptic' on other issues, indeed some – for example, Lord Owen – are strongly pro-European.

64. HC Deb, 21 July 1994, cc. 595–604 (Bernard Jenkin), 19 July 1995, cc. 1586–1589 (Teddy Taylor), 24 January 1996, cc. 286–308 (Christopher Gill), 13 March 1996, cc. 895–917 (Christopher Gill, ostensibly on the Inter-Governmental Conference but most of his speech was about the single currency), 1 May 1996, cc. 1274–1280 (Llew Smith), 3 March 1996, cc. 993–1016 (Vincent Cable), 30 January 1997, cc. 269–290 (William Cash).
65. See Bill 55, 1994/95 (Bill Cash) and HC Deb, 24 February 1995, c. 592 (Teresa Gorman).
66. HC Deb, 3 March 1999, cc. 993–1016.
67. HC Deb, 26 January 2000, c. 83WHff.
68. HC Deb, 10 January 2001, c. 217WHff. and 28 March 2001, c. 253WHff.
69. HC Deb, 5 July 2000, c. 43WHff.
70. HL Deb, 20 January 1999, cc. 600–601.
71. Ibid., cc. 599–667.
72. HL Deb, 18 June 1999, c. 592.
73. HL Deb, 17 March 2000, c. 1805.
74. Lords Vivian (Ibid., cc. 1844–1845), Willoughby de Broke (cc. 1851–1852), Moran (c. 1833) and Monson (c. 1816).
75. The nine motions were EDM 136, 1997–98, *EMU and Independent Economists* (Ken Livingston, 18 June 1997, 8 signatories, all Labour); EDM 340, 1997–98, *Conduct of the Chancellor of the Exchequer and His Advisers* (Peter Lilley, 27 October 1997, 121 signatories, all Conservatives); EDM 1361, 1997/98, *Conduct of the Leader of the Opposition and the European Single Currency* (Bill Rammell, 21 May 1998, 21 signatories, 20 Labour and 1 Lib Dem; a 'pro-Hague' amendment attracted 4 Conservative signatures); EDM 1438, 1997/98, *The Euro and Millennium Compliance* (David Atkinson, 16 June 1998, 14 signatories, 12 Conservative, 1 Labour and 1 UUP); EDM 1541, 1997/98, *Co-operation in Europe* (Tony Benn, 13 July 1998, 13 signatories, 10 Labour, 2 Conservative and 1 UUP); EDM 185, 1998/99, *White Paper on Europe* (Bill Cash, 107 signatories, 82 Conservative, 12 Labour, 3 Lib Dem, 8 UUP, 1 DUP and 1 UKUP); EDM 713, 1998/99, *Leader of the Opposition* (Teddy Taylor, 14 June 1999, 7 signatories, all Conservatives); EDM 253, 2000/01, *Public Spending and the Euro* (Austin Mitchell, 25 January 2001, 13 signatories, all Labour); EDM 352, 2000/01, *Democracy in Europe* (Tony Benn, 14 February 2001, 15 signatories, all Labour).
76. Eleventh Report of the Select Committee on the European Communities, *An EMU of Ins and Outs*, HL 86, 1995–96, July 1996.
77. Lord Barnett, HL Deb, 24 July 1996, c. 1416.
78. Ibid., c. 1419.
79. Second Report of the European Communities Committee, *Preparations for EMU*, HL 18, 1996–97, November 1996. The debate was held on 4 December 1996, HL Deb, c. 673ff.
80. Ibid., c. 746.

81. Twenty-fourth Report, *The European Central Bank: will it work?* HL 112, 1997/98, June 1998.
82. Ibid., para. 134.
83. Witnesses listed in Appendix 2 of the Report included the Chancellor of the Exchequer; Commissioner Yves-Thibault de Silguy from the European Commission; Members of the EU Committee and of the Finance Committee of the Deutsche Bundestag; the EMI President, Dr Duisenberg, the Governor of the Bank of England; Professor Goodhard from LSE; the General Secretary of the TUC, the Director General, European & International Affairs of the German Ministry of Finance; the President of the Deutsche Bundesbank; the Governor of the Banque de France; the Director General of the CBI; the Chairman of the EP's Committee on Economic and Monetary Affairs and Industrial Policy; the UK representative on the board of the EMI; a previous Chairman of the US Federal Reserve Bank, Paul Volcker; and the Economics Commentator of the Financial Times.
84. Lord Barnett, HL Deb, 13 October 1998, c. 788.
85. Fifth Report of the Treasury Committee, *The UK and Preparations for Stage Three of Economic and Monetary Union*, HC 503, 1997–98, April 1998.
86. Sixth Special Report of the Treasury Committee, *The UK and Preparations for Stage Three of Economic and Monetary Union: the Government's Response to the Committee's Fifth Report of Session 1997–98*, HC 905, 1997–98, July 1998, opening paragraph.
87. The Chancellor's letter is printed in full in the Committee's Sixth Special Report, July 1998.
88. Fifteenth Report of the Select Committee on the European Communities, *Taxes in the EU: can co-ordination and competition co-exist?* HL 92, 1998–99, July 1999. The ECC had launched an enquiry in the previous session, but as it was overtaken by events it reported only the evidence it had received. See Twenty-eighth Report of the Select Committee on the European Communities, *Tax and Competition Policy in the Single Market*, HL 117, 1997–98.
89. Ibid., para. 9, summarising paras 78–80.
90. Ibid., para. 20, summarising paras 129–136.
91. From, amongst others, Commissioner Monti, the CBI, the Institute of Directors, the Bank of England, the private banking sector, the financial markets and the City of London, the Treasuries of France, Germany and Ireland, as well as UK Treasury, and Revenue officials.
92. Ibid., para. 26.
93. Ibid., para. 50 and see Lord Grenfell, HL Deb, 3 November 1999, c. 916.
94. Ibid., paras 24–32.
95. HL Deb, 3 November 1999, c. 972.
96. Ibid., c. 974.
97. Ibid., c. 977.
98. Ibid., para. 3.
99. For a list of oral witness, see loc. cit., para. 4.
100. Ibid., *Proceedings of the Committee relating to the Report*.

101. Tenth Special Report of the Treasury Committee, *Economic and Monetary Union: The Government's Response to the Committee's Eighth Report of Session 1999–2000*, HC 983, November 2000.
102. Eighteenth Report of the European Union Committee, *How is the euro working?* HL 124, 1999–2000, December 2000.
103. Ibid., paras 3 and 18; see also Lord Tomlinson, HL Deb, 5 February 2001, c. 942.
104. Ibid., Appendix 2, *List of Witnesses*.
105. The list is set out in full in paragraph 8 of the Report.
106. Ibid., paras 12 and 13; HL Deb, 7 February 2001, cc. 943–944.
107. Ibid., para. 14; HL Deb, 7 February 2001, c. 944.
108. Ibid., para. 19.
109. Second Report of the Select Committee on European Union, *Memorandum from the Treasury*, HL 13, 2001–02, 16 November 2001 (but written in February 2001).
110. HL Deb, 7 February 2001, Lord Tomlinson (c. 943), Lord Renton of Mount Harry (c. 945) and Lord Tordoff (c. 994).
111. Ibid., c. 993.
112. Fourteenth Report, 1999–2000, HC 755, 16 November 2000.
113. Ibid., paras 13, 38.
114. Ibid., para. 61.
115. Second Special Report from the Select Committee on Trade and Industry, *Government Observations on the Fourteenth Report from the Committee*, HC 170, 2000–01, 29 January 2001, *Appendix*, especially para. 11.
116. For example, Lord Owen and Peter Lilley. For a recent statement of the latter's view, see HC Deb, 12 June 2003, c. 821.

# 8
# Second Pillar Challenges: Foreign, Security and Defence Policies

*Richard Ware and Joanne Wright*

The 'second' and 'third' pillars of the European Union remain fundamentally different in nature from the 'first' in ways which significantly affect the ability of national parliaments to monitor and influence them. If we consider the second pillar (the subject of this chapter) then, to put it bluntly, neither the Common Foreign and Security Policy (CFSP) nor the Common European Security and Defence Policy (CESDP) have replaced national prerogatives in the way that, for example, EC fisheries policy has replaced national regimes. The extent to which the fifteen Member States are able and willing to pool their diplomatic and security resources for a sustained effort in a particular cause is a matter of almost infinite negotiation. The degree of coherence actually achieved in diplomacy and international security co-operation continues to fluctuate from week to week and issue to issue: the record of the CFSP is patchy at best; CESDP has barely got off the ground.

For national parliaments this means that there is, inevitably, a continuous switching between the older habit of viewing foreign policy and defence through national filters and the newer one of viewing them as aspects of European co-operation. In the case of the United Kingdom the dichotomy is particularly apparent: the same issue, be it Afghanistan, Chechnya or Zimbabwe, can be viewed one minute in terms of 'traditional' British relationships with the United States, Russia or the Commonwealth and the next as the subject of a delicately negotiated EU common strategy or common position.

For the government, this presents opportunities rather than problems. Diplomats and ministers are used to working the same problem in different contexts and at different levels from one day to the next. The UN, NATO, the G8, the Commonwealth and the EU: all are grist to the mill.

Is there a problem for Parliament? On the face of it, there should not be. The 'traditional' mechanisms of debates, statements and questions in both Houses are flexible and can address each issue in multiple contexts. And yet, there is felt to be a problem, perhaps a serious one, for national accountability in relation to the European dimension. The House of Lords Committee commented on CFSP scrutiny in July 2000, endorsing the conclusion of Professor Jorg Monar that 'it will be increasingly difficult for national parliaments to exercise adequate democratic scrutiny of the collective elements of decision-making at the European level'.[1] Similar concerns were raised by government and opposition members in the House of Commons.[2] There was particular anxiety, as the Nice Convention and Intergovernmental Conference (IGC) loomed, that if national parliaments could not take a firmer grip of the CSFP and CESDP in all their aspects, then accountability and influence might be ceded by default to the European Parliament.

Given their highly executive nature and the fact that both the CFSP and the CESDP are relative new comers to the formal parliamentary scrutiny processes, there is much less in the way of formal documentation than there would be for, say, agriculture or fisheries. Nonetheless, the reports of select committees and parliamentary debates and questions will form the core material of this chapter. It should also be noted that this material reflects a clear party political divide on many of the issues discussed, making it difficult to isolate the impact or effect of cross-party parliamentary scrutiny. After briefly outlining relevant historical developments, the chapter looks first at the CFSP. The following section concentrates on the CESDP and has a different structure. It concentrates on four major themes that have dominated parliamentary consideration of the CESDP – the relationship with NATO, the 'exclusivity' of the CESDP, its capabilities and the ability of the Westminster Parliament to exercise appropriate oversight. The chapter concludes that key issues of accountability remain to be addressed at the 2004 IGC and that consideration of the CFSP and the CESDP cannot be divorced from broader questions of foreign policy orientation.

## The development of the CFSP and CESDP

The aspiration to harmonise the foreign policies of what were then the six members of the European Economic Community can be traced back to the 'Luxembourg Report' of 1970. The six foreign ministers reported jointly to their heads of state and government:

> The present development of the European Communities requires Member States to intensify their political co-operation and provide in an initial phase the mechanism for harmonising their views on international affairs.[3]

For the next 20 years the process known as 'European Political Cooperation' developed gradually, if fitfully, outside the formal structures created by the European treaties. From 1975 the newly created 'European Council' (the meeting of heads of government, plus, in the case of France, the President of the Republic) met in dual mode, 'in the Council of the Communities and in the context of political co-operation'. In 1986, the Single European Act gave the European Council a distinct treaty base and defined the objective 'to formulate and implement a European foreign policy'.

After much further deliberation, the Maastricht Treaty of 1992 combined the diplomatic work done under 'political co-operation' with a new defence and security dimension founded on the existing (but hitherto quite separate) Western European Union (WEU). Together these were to form a CFSP pillar of the new overarching Treaty on EU. The Amsterdam Treaty of 1997 took the 'second pillar' process a stage further, adding new instruments and infrastructure. Since the Amsterdam Treaty, most of the major innovations and developments have been more specifically in the areas of defence and security.

At Maastricht and Amsterdam, the British had insisted that the WEU and NATO needed to be kept separate, largely because they felt that any merger would damage NATO and that the EU's bureaucracy would stifle the ability to act swiftly in a crisis. However, it was this stance that Tony Blair's Labour Government began to change in the later part of 1998 and which set off a chain of very rapid developments.

Indications of a change in British thinking began to emerge in the press in the autumn of 1998.[4] Official confirmation of change came at an informal European Council meeting in Austria on 24 October 1998, where the British prime minister called for 'fresh thinking' on defence and mentioned the possibility of a gradual merger of the WEU into the EU. This was taken a step further at an Anglo–French Summit on 3–4 December 1998, when Tony Blair conceded that the EU needed a defence capability autonomous from NATO, and the French conceded the primacy of NATO in European security and especially in relation to collective defence.[5]

The 50th anniversary summit of NATO in Washington in April 1999 is also significant. It talked of NATO lending its assets for European-led operations to the EU rather than to the WEU (as had been the case since 1994 under NATO's Combined Joint Task Force Concept).[6] The formal establishment of the CESDP came with the EU's Helsinki Summit in December 1999. Essentially two major decisions were taken at Helsinki. The first of these was to create a European Rapid Reaction Force (ERF) which was to be comprised of 60,000 personnel, be deployable within sixty days and sustainable for up to one year. By 2003 this force was to have the capability to carry out 'Petersberg' tasks[7] on behalf of the EU. The second was the creation of three new military bodies, modelled on NATO structures, within the EU. These were the Political and Security Committee, the European Military Committee and the European Military Staff.[8]

These new committees, meeting initially as interim committees, worked throughout 2000 towards first creating a capabilities catalogue and then holding a Capabilities Commitment Conference. At this conference in November 2000 all members of the EU, with the exception of Denmark, committed something to the Helsinki goals, including ERF.[9] Also in November 2000, the WEU agreed to the transfer of most of its tasks and resources to the EU.

The Treaty of Nice, negotiated in December 2000, did not say much in relation to defence and security. However, the simultaneous Conclusions of the Presidency did contain a report on European Security and Defence at Annex VI, which outlined developments since Helsinki.[10] In November 2001, a Capabilities Enhancement Conference aimed to provide the CESDP and its ERF with additional resources, and by the Laeken Summit of December 2001, the EU felt able to declare itself ready to undertake some, but not all, elements of crisis management, although practical realisation continued to be hampered by Greco–Turkish tension.[11]

## Scrutiny of Common Foreign and Security Policy documents

Foreign policy in the broad sense (including external security policy) has two characteristics which distinguish it from domestic policy and make it an awkward candidate for European scrutiny as previously understood at Westminster: it is only occasionally expressed in formal documents; and, for reasons of discretion and security, it tends to be conducted by the executive branch with only rather sporadic and general political accountability to Parliament. Tony Blair's comfortable parliamentary position compared to that of his immediate predecessor heightens the sense of executive control.[12] An additional difficulty is that decisions, even when expressed in legal texts, are frequently taken as a matter of urgency in response to fast moving events.

The House of Lords Committee began to carry out 'informal scrutiny' of second pillar documents after the Maastricht Treaty came into force in 1993, but the shift to formal scrutiny by the committees of both Houses came only in 1998 following the Amsterdam Treaty. The terms of reference of the Commons Committee were altered in December 1998 to incorporate 'any proposal for a common strategy, a joint action or a common position under Title V of the TEU'. As with domestic and economic matters, the Commons Committee can refer CFSP documents that it regards as being of legal or political importance for debate in one of the European Standing Committees, or can recommend debate on the floor of the House. The House of Lords followed suit a year later, creating its new sub-committee to cover CFSP. The first chairman was Lord Howell, a former chairman (as David Howell) of the Commons' Foreign Affairs Committee. The three main categories of documents which are subject to the Westminster scrutiny procedure are the three principal instruments designed to carry forward the CFSP: common strategies, joint actions and common positions. Miscellaneous statements and press releases issued by the CFSP 'High Representative', of which there are a great many, are not binding expressions of policy and are not included in the scrutiny process, although they may be referred to in parliamentary debates. The revised Commons terms of reference of 1998 also allow matters to be referred to departmental committees for an opinion. This provision has not been much used to date in CFSP fields, but in

April 2000 the Defence Committee was asked for (and gave) its opinion on a presidency progress report on the CESDP.[13]

Common strategies were a new instrument, created by the Amsterdam Treaty. They were intended to cover very broad regions or areas of EU external policy where decisions were likely to be needed under all three pillars of the Union. It was felt that the post-Maastricht system had not taken sufficient account of the need to integrate 'cross-pillar' policy-making. In particular, common strategies were intended to bring together 'community' instruments (such as trade agreements) on the one hand, and political or security initiatives on the other. Such high level integrating strategies would be developed by the Council of Ministers, but decisions would have to come from the European Council and be agreed unanimously.

Common positions and joint actions are lower level instruments, which may be free-standing or implement an existing strategy. Common positions are expressions of an agreed EU approach; joint actions are matters for operational implementation. The voting rules in the Council of Ministers are complex.[14] In brief, if the subsidiary instruments are non-military in nature and in furtherance of an existing common strategy, than they may be agreed by qualified majority voting (QMV) in the Council; but if any single Member State should express opposition for 'important and stated reasons of national policy' then the decision would be blocked; if sufficient number of states to form a qualified majority continue to support the decision then it will be referred up to the next European Council. Common positions and joint actions of a military nature and/or not arising from an adopted common strategy would always be subject to unanimous agreement in the Council, with the proviso that Member States not wishing to take part, but also not wishing to frustrate the others, may register a constructive abstention.

In practice, this delicate web of rules and exceptions was not likely to result (and to date has not resulted) in frequent use of QMV in controversial circumstances. At most it could persuade governments which wished to block EU action in a particular area to state their reasons more openly and to be prepared to argue their case at the Summit level.

### Experience of scrutiny of the common strategies

The EU has so far adopted common strategies on Russia (June 1999), Ukraine (December 1999) and the Mediterranean (June 2000). A common strategy on the Balkans has been discussed, but had made little progress as of early 2002, partly because of Greek sensitivities concerning Macedonia and strains over the role of NATO in the region.[15] Indeed, after the initial burst of activity there has been some frustration and disappointment with the 'common strategy' concept and calls for any future common strategies to have more limited and practical foreign policy objectives.[16]

The setting up of Sub-Committee C in the House of Lords came too late for it to reflect on the first two Common Strategies, on Russia and Ukraine, but the third, the Common Strategy on the Mediterranean, was the subject of a full-scale inquiry by the sub-committee, despite the fact that it had been adopted in haste before the sub-committee had time to take evidence. The report took the opportunity to comment more generally on the concept of common strategies as well as on the particular issues raised by the Mediterranean strategy.[17]

In the Commons, the Foreign Affairs Committee had commented in passing on the EU Common Strategy on Russia (adopted 4 June 1999) and on other aspects of EU activity relating to Russia in its report on *Relations with the Russian Federation*,[18] but made only three recommendations related to the strategy (criticising the inefficiency of the Technical Assistance to the Commonwealth of Independent States (TACIS) programme, calling for a reassessment of restrictions on trade and asking for regular reports on UK contributions to the weapons disposal programme).

The Common Strategy on Ukraine was referred by the Commons European Scrutiny Committee to a European Standing Committee. Indeed, as of June 2002 it was still the only CFSP document to have been examined in this way. However, as with the House of Lords and the Mediterranean strategy, the examination came in European Standing Committee B on 9 February 2000 after the Ukraine strategy had been formally adopted by the European Council on 11 December 1999.

The proceedings in European Standing Committee B opened with the then Minister for Europe, Keith Vaz, explaining that the objectives of the strategy 'closely resemble and complement our bilateral objectives'. Members of the committee expressed concerns about Ukraine's political stability, its economic progress and commitment to human rights (including the abolition of the death penalty). It became clear in the course of the questions and debate that conditional funding for technical assistance through TACIS formed a major element of the strategy.

### Scrutiny of common positions and joint actions

The European Scrutiny Committee and its advisers have diligently examined a considerable variety of CFSP common positions and joint actions since they were included in the terms of reference in 1998, but none has been recommended for further consideration in European Standing Committee or on the floor of the House.

These documents tend to be either very minor, or very urgent, in neither case offering easy targets for scrutiny. The Committee has often expressed frustration about this. Some of the issues covered, for example, EU sanctions against Zimbabwe following criticism of its election and human rights record, are of considerable interest to UK parliamentarians, but the latters' focus tends to be on current events and policies rather than on the technical agreements needed to implement or renew sanctions. It would almost certainly be fruitless to recommend debates on these documents to be held several weeks or months later when devices such as statements, parliamentary questions and adjournment debates offer more immediate opportunities to react to the political events that have prompted the sanctions. Many documents relating to EU external matters are cleared by the European Scrutiny Committee not only without any recommendation for debate, but on the basis that they do not raise questions of sufficient legal or political importance to be reported substantively. These include appointments of individuals to be Special Representatives in troubled regions of the world and renewals of previous decisions that were time limited. In its May 2002 review of procedures the Committee suggested that some of these routine decisions might be submitted in the form of quarterly lists, rather than individually deposited as hitherto.[19]

There have been frequent examples of decisions being made in the Council of Ministers before there has been any opportunity for Westminster scrutiny. The Committee accepts this with varying degrees of fortitude. In its Third Report of 2001–02[20] the ESC cleared a document extending the EU Common Position on Burma, which had actually been agreed in the General Affairs Council four weeks later . The Committee acknowledged that the document was of political importance and some sensitivity (because it balanced a decision to prolong the political sanctions contained in the Common Position with some modest supplementary concessions designed to signal approval of small improvements in the political and human rights stance of the Burmese government), but also conceded that the Government had been right to agree to the decision without prior scrutiny. It accepted the Minister's argument that work by officials on the decision had continued right up to the General Affairs Council at which it had to be adopted, were the previous Common Position not to lapse.

On another occasion, a Common Position on ballistic missile proliferation was adopted before the committee could report on it. The Committee accepted the reasons for this, but declined to give formal clearance pending clarification of some points by the Foreign and Commonwealth Office (FCO).[21] The Committee has often commented on what it regards as inadequacies in the administration of the scrutiny process. For example, in October 2001 the Committee agreed to clear retrospectively two documents concerned with the extension of EU financial support for confidence-building measures on the Russian-Georgian borders, on which political agreement had actually been reached in the Council of Ministers in July, but it also asked the FCO to make sure that the requirements of parliamentary scrutiny were more strictly observed in the future.[22]

The Minister for Europe, Peter Hain, told the Committee on 11 March 2002:

> We have had a spate of recent initiatives on common foreign and security policy, and I know there have been problems with that which you have written to me about, Chairman, and I think our officials are going to meet... to seek a way forward, and we genuinely want to find a way forward. It is not in my interests as a Minister to have your Committee dissatisfied on this point. We want to be open and accessible to you, and I hope we can agree that.

## Common European Security and Defence Policy

While his comfortable parliamentary and party positions combined with the highly executive nature of defence and security policy present Mr Blair with an unparalleled opportunity, they also draw attention to issues of accountability and scrutiny. The ability of

Parliament to exercise scrutiny in these areas is further hampered by the fact that the CESDP coexists with other defence and security institutions in an often bewilderingly complex fashion.

A survey of various parliamentary debates and select committee reports since the Treaty of Amsterdam suggests that there are a number of issues in relation to the CESDP that consistently concern parliamentarians. The first of these not surprisingly relates to the relationship between the CESDP and NATO and the possible impact this might have on the United Kingdom's relations with the United States. The second concern relates to the 'exclusivity' of the CESDP and, especially, what it means for the European members of NATO who are not EU members. A third concern relates to the capabilities of the CESDP and how adequate they might be in carrying out the Petersberg tasks. A particular consideration here is the possibility that the EU might become involved in the 'sharp-edge' of peacemaking and peacekeeping for which it is ill equipped both organisationally and logistically. These are all exceptionally important issues and failure to consider them judiciously with democratic accountability has the potential to impact negatively on the United Kingdom, the EU, the rest of Europe, NATO and the United States.

## NATO and the United States

Given that the United Kingdom's strongest objection to the development of any sort of autonomous EU defence and security capability before 1998 was that it might harm relations with NATO and the United States, it is perhaps not surprising that this possibility remains a consistent concern among parliamentarians. The First Report of the House of Lords EU Select Committee's Sub-Committee C published in July 2000, contains the opinion '[w]e cannot express too strongly our anxiety at the danger of the CESDP turning into a damp squib and consequently into seriously deteriorating relations with the United States'.[23] This concern was repeated in an update produced by the House of Lords Select Committee after the November 2000 Capabilities Commitment Conference.[24] There are three related areas of the CESDP's relations with NATO and the United States that cause particular difficulty for parliamentarians, and in all of them there is some dispute over the wording and interpretation of key texts. These three areas correspond to three quite fundamental questions: who would command a European-led operation; who would plan a European-led operation and who would decide on a European-led operation?

In a March 2001 motion in the House of Commons to 'welcome the Government's approach to a Common Security and Defence Policy', the then Minister of State for the Foreign and Commonwealth Office, Keith Vaz, outlined the Government's view of developments since Amsterdam. Mr Vaz told the Commons that the CESDP and the Helsinki Conclusions were supported by the United States and NATO and that there was no duplication of NATO resources. He went on to say that this was not a European army and that EU nations would decide on an operation 'only after consultations with NATO and once it was clear that NATO was not going to act'. In those situations where NATO did act, or for any EU-led operations using NATO assets, 'the operational planning and command structures will come from NATO'.

The Minister conceded that the EU would only be able to act on its own in limited circumstances and for these 'small EU-led operations, the alternative exists of planning done by national Headquarters'. According to the Minister, 'EU nations will determine the objectives for an EU operation and will be responsible for its strategic control and political direction.' Finally, the Minister promised full consultation with non-EU countries and suggested that when they made a 'significant contribution' to any operation, they 'will take part in its day-to-day management on the same basis as participating member states'.[25]

Several parliamentarians pressed the Minister for clarification and pushed different interpretations of the Nice documents. William Cash, Iain Duncan Smith and Quentin Davies all questioned whether the initiative had US support and whether the Prime Minister had spoken with a 'forked tongue'[26] to President Bush, stressing an interpretation that was not supported in the documentation. According to these members of the Conservative Opposition, President Bush was told by Tony Blair that 'there would be a joint command and that planning would take place inside NATO'.[27] But as Quentin Davies and Iain Duncan Smith both pointed out, there is no mention of joint commands in the Nice document. John Redwood, in the same debate, claimed that CESDP is 'a scheme for a comprehensive military force that does things that NATO does not want to do – not under NATO command and not in cooperation, but separate and deliberately so' and that is why the EU has set up military structures.[28]

Planning within NATO is also not unambiguously supported in the documentation. Quentin Davies claimed that there would be problems with using any sort of European or national Headquarters, or, indeed with using NATO's planning capabilities anywhere because of the possibility of a veto from the Turkish Government. (Mr Davies also accused the Government of systematically attempting to 'conceal from Parliament' this latter problem.)[29]

The involvement of NATO in planning presupposes that it will have the opportunity to become involved, and concern that it would not have such an opportunity had been raised on 11 December 2000, immediately after Nice, by Michael Howard. Mr Howard claimed that the Nice documentation did not support the Government's contention that the EU would only become involved in operations where NATO as a whole decided not to act. According to Mr Howard, the wording 'where NATO as a whole is not engaged' can be interpreted in only one way. According to those documents, the EU – not NATO – will decide whether or not NATO is to be engaged. There is no question of NATO having the option to decide or having choice. There is not a word to that effect in the documents, which represent the text to which the Prime Minister and the Foreign Secretary have put their signatures. With a stroke of a pen, they have put at risk the greatest peacetime alliance that the world has ever seen.[30]

This is also a concern that has been picked up by the Liberal Democrats and has consistently been a central platform of their contributions to parliamentary debates. For example, Menzies Campbell told the House of Commons on 11 July 2001 'I adhere strongly to a view that I have persistently expressed here in the House…we need a formal protocol between NATO and the EU in which NATO is given a formal right of first refusal.…I would go further and argue that strategic planning should also be located in NATO.'[31]

Given that some of the most vocal critics of the CESDP in these parliamentary debates are also on the Euro-sceptical wing of the opposition Conservative Party, their comments may also serve partisan and ideological purposes. However, it is also true that many of the concerns they raise are voiced in the generally less partisan atmosphere of the Select Committees. For example, the relationship between NATO and EU planning is a central concern of the Eighth Report of the 1999–2000 session of the Commons Defence Select Committee (chaired by Labour MP Bruce George). In order to ensure no duplication between the two organisations and to ensure appropriate coordination, the Committee made two recommendations in the run up to Nice. The first was that the inaugural Chairman of the European Military Committee should be from a European Union NATO country, and the second was that NATO's Deputy Supreme Allied Commander Europe should have the right to attend all meetings of the European Military Committee.[32] These recommendations were acknowledged in broad terms by the Government in its response to the report,[33] but not fully adopted by the EU. However, it is clear from questions asked at the Defence Committee evidence session in December 2001 that the concerns persist.[34] The importance of a properly functioning and resourced CESDP to relations with the United States and NATO was also raised in a recent report by the Select Committee on Foreign Affairs.[35]

Similarly the Foreign Affairs Select Committee in its report on *European Enlargement and Nice Follow-up* in the 2000–01 session was concerned about the potential veto over the use of NATO's facilities by non-EU NATO members such as Turkey. The Committee was so dissatisfied by the Minister's comments on this issue that it 'recommended that the Department in its Response to this Report clarifies whether it considers that any single NATO member will have a veto over provision of NATO assets and capabilities for an EU-led military operation'.[36] (Three months later in July 2001, the Government replied that all non-EU NATO members had a right of veto.) The possibility of veto however, is not the only difficulty in relation to the non-NATO members.

### 'Exclusivity' of CESDP

The membership of the EU coincides with neither that of NATO nor the wider European set of nation-states, and this has also caused some parliamentary anxiety. The EU has set up mechanisms by which these non-EU members can be associated with the CESDP and it is these arrangements which have been the subject of debate. These non-EU members can be divided into two sub-sets:

1. European members of NATO that are not members of the EU.
2. States that are currently members of neither NATO nor the EU.

It is the former category comprising the Czech Republic, Hungary, Iceland, Norway, Poland and Turkey that are generally considered the most important and are often referred to in the format of EU + 6. As early as the Helsinki Summit in 1999, the EU recognised the need to involve the non-EU members of NATO. The Summit Declaration stated that:

> Modalities will be developed for full consultation, cooperation and transparency between the EU and NATO, taking into account the needs of all EU Member States . . . [A]ppropriate arrangements will be defined that would allow, while respecting the Union's decision making autonomy, non-EU European NATO members and other interested States to contribute to EU military crisis management.[37]

This commitment was strongly supported by the Defence Select Committee in its consideration of Helsinki and associated developments. It warned that even though 'in operational circumstances' institutional arrangements may have to be fluid it was nonetheless 'vital to the success of the [C]ESDP . . . that the special status of the six is formally and fully acknowledged. There must be a structure for the non-EU European allies which exists alongside but is fully integrated with the EU'.[38] The Committee went on to recommend regular consultation between the EU and the six NATO members. Regular meetings in peacetime and more frequent meetings during a crisis were subsequently established by the Nice Summit.[39]

However, it does remain uncertain how the NATO six and the others will fit into the CESDP in a crisis. Concern also remains about how the input of others can be reconciled with 'full respect for the decision making autonomy of the EU and the single institutional framework of the Union' on any really inclusive basis. It is this that some parliamentarians feel relegates these countries to 'second class citizens within the security apparatus of their own continent. . . . The non-EU countries have just as great an interest in the security of our continent as do the EU nations'.[40]

### European Rapid Reaction Force – capabilities and commitments

In terms of the potential commitments of the ERF, the concerns of parliamentarians centre on definitions of the Petersberg tasks and the geographic scope within which the ERF could be deployed. According to Oakes, the capabilities catalogue, although it contained mostly classified information, was structured around four scenarios. These were separation by force of belligerent parties, peacekeeping, humanitarian aid and the evacuation of nationals.[41] The Defence Select Committee sought a clarification of what this meant in practice from Defence Secretary Geoff Hoon. The Committee was also unimpressed by Mr Hoon's argument that a certain vagueness was necessary 'in order to avoid artificial constraints'.[42] What worried the Committee most were operations at the 'upper end' of the Petersberg missions, meaning those deemed 'most demanding', and as an example of such a mission Mr Hoon offered Operation Allied Force in Kosovo during 1999. The Committee stated:

> [w]e should not be too ready to accept the Secretary of State's admonition against 'esoteric' discussions about the nature of the Petersberg tasks. The first duty of a commander must be to understand the nature of the war in which he is about to become engaged.[43]

This concern was echoed by the House of Lords Select Committee in its update on European security and defence after the November 2000 capabilities commitment conference.[44] There was also some anxiety, and a sharp party political divide, over the capabilities committed and what they signify. On the one hand, several prominent members of the Conservative Party, including Iain Duncan Smith, expressed the opinion that the capabilities committed were far in excess of those needed for Petersberg tasks and thus the ERF was a European army.[45] On the other hand, there have been several expressions of concern that the capabilities committed to the ERF are insufficient both in terms of tasks it may be expected to do and in terms of defence expenditure. At a very early stage the House of Lords Select Committee on the EU expressed its opinion that the Helsinki targets of deploying 60,000 within 60 days and sustaining the force for up to one year were insufficient.[46] Other parliamentarians expressed their doubts that the levels of defence expenditure across the EU were not able to support the proper development of the ERF.[47] Menzies Campbell also raised the issue of efficiency in defence expenditure:

> The real question is not what is being spent, but what we are getting for the money that is being spent; to use an expression

that was current about 10 or 15 years ago, how big a bang are we getting for the buck?...Those of us who support a European defence and security policy...must also argue the case as persuasively as we can – within our Parties and this House, and outside – to ensure that sufficient expenditure is made available to make a European security and defence policy a reality.[48]

From the evidence sought at the December 2001 Defence Select Committee hearing on European defence and security it seems that the issue of matching capability to threat remains of concern to parliamentarians.[49] It is correct, of course, that parliamentarians should be concerned with such issues given the potential of the ERF to commit UK citizens to arenas of intense conflict. This leads into the final area to be considered here.

### Parliamentary oversight and scrutiny: the wider issues

The issue of parliamentary oversight of the CFSP has been a consistent subject of interest to members of both Houses. In early 2000, the Defence Select Committee pointed out that the development of the CESDP and the ERF had heightened concerns. The Committee questioned the Secretary of State for Defence on the issue of democratic accountability and was told that since any decision to commit British forces to an CESDP action would be made solely by the British Government 'the scrutiny of that decision will continue to rest firmly in Parliament'.[50] But the issue is much more complicated than this. There are questions relating to the role of both the parliamentary assembly associated with the WEU (and less directly the North Atlantic Assembly associated with NATO) and EU institutions.

The Defence Select Committee and the House of Lords Select Committee on the EU emphasise the primacy of Westminster scrutiny. However, they also state that this does not exclude other bodies from playing a role too, although the Lords appears to be more open to the European Parliament playing a role than does the Defence Select Committee.[51] The Parliamentary Assembly of the WEU has also been defended in the House of Commons debates on the grounds that it provides a mechanism of scrutiny as well as information coordination. Indeed, pleas have been made for its continued existence on these grounds despite the fact that the EU has essentially taken over all the functions of the WEU.[52]

In terms of the European Parliament, or other EU institutions, parliamentarians raise two related issues. First that the Treaties do give the European Parliament and the Commission a role in the CFSP and the CESDP, and second that this role is inappropriate. As the Defence Select Committee points out, the Treaty on EU requires that the Presidency of the Council consult the European Parliament on the major aspects and choices of the CFSP and take the views of the Parliament into consideration. The Parliament is also able to ask questions of the Council and make recommendations to it in addition to holding an annual debate on the progress of the CFSP.[53] Although the decision to commit forces to any particular action may be the prerogative of national governments and thus subject to scrutiny and accountability at Westminster, there is concern that once an action is under way this role is lost as 'the operation commander will report on the conduct of the operation to EU bodies only'.[54]

As this suggests, the European Parliament is already active in the field of CFSP. There are occasional debates in plenary sessions and question-and-answer sessions with CFSP 'High Representative' Solana, but the main instrument is the committee which now carries the unwieldy title 'EP Committee on Foreign Affairs, Human Rights, Common Security and Defence Policy' (FAHRCSDP). Nor does the European Parliament any longer steer clear of 'purely' military matters. In a plenary debate on 24 October 2001 the FAHRCSDP chairman (Elmar Brok) stressed the need for the Rapid Reaction Force, expanded military transport capability and 'our own' satellite system, as essential for the credibility of the CFSP.[55] However, the Parliament has no budgetary responsibility for such matters.

Whereas the machinery at Westminster is designed primarily to scrutinise laws and policy instruments before they are adopted, the European Parliament focuses instead on monitoring implementation after the event, and therefore does not feel the same sense of frustration when commitments are made without prior consultation. Thus, the FAHRCSDP committee appointed a rapporteur on the Common Strategy on Ukraine after it had been adopted in December 1999 and proceeded to carry out an investigation, reporting in February 2001. On 15 March 2001 the Parliament passed a resolution on the Common Strategy on Ukraine, on the basis of the committee's report.[56] The lengthy resolution supported High Representative

Solana's conclusion that 'the common strategies will become more credible if their goals become more specific, if priorities are clearly formulated, if there is a vision on added value and if sufficient means are available for implementation'. Its political effect was to reinforce the message to Ukraine that continuing EU goodwill would be dependent on progress in political democracy, economic modernisation and human rights.

A good deal of the CFSP is financed from trade and aid provisions in the Community budget, over which the European Parliament has well-established oversight. External Affairs commissioner Patten, for example, has acknowledged in relation to the Balkans that 'aid as a supportive part of our policy is exceptionally important'.[57] Moreover, under the Interinstitutional Agreement of 1999, the Council has undertaken to report annually to the Parliament on 'the main aspects and basic choices of CFSP, including the financial implications for the general budget of the European Communities'.[58] The Parliament can also amend the EC external relations budget. The UK Treasury Minister Ruth Kelly reported to the Commons European Scrutiny Committee as a *fait accompli* that in the aftermath of September 11, the European Parliament had approved a major switch of funding from the Balkans to Afghanistan.[59]

In evidence to the Lords EU Committee (Sub-Committee A) on the role of EU aid in the Balkans, the Dutch MEP Arie Oostlander noted that there were MEPs who followed Balkan developments very closely and were very well-informed. He also applauded the work of national parliaments, not least because 'not only the money of the Union as such is involved in these plans but also money coming from the Member States themselves separately'.[60] He suggested that the European Parliament and national parliaments should 'pool our knowledge and play the ball to each other'.[61]

In many ways the European Parliament would be in a strong position to accept a larger degree of responsibility for foreign policy and security, if not for specifically military matters. It has the mechanisms for closely monitoring and influencing the community budget, ready access to both Commissioner Patten and CFSP High Representative Solana, and a rapporteur system that allows committees to keep track of multiple issues at the same time.

On the other hand, many EU Governments (not only the UK) would be nervous about giving the European Parliament direct competence in defence matters, especially when, in practice, the major military contributions to future projects are likely to come from a handful of countries. And, despite the high proportion of aid that is administered by the Commission, there is still a significant component that is contributed by national governments. For example, in the case of the Ukraine strategy, the United Kingdom provides around £13 million as its share of European Community programmes supporting Ukraine, but it also provides around £9 million in bilateral technical assistance.[62]

For the moment, the British Government and Parliament are in agreement that Westminster should have the primary scrutiny role and the Government admits that there is a need for much more to be done in the area of scrutiny and accountability. In its response to the Defence Select Committee's report, the Government stated:

> We agree that the question of democratic scrutiny of European defence arrangements needs to be tackled. As Member States will remain individually responsible for decisions about the deployment of their armed forces, the primary responsibility for parliamentary scrutiny of European defence will rest with national Parliaments. At the European level, we believe that it is more important to get future parliamentary oversight right than to rush through changes that might have treaty implications. It will be better, therefore, to address this question once the permanent arrangements are in place in the EU.[63]

These arrangements have subsequently been put in place, although some decisions regarding the WEU were still outstanding in mid-2002. The issue of CFSP scrutiny was not addressed at Nice but is very likely to be part of the agenda at the 2004 IGC.

## Conclusions

Parliamentary scrutiny of the CFSP and the CESDP is relatively new and for a variety of reasons somewhat different from scrutiny in other areas. However, parliamentarians have engaged with both the processes and mechanisms of scrutiny, and the complex and important issues thrown up by the policies. In terms of processes and mechanisms, there is general agreement that these are inadequate, but some difference of views as to the reasons. For some the problem is that the second pillar does not easily lend itself to document-based scrutiny; others point to the traditional reluctance of governments to involve Parliament in the detail of external and security policy any more than is politically expedient; others again might question whether sufficient MPs at Westminster any longer have the appetite and the knowledge to specialise in such matters.

Although there is great reluctance to hand new powers to the European Parliament in these areas, a Lords report has pointed out that the European Parliament is likely to acquire some competence by default if political obligations relating to security initiatives are to be funded out of the EU budget.[64] This could lead to a sharing of accountability between national parliaments and the democratic institutions at the European level which is very much part of the general 2004 IGC agenda. The desirability of shared accountability is a matter of personal and political judgement, but at this time, as this chapter has shown, it would not be a development consciously willed by the British Government or Parliament.

In its report on the idea of a European second chamber, the House of Lords European Union Committee acknowledged that there were weaknesses in the scrutiny of the second pillar and that some policies in this area were agreed without reference to national parliaments. However, it was not immediately convinced that a new second chamber would solve the problem and concluded that 'those preparing the IGC should examine the mechanisms of CFSP scrutiny in depth'.[65]

The Commons European Scrutiny Committee has also acknowledged the problem and is also sceptical about the second chamber idea, on the grounds that such a chamber would not necessarily contain defence and foreign affairs specialists. Its preferred solution is that the primary scrutiny role should rest with national parliaments, but that there should be regular joint meetings of the defence, foreign affairs and European affairs committees of national parliaments to achieve what is described in the committee's report as 'collective scrutiny'.[66] If the primary responsibility remains with Westminster, then perhaps more consideration should be given to mechanisms for systematic ongoing scrutiny and review, alongside the existing system for tracking draft documents in the run-up to decision-making.

In terms of issues, parliamentary consideration of CFSP and especially CESDP has raised questions of fundamental orientation and priority. The Foreign Affairs Committee's first report after the Blair Government's re-election in 2001 was on relations, not with the EU, but with the United States. It declared '[n]ot withstanding Britain's membership of the European Union, the United Kingdom's diplomatic and marketing operations in the United States constitute by far the Foreign and Commonwealth Office's most important single overseas operation'.[67] Though this was written just after the events of September 11, it shows that in British eyes at least, CFSP and CESDP are still to be seen in the context of more traditional strategic relationships. It remains to be seen how the aftermath of September 11 and the subsequent Afghanistan and Irag wars will affect the longer-term viability of 'second-pillar' Europe.

While more effective scrutiny of EU efforts at concerted foreign and security policy might give CFSP and CESDP greater credibility with the British Parliament and public, a more integrationist mood in the United Kingdom in the years ahead might enable an eventual shift of responsibility and focus to the European Parliament. None of this is likely to gain real substance and significance until CFSP and CESDP are seen to work on a practical level and to achieve more tangible results. Only then will it become apparent whether or not the EU has finally grown into a fully coherent diplomatic and military coalition requiring systems of democratic accountability to match.

## Notes

1. House of Lords Select Committee on the European Union, Fifteenth Report, *The Common European Policy on Security and Defence*, HL 101, 1999–2000, paras 90–93. (Hereafter cited as House of Lords Select Committee on the European Union, HL 101.)
2. See, for example, defence questions in HC Deb, 27 November 2001, cc. 814–815 and during the Prime Minister's statement on the Laeken European Council, HC Deb, 17 December 2001, c. 20.
3. C. Carstairs and R. Ware (eds), *Parliament and International Relations*, Milton Keynes: Open University Press, 1991, p. 141.
4. R. Preston, 'Premier Tiptoes through EU Defence Minefield'. *Financial Times*, 1 October 1998, p. 12.
5. See http://www.fco.gov.uk/news/newstext.asp?1795.
6. See http://www.nato.int/docu/comm/1999/9904-wsh/9904-wsh.htm.
7. Essentially these are peacemaking, peacekeeping, humanitarian and rescue tasks.

8. See   http://ue.eu.int/Newsroom/LoadDoc.asp?BID=76&DID=59750&LANG=1 (hereafter cited as Helsinki Conclusions).

9. See http://ue.eu/pesc/military/en/CCC.htm.Other non-EU countries also made some contributions.

10. http://ue.eu.int/Newsroom/
    related.asp?max=1&bid=76&grp=3018&Lang=1 (hereafter cited as Nice Conclusions). It is often these Presidency conclusions that provide the information considered by the various bodies at Westminster.

11. http://ue.eu.int/Newsroom/
    related.asp?max=1&bid=76&grp=4061&Lang=1 (hereafter cited as Laeken Conclusions).

12. In recent times, only Mrs Thatcher was relatively unconstrained by her backbenchers on issues of Europe. See B. Soetendorp, *Foreign Policy in the European Union*, London: Routledge, 1999, p. 31.

13. House of Commons Select Committee on Defence, Eighth Report, *European Security and Defence*, HC 264, 1999–2000.

14. For a full explanation see House of Commons Library Research Paper 97/ 112: *The European Communities (Amendment) Bill: Implementing the Amsterdam Treaty*, pp. 26–27.

15. There is an EU strategy on aid to the Balkans, on which the Lords European Union Committee reported in April 2002 (House of Lords European Union Committee, Twentieth Report, *Responding to the Balkan Challenge: The Role of EU Aid*, HL 107, 2001–02 – but this is not a Common Strategy under Title V and does not cover security aspects.

16. House of Commons European Scrutiny Committee, Twentieth Report, HC 152-xx, 2001–02, para. 21.

17. House of Lords Select Committee on the European Union, Ninth Report, *The Common Mediterranean Strategy*, HL 51, 2000–01.

18. House of Commons Select Committee on Foreign Affairs, Third Report, *Relations with the Russian Federation*, HC 101, 1999–2000, xxvii.

19. House of Commons European Scrutiny Committee, Thirtieth Report, *European Scrutiny in the Commons*, HC 152-xxx, 2001–02, para. 111.

20. 12 November 2001, HC 152-iii.

21. House of Commons European Scrutiny Committee, Second Report, HC 152-ii, 2001–02.

22. House of Commons European Scrutiny Committee, Fourth Report, HC 152-iv, 2001–02, para. 15.12

23. House of Lords, Select Committee on European Union, HL 101, op. cit., para. 103.

24. House of Lords, Select Committee on European Union, First Report, *The Common European Policy on Security and Defence – an update*, HL 3, 2000–01, para. 96.

25. HC Deb, 19 March 2001, cc. 39–145.

26. Quentin Davies, HC Deb, 19 March 2001, c. 149.

27. George Bush as quoted in HC Deb, 19 March 2001, c. 147.

28. HC Deb, 19 March 2001, c. 143.

29. Ibid., c. 151.

30. HC Deb, 11 December 2000, c. 412.
31. HC Deb, 11 July 2001, c. 883.
32. House of Commons Select Committee on Defence, HC 264, op. cit., paras 62–63.
33. House of Commons Select Committee on Defence, *Government Observations on the Eighth Report from the Committee*, 3 August 2000, HC 732, 1999–2000, paras 7–10.
34. House of Commons Select Committee on Defence – Minutes of Evidence, HC 487-i, 19 December 2001.
35. House of Commons Select Committee on Foreign Affairs, Second Report, *British US Relations*, HC 327, 2001–02.
36. House of Commons Select Committee on Foreign Affairs, Fifth Report, *European Union Enlargement and Nice Follow-up*, HC 318, 2000–01, para. 33.
37. Helsinki Conclusions.
38. House of Commons Select Committee on Defence, HC 264, op. cit., paras 71, 74.
39. Nice Conclusions – see especially Annex VI.
40. John Wilkinson, HC Deb, 11 July 2001, c. 868.
41. M. Oakes, 'European Security and Defence Policy: Nice and Beyond', *Research Paper_01/50*, House of Commons Library, May 2001, p. 10.
42. House of Common Select Committee on Defence, HC 264, op. cit., para. 41.
43. Ibid., para. 42.
44. House of Lords Select Committee on the European Union, HL 3, op. cit., para. 6.
45. See for example, HC Deb, 22 November 2000, c. 314, HC Deb, 19 March 2000, cc. 141, 143.
46. See House of Lords Select Committee on the European Union, HL 101, op. cit., para. 101. See also HC Deb, 19 March 2001, c. 141.
47. See for example, HC Deb, 19 March 2001, cc. 155, 159.
48. HC Deb, 11 July 2001, cc. 882–883.
49. See House of Commons Select Committee on Defence, Minutes of Evidence HC 487-i, 19 December 2001.
50. House of Commons Select Committee on Defence, HC 264, op. cit., para. 81.
51. Ibid., and House of Lords Select Committee on the European Union, HL 101, op. cit., para. 106.
52. See, for example, HC Deb, 15 March 2001, c. 1257.
53. House of Common Select Committee on Defence, Eighth Report, HC 264, op. cit., para. 81.
54. See HC Deb, 17 October 2001, c. 1256.
55. European Parliament Debate of 24/10/02 – from europarl.eu.int/.
56. European Parliament Committee on Foreign Affairs, Human Rights, Common Security and Defence Policy, 28 February 2001, A5–83/2001.
57. House of Lords Select Committee on the European Union Committee, HL 107, op. cit., evidence p. 23.
58. H. Point, para. 40 of the Interinstitutional Agreement of 6 May 1999, Official Journal C 172, 18 June 1999.

59. House of Commons European Scrutiny Committee, Fourteenth Report, HC 152-xiv, 2001–02 (on the 02 budget).
60. House of Lords Select Committee on the European Union Committee, HL 107, op. cit., evidence para. 19.
61. Ibid., 22.
62. HC Deb, 10 January 2001, c. 579W.
63. House of Commons Select Committee on Defence, HC 732, op. cit., para. 13.
64. House of Lords Select Committee on the European Union, Fifteenth Report, *The Common European Policy on Security and Defence*, HL 101, 1999–2000, para. 92.
65. House of Lords Select Committee on the European Union, Seventh Report, *A Second Parliamentary Chamber for Europe: An Unreal Solution to Some Real Problems*, HL 48, 2001–02, paras 44–45.
66. House of Commons European Scrutiny Committee, *Democracy and Accountability in the EU and the role of national parliaments*, HC 152-xxxiii, 2001–02, para. 147.
67. House of Commons Select Committee on Foreign Affairs, HC 327, op. cit.

# 9
# Immigration and Asylum: Law and Policy in Action

*Gavin Drewry, with Gabrielle Garton Grimwood and Edward Wood*

## Introduction

> For an area that has on occasion [in the 20th] century seen little legislative action the 1990s has signalled a significant change of direction. Migration has become a key theme in national, regional and international debates.[1]

The chapter will discuss some of the most prominent debates in recent years surrounding asylum and immigration (closely linked and often considered together, but not in fact synonymous) and, in particular, the role of Parliament in both shaping and responding to those debates. This is a subject-area the history of which long predates the Treaty of Rome. But in recent years the progress of European integration and the quest for harmonisation of law and practice among EU Member States (with the European Convention on Human Rights as a significant part of the backcloth) have increasingly impinged upon it. But in some respects – ones that have at least as much impact on the day-to-day agendas of Westminster parliamentarians – Europe itself may be seen as the source of "the problem" with immigration and asylum. Conversely, EU policies in this area sometimes resonate with Eurosceptic concerns about whether policies that are good for continental Europe are necessarily appropriate for the geographically insular United Kingdom. Thus the Commons

Home Affairs Committee (HAC) observed, in its report on *Border Controls* that:

> Geography has endowed Great Britain with a natural barrier between it and other countries; economics has dictated that entry and departure occurs mainly through major sea and air ports; history means that there are people living in many parts of the world who have family links with the UK. Consequently the UK has a very different approach to its immediate neighbours, most of whom are now part of the Schengen Convention for free movement of people between countries.[2]

Moreover, immigration and asylum are tightly intertwined with other issues, such as housing, welfare and security, as, for instance, the Sangatte refugee centre near Calais (closed at the end of 2002). At a European macro-policy level lies the prospect of EU enlargement – inevitably bringing with it further cross-border and security issues – discussed later in this chapter, and elsewhere in this book (see in particular Chapter 8). And beyond Europe the outrages of September 11th 2001 have prompted alarm about the possibility of terrorist infiltration under the guise of asylum-seeking that is still rumbling on at the time of writing.

So far as the implications of immigration and asylum on public services are concerned, the same HAC Report just quoted concludes that:

> Few if any countries are organised to provide housing, education, health and other public services for large movements of genuine refugees and economic migrants. There needs to be a national debate about the implications of greater movement of people around the world and this should take place in a wider context than just the issues of asylum-seeking and illegal immigration.[3]

So this is a multi-layered subject – in which the impact of Europe on Westminster is interwoven with domestic and party politics, and the subject area itself has elastic and permeable boundaries. So it is necessary to begin with an account of the emergence of asylum and immigration as two of the most contested and emotive areas of domestic politics and to reflect on how they may have impinged on Parliament by their prominence in recent general election campaigns.

## The post-war politics of race, immigration and asylum

The politics of immigration and asylum generally, and specifically in the EU context, embrace many issues – territorial integrity, frontier security, protection of the domestic labour market – and of course the profoundly sensitive and difficult issues to do with race (itself a controversial term, though it is retained for the purposes of this discussion) and ethnicity.

Mainstream party politics in modern Britain has generally eschewed exploiting racial prejudice for electoral advantage, and far right parties such as the National Front and the British National Party have had much less electoral impact even at local, let alone national, level than some of their counterparts in continental Europe – in May 2002, three BNP candidates won local council seats in Burnley, shortly after the French National Front leader, Jean-Marie Le Pen came second in the first round of the French Presidential election. This has tended to camouflage the importance of race – and immigration – as a recurrent sub-plot of post-war British politics. This part of the story begins long before UK membership of the EU, with the end of Empire and the passing of the British Nationality Act 1948, which allowed Commonwealth citizens to settle freely in the United Kingdom.

Layton-Henry (1992) points out that by the beginning of the 21st century, emigration was an important part of British imperialist policy.[4] The depression between the two world wars propelled many disappointed emigrants to return to the United Kingdom but the trend towards emigration resumed after the Second World War and – coupled with the post-War labour shortage – caused such concern that the Royal Commission on Population was established in 1944. The Government of the day worked hard to recruit workers from displaced persons camps in Germany and migrant workers from Italy.

Although it was widely assumed that citizens of newly independent countries would have neither the inclination nor the resources to migrate to Britain, the continuing shortage of unskilled labour during the 1950s led British employers actively to recruit from the Caribbean and Indian subcontinent, which produced a substantial inflow of immigrants. The Commonwealth Immigrants Act 1962 reversed the policy of the 1948 Act by introducing a strict regime of immigration controls, and a system of employment permits. It was strengthened by a further Act of the same title, passed in 1968, and substantially replaced by the Immigration Act 1971. The British Nationality Act 1981 comprehensively recast the definition of British nationality, creating in all six categories of citizenship, with the right of abode in the United Kingdom attached only to one.

In addition to seeking to control immigration, governments also sought to tackle the growing problem of racial discrimination. Race Relations Acts in of 1965, 1968 and 1976 marked legislative attempts by successive governments to reduce the incidence of discrimination on the basis of nationality, citizenship and ethnic origin. In this context the language of public debate was very sensitive. Enoch Powell was dismissed from the Conservative Shadow Cabinet in 1968 following his notorious "rivers of blood" speech. Nevertheless, ten years later the next Conservative Leader Margaret Thatcher, felt able publicly to align herself with those who feared that the British character might be "swamped" by immigrants from different cultural backgrounds. Any reference to "swamping", however innocently intended, has particularly sensitive overtones in this context. In 2002, the Labour Home Secretary, David Blunkett, had to apologise for a "slip of the tongue" on the *Today* programme, when he explained proposals in the Nationality, Immigration and Asylum Bill, to introduce special schools for asylum seekers' children as being intended to prevent the "swamping" of local schools.[5]

In the post-Thatcher era, racial issues have intermittently re-surfaced in electoral politics. In 1992, in Cheltenham, the local Conservative Party selected a black candidate, John Taylor, but only after a bitter internal row in which racist attitudes were openly expressed. Elsewhere, Lord Whitelaw declined to speak in support of Sir Nicholas Fairbairn, campaigning in Perth, after he had claimed that "under a Labour government this country would be swamped (that word again) with immigrants of every colour and race and on any excuse of asylum or bogus marriage or just plain deception".[6] Although Butler and Kavanagh note that "immigration and race hardly came into the 1992 election at the national level",[7] within ten years asylum issues had become one of the hottest of political hot potatoes of the early years of the 21st century. Asylum, and its racial connotations, formed an important part of the backcloth to the 2001 general election.

Labour's manifesto for the 2001 general election offered a 5-point plan for dealing with asylum, with a mixture of policies to help the integration of those fleeing persecution and firm action against those seen to be abusing the system.[8] The Conservative manifesto, meanwhile, was committed to making the United Kingdom "a safe haven, not a soft touch, for asylum",[9] whilst the Liberal Democrats pledged to "reform the asylum system so that applicants are dealt with fairly and quickly".[10]

## The Blair Government's agenda

In July 1998, the Blair Government published a White Paper, *Faster and Firmer – A Modern Approach to Immigration and Asylum*[11] – which was the basis of the Immigration and Asylum Bill of the following session. At second reading, Jack Straw, the Home Secretary, claimed that his aim was "to make the system fairer, faster and firmer".[12] An interesting feature of the Bill's passage – it received the royal assent in November 1999 – was its reference to a special standing committee, empowered to take up to four sessions of oral evidence before undertaking clause-by-clause scrutiny. One of those who gave evidence was the Home Secretary himself, who said that he "strongly supported the setting up of a Special Standing Committee because it genuinely adds to the way in which Parliament scrutinises a Bill of this nature".[13] A formidable array of individuals and interest groups also gave evidence – much of it highly critical of various aspects of the Bill.

And the Government's policies attracted more general criticism. In April 2000, Bill Morris of the Transport and General Workers' Union criticised the institutional racism at the heart of Government and the climate of hostility towards asylum seekers which (he said) the Government had stirred up.[14]

In February 2001 Jack Straw, in a speech to the Institute for Public Policy Research, referred to the need to deter so-called "asylum shopping" (whereby asylum seekers make applications in more than one country) and other abuses of the asylum system.[15] This prompted accusations that the Home Secretary was seeking to undermine the internationally agreed (and widely accepted) concept of what it means to be a refugee and of inflaming hostility towards asylum seekers. He was accused of stoking controversy again in April 2001, when he suggested that the Amsterdam Treaty would provide an opportunity to revisit the Dublin Convention (see below) which had not worked as had been hoped. A month later, the Prime Minister, Tony Blair himself entered the debate. Writing in *The Times*, he too argued that reform of the 1951 Convention on Refugees was necessary, and should Labour win the forthcoming election, this would be a priority. What was needed, however, was reform of the way the convention operated, rather than its basic values.[16]

## The European dimension – the role and influence of the European Union

Since 1990 domestic policy on immigration and asylum has increasingly been shaped by EU initiatives. As a result of the fall of the Iron Curtain, the Member States of the European Community saw a dramatic increase in numbers of asylum seekers from Eastern and Central European states. At the same time, the number of asylum seekers from developing countries also increased. This coincided with the creation of the single European market, which required Member States to remove all internal barriers to commerce and free movement of people within the EC. In response to these developments (and also, some would add, to increased levels of racism and xenophobia in Europe), European Member States began the long process of harmonising their border controls and immigration and asylum policies. As the 2000 edition of the UNHCR publication *The State of the World's Refugees* put it:[17]

> The wish to remove obstacles to trade and other flows within the EU went in parallel with the desire to maintain control over the movement of people from non-member countries. At the same time, governments feared that freedom of movement within the EU would create numerous new problems in the immigration and asylum arena.

The Maastricht Treaty established the third pillar – Justice and Home Affairs (JHA) – as part of the new European Union in order to increase inter-Governmental co-operation on these issues. When Maastricht came into force in November 1993, the provisions of this Third Pillar subsumed the previous arrangements for discussing security, border controls and immigration at a pan-European level.

The Treaty of Amsterdam 1997 (some aspects of which are also discussed in Chapter 4) further extended EU competence on JHA matters. By Title IV of the Treaty, the EU gained powers to pass community legislation on immigration and asylum for the first time. The Treaty came into force in 1999. The UNHCR publication describes the Treaty in the following terms:

> The Treaty of Amsterdam ... represents a milestone in the development of European Union asylum policy. It sets out an agenda to move asylum matters over a five year period from an area where they are subject to inter-governmental agreement by the member states to one where policy development and decision-making fall clearly within the competence of the EU institutions.

A key feature of the change is that once the responsibility for policy and decision-making has passed to the European institutions, unanimity will not always be required. In addition, the European Parliament has a consultative role in developing the common policies. The European Court of Justice is permitted to issue preliminary rulings and to act as the last court of appeal in interpreting the relevant EU treaty provisions. The Treaty of Amsterdam lists six areas of refugee policy on which minimum standards must be agreed. These are areas on which Directives are now in force, or on which draft Directives or Regulations are under consideration. The target date for total agreement is 2004. However, the United Kingdom, along with Ireland and Denmark, negotiated an "opt in opt out" protocol to the immigration provisions of the Amsterdam Treaty, which means that it can, in effect, choose not to be bound by EU legislation on this subject.

We will examine some of the specific measures stemming from Amsterdam later. First, however, we will look at two important initiatives involving Member States which developed outside the EU framework, namely the Schengen and Dublin Conventions.

## The 1990 Dublin Convention

The Dublin Convention established common criteria for all EU Member States to determine which state is responsible for examining an asylum request. It also created a procedure for deciding which EU state is responsible. Another EU state can assume responsibility for an asylum claim under the Convention, although this rarely happens. Although the Dublin Convention was signed in 1990, insufficient countries had ratified the agreement to enable it to come into force until 1997. The rationale behind the Dublin Convention was to prevent the problem of "asylum shopping" whereby an asylum seeker who had been refused asylum in one state could make a series of further claims in other states with more favourable asylum laws. It was also designed to address the problem of "refugees in orbit". This term referred to those who arrived in an EU state, which then refused to consider the claim, but instead sent the asylum seeker back to another country. Frequently, the asylum seeker was passed around from country to country without his claim being determined at all.

There has been general dissatisfaction with the way in which the Dublin Convention works in practice on the part of Member States. Several problems have arisen: the high financial cost of administering the returns system under the Convention (for example Germany); the disproportionately high number of claims on those countries on the borders of the EU (for example Italy); and the asylum seekers who travel clandestinely through Europe with no documents and thus no evidence to show which country is responsible for determining the claim. That problem is compounded by the fact that illegal traffickers of asylum seekers destroy identity documents and other such evidence en route.

In the light of these problems, and following the coming into force of the Amsterdam Treaty, the Council of Ministers agreed in December 2002 on a Commission proposal to amend the original Dublin Convention and to transform it into an EC Regulation. Dublin II[18] is based on the same principle found in the Dublin Convention that people should only have one chance of making an asylum application within the area of the EU. This is the first EU country they enter, or the country which played the largest part in their gaining entry to the EU. Asylum seekers do not have the right to pick the country in which they want to apply for asylum. However, family reunion for unaccompanied minors, and for the family members of recognised refugees are priorities. It creates penalties for governments tolerating illegal residents without either trying to send them back, or dealing with their asylum applications. It also shortens the timetable for people to be transferred between countries.

## The 1990 Schengen Convention

This Convention, known as Schengen II, sought to reinforce external border controls to permit free movement within participating states. It includes provisions to strengthen police and judicial co-operation, and to introduce common visa policies and carrier sanctions, and was subject to parliamentary ratification in each state. It followed the similar 1985 Schengen Agreement (Schengen I) between five European States (not including the UK). Schengen II came into force on 1 September 1993 and began to be implemented in Member States from March 1995. Italy joined the group later in 1990, followed by Spain and Portugal in June 1991, Greece in 1992, Austria in 1995 and Denmark, Finland and Sweden in 1996. Thus, all EU members states except Ireland and the United Kingdom are now parties to the Convention. In addition, Iceland and Norway are associated with the implementation of the Schengen *acquis* and its further development.

The United Kingdom has adopted a position whereby it will opt in to those parts of the Schengen Agreement which it finds palatable. Thus, as a non-participant, the United Kingdom has stood aloof and remains free to maintain its own controls at national borders. Conversely, other states can impose controls on people arriving from the United Kingdom. British Governments have consistently argued that the United Kingdom should not surrender the advantage conferred by its island status in being relatively easily able to check people's identity and bona fides before they enter the United Kingdom rather than after, as is generally the case in other Member States where land borders are more porous. This (they argue) offers a more robust form of control.

Under the provisions of the Amsterdam Treaty, a protocol has been established for integrating Schengen into the framework of the EU. The Member States that have signed up to the Schengen Agreements now conduct their co-operation on abolishing internal borders under the institutional and legal framework of the EU. The Council has taken the place of the Executive Committee established by the Schengen Agreements. Ireland and the United Kingdom may take part in some or all of the arrangements under the Schengen *acquis* after a unanimous vote in the Council by the thirteen participating Member States plus the representative of the government of the State concerned.[19]

## Other measures adopted during the 1990s

In 1992, European Community ministers responsible for immigration approved three resolutions in London, known as the London Resolutions. They defined three concepts aimed at accelerating procedures for assessing asylum claims:

1. "manifestly unfounded" asylum applications;
2. safe third countries which asylum seekers passed through in transit to which they can be returned; and
3. countries where there is no serious risk of persecution.

The resolutions are not binding, but they have been applied in EU states and beyond. During the 1990s, the EU Council of Ministers approved a series of resolutions, recommendations and joint positions, which are also not legally binding. Among the instruments adopted were two recommendations on re-admission agreements, approved in 1994 and 1995. These established a model agreement for returning asylum seekers whose applications had been rejected or deemed unfounded. Between 1993 and 1996, the Council of Ministers agreed a series of "burden-sharing" measures to deal with situations where there was a large-scale influx of refugees (as during the conflict in Yugoslavia, for example). In June 1995, the Council of Ministers approved a resolution on minimum guarantees for asylum procedures. This outlined procedural rights and obligations. In March 1996, a joint position was agreed on the harmonisation of the term "refugee". The UNHCR publication observes that many of these measures have been criticised as representing harmonisation on the basis of the lowest common denominator.[20]

## Tampere

Article 63 of the Treaty of Amsterdam provides that new measures on asylum, introducing minimum standards on procedures, common criteria and mechanisms for determining which Member State is responsible for considering asylum applications, should be adopted within five years of the entry into force of the Treaty – that is, 1 May 1999. In fact it was not until October 1999 that the European Council at Tampere, Finland, agreed to work towards a common asylum policy.

The system envisaged at Tampere would lead to a common asylum procedure and a uniform status, valid throughout the Union, for those granted asylum. The system was initially to work towards "a clear and workable determination of the State responsible for the examination of an asylum application, common standards for a fair and efficient asylum procedure, common minimum conditions of reception of asylum seekers, and the approximation of rules on the recognition and content of the refugee status". The challenge following Tampere is to ensure these objectives are translated into reality – "a difficult task given the range of measures which the same governments have introduced to prevent asylum seekers from gaining access to their territory".[21]

## Aspects of Westminster scrutiny

Apart from primary legislation such as the Immigration and Asylum Act 1999, the starting point for any discussion of the impact of Europe on Westminster must be the committee system. This is where members and peers have an opportunity to select issues of particular interest and perceived relevance and subject them to a measure of specialist scrutiny, in some depth. The obvious committee players in this context are the Commons Home Affairs Committee (though other Commons Committees, such as Foreign Affairs,[22] and even the Public Accounts Committee (PAC)[23] have been known to enter the immigration and asylum arena) and the House of Lords Committee on the EU.

### Home Affairs Committee Report on Border Controls

So far as the HAC is concerned, its substantial report on Border Controls[24] was prompted in particular by the deaths of 59 illegal immigrants from China, found in a lorry at Dover in June 2000:

> There have been near tragedies on a similar scale in other European countries in recent years. 2,180 illegal entrants to the UK were identified in May 2000 – nearly twice as many as in the same month a year before. The fact that so many people take such risks and try to reach the UK, and that so many succeed, has caused us to examine the effectiveness of border controls.

The Committee took evidence from a wide range of sources, and made several overseas visits, including one to the Sangatte Red Cross refugee centre at Calais. It recommended *inter alia* an urgent revision of the Dublin Convention, the closure of the Sangatte Centre and, in the longer term, updating of the 1951 Convention on the Status of Refugees. The Government's reply – as is so often the case, a mixture of the positive and the defensive – was published as a special report of the Committee.[25] It accepted the need to revise the Dublin Convention, but denied any need to rewrite the 1951 Convention; and it flatly rejected the Committee's claim that the Home Office had been dilatory in enforcing the removal of illegal immigrants and of people whose claims for asylum had been denied.

Two of the most significant contributions to parliamentary engagement with immigration and asylum issues during our period of study came from the House of Lords European Union Committee (EUC) – and major inquiries by its Sub-Committee F (Social Affairs, Education and Home Affairs).

### European Commission report on minimum standards in asylum procedures: Report of the European Union Committee

The *Draft Directive on minimum standards for procedures in the asylum decision making process* was published in September 2000 and has not been agreed at the time of writing. It includes fast-track procedures for dealing with "manifestly unfounded asylum applications", a suggested procedure for other applications, and the criteria for appeals.

In its explanatory memorandum, the Commission observed that:

> This measure will not require Member States to apply uniform procedures. Nor will it oblige them to adopt common concepts and practices which they do not wish to apply. For example, if a Member State does not wish to apply the safe third-country concept to reject asylum applications, the measure will not oblige this Member State to adopt the concept. Moreover, all standards for operating a fair and efficient procedure are laid down without prejudice to Member States' discretionary power to prioritise cases on the basis of national policies.

In March 2001, having considered the Commission's proposals, the EUC published its report.[26] The Committee noted that the proposed

Council Directive on procedures in Member States for granting and withdrawing refugee status formed part of a package of measures whose longer-term purpose was to establish a common European asylum policy and so had to be considered against the backdrop of forthcoming measures on the reception of asylum seekers and the status of refugees. The Committee remarked that the Directive could do much to raise standards throughout the Union, but still provoked substantial concern as to whether it went far enough on safeguarding the rights of the asylum seeker under international law.[27]

### European Union Committee's report on community immigration policy

Another recurrent theme in the debate has been whether the United Kingdom's policies on asylum (and those of its EU partners) will be adequate or appropriate for the 21st century. Questions have been raised about how better to co-ordinate UK policies with those across the EU to create a coherent and uniform policy and how to ensure that the United Kingdom has enough skilled workers to fill jobs in shortage areas. The European Commission's proposals for a common approach to immigration were published in November 2000.[28] The EUC's report on community immigration policy published in April 2001[29] noted the United Kingdom's unique position in respect of Title IV of the EC Treaty and suggested that the Government's position was both ambiguous and at odds with the European Parliament and Commission:

> Mrs Roche confirmed that the preservation of the United Kingdom's frontier controls remained the central pillar of Government policy, and accepted that "it is extremely unlikely that we would want to opt in to any of the proposals" emerging from the Communication. Nevertheless, she claimed that this "does not stop us, and indeed our European partners welcome our contribution, from playing a constructive role in discussions around the Communication about anything that may arise from it". The perspective from the European Parliament and the European Commission is rather different. According to Mr Watson, "What one can say undoubtedly is that the United Kingdom's influence on the shaping of policy is reduced by the fact that it seeks not to participate in quite a lot of policy". Mr Fortescue cited the specific

212 Law and Policy in Action

example of the Regulation establishing a common visa list, which the United Kingdom did not opt into: "Of course, by staying out of the discussions you have less influence on the list that the other 13 will adopt very soon, but that was a political choice and it was made".

We have already drawn attention to the Government's somewhat ambiguous position on the relationship between measures to control illegal immigration and the opening up of avenues of legal immigration.[30]

The EUC also highlighted the difficulty for the UK Government – committed as it was and is to maintaining immigration controls at national borders – in granting rights of free movement, as the Commission proposed, to third party nationals legally resident in the EU. This was not the first time, the Committee remarked, that it had been unconvinced by the Government's arguments in favour of comprehensive immigration controls at UK borders. Now, the Committee foresaw that the United Kingdom's influence would be weakened by its non-participation in European initiatives:

> We are therefore concerned that the Government's insistence on maintaining an artificial distinction between "control" measures and "positive" measures may hinder it from making a useful contribution to this debate. We are disappointed that the United Kingdom has set its face against a number of positive measures, including the proposed Directive on family reunification. We believe that the Community should grant legally resident third country nationals a core of clearly defined rights. The United Kingdom, which has a proud record of welcoming and integrating immigrant communities, should be playing a full part in shaping such European-wide rights.[31]

In conclusion, the EUC argued that, in a free society and in an era of globalisation, immigration was inevitable. Managed immigration could go some way towards addressing problems within the Western European labour markets, yet governments had failed to keep pace with economic and labour market trends. Community immigration policy should, it argued, be designed so that businesses could rapidly respond to labour shortages. It went on:

> We recognise that there are serious fears in some quarters about any proposal to extend free movement rights to third country nationals. We believe these fears are over-stated. The experience of successive enlargements has shown that EU citizens from poorer Member States have not by and large taken advantage of their right of free movement in order to "shop around" for more generous social provisions elsewhere. We see no reason to believe that long-term resident third country nationals will do so either.[32]

## Parliamentary questions and debates

Although parliamentary questions lack the sharp cutting edge and cumulative effectiveness of select committee inquiry they do provide some indication of the nature and intensity of political interest in a given subject area. Debates in Parliament consume much more time than PQs and therefore tend to be spread thinly over quite long periods. But they too give some useful indication of parliamentary interest. So we undertook a search of the parliamentary database, Parliamentary On-Line Indexing Service (POLIS), focusing in particular on PQs and debates concerning some of the major European initiatives relating to immigration and asylum, mentioned earlier in this chapter.

The meeting of the European Council in Tampere in October 1999 agreed *inter alia* a common approach to the way in which Member States deal with applications for asylum. According to POLIS, there were 31 written and oral PQs on the Tampere meeting. The agreement on asylum was relatively uncontroversial, and only two of the PQs on Tampere refer specifically to immigration or asylum. A statement in the Commons immediately after the summit provided an opportunity for questions to the Prime Minister. The statement was repeated in the Lords, as is the custom. In the run-up to Tampere the EUC held an inquiry on the prospects for progress at the summit; there was also an hour's debate in the Lords on the likely significance of Tampere arising from an "unstarred question" (a procedure whereby Peers may table a question for debate on the floor of the House).

The "Schengen II" Convention on border controls sought to reinforce external border controls to permit free movement within participating states. This was, and is, a more contentious subject than the asylum framework agreed at Tampere, and in the 1997 Parliament there were 155 PQs on Schengen-related matters. In addition, there were three debates in the House of Lords (ranging from one and a half to two and a half hours) on motions to take note of European Communities Select Committee reports on Schengen. As noted earlier, the Amsterdam Treaty paved the way for Schengen to be integrated into the framework of the EU; consequently, debates during the passage of the European Communities (Amendment) Bill provided further opportunities for Parliament to consider the issues raised by Schengen.

Parliamentary On-Line Indexing Service records only 28 PQs on the Dublin Convention during the 1997 Parliament (and only a handful since then), which seems a remarkably small number given the controversy it has generated since its implementation in 1997. The convention was also considered during an Opposition Day debate on asylum in April 2000.

## Conclusions

Immigration and asylum have been high-profile issues both inside and outside Parliament, and the European dimensions of these issues have been evident throughout. The period 1997–2001 saw several weighty and highly relevant select committee reports in both Houses, and a major item of primary legislation. Even in the (unlikely) absence of an EU agenda on these subjects, immigration and asylum would certainly be impinging on UK politics, and on the work of the Westminster Parliament, as they frequently did before 1973. However, Europe has introduced new pressures and additional layers of complexity in which the boundaries between domestic policy (the uncontested territory of a national legislature, in its role as active scrutineer of the executive) and foreign and diplomatic policy (where parliaments tend to play a more passive role) having become blurred.

Westminster has a hard time of it influencing major areas of policy: in this and other EU-relevant fields its direct influence is marginal. Indirect influence is another matter, however: governments have to retain the confidence of the House of Commons – and they also have to win elections. Given the public and media profile given to immigration and asylum, and the strong feelings (sometimes palpably tainted by racism) these subjects arouse, the voice of rank-and-file parliamentarians cannot be ignored.

That voice is not confined to small contributions to set-piece, executive dominated, legislative debates, or to the collective work of investigative select committees which can be ignored by ministers. It is also heard in the day-to-day interventions and questions of back-benchers. The raw statistics of PQs tabled during the Parliament, as logged in POLIS, look like this:

|  | Asylum | Immigration | A *or* I | A *and* I |
|---|---|---|---|---|
| 1997–98 (long session) | 263 | 693 | 776 | 180 |
| 1998–99 | 374 | 567 | 813 | 128 |
| 1999–2000 | 606 | 557 | 970 | 193 |
| 2000–01 (short session) | 435 | 250 | 616 | 69 |

The figures should be taken as roughly indicative only. The categories reflect the coding conventions used by the managers of POLIS, and they are a mixed-bag of sub-categories – the great majority being Commons written questions, but with a sprinkling of oral questions, and some Lords questions. Moreover, there is a lot of overlap and duplication – same questioner asking much the same thing repeatedly in different ways.

Bearing these caveats in mind, three cautious conclusions may be drawn. First, the number of questions is substantial; secondly, the ratio of "asylum" to "immigration" increased significantly over the course of the Parliament (reflecting our impression that the political salience of asylum issues has steadily grown in recent years); but, thirdly, that these are very much overlapping categories – the overlap being indicated in the fourth column, which shows the numbers of questions classified by POLIS as raising both immigration and asylum issues.

Parliamentary questions are part of the background noise of policy debate. The main action may be happening elsewhere – in White-hall, in Brussels and in extra-parliamentary policy networks – but the constant muttering from the sidelines is heard by those on the field of play. We are reminded of a metaphor used by Maurice Kogan, when writing about educational policy-making: Kogan depicted the policy-making process as an interaction between the "low frequency" policy waves generated by officials and the "high frequency" policy waves emanating from ministers.[33] Transposing this into the present context, we might characterise the development of policies on immigration and asylum as being primarily in the hands of "low frequency" transmitters – Whitehall ministries, Brussels and established networks of professional groups and NGOs – but with high frequency signals – from national parliaments, the media and critical pressure groups – constantly impinging. The executive may dominate the parliamentary agenda, but in a politically sensitive area like this one there is a significant amount of parliamentary influence as well – difficult though it may be to quantify it.

## Notes

1. C. J. Harvey, "Immigration and asylum law: new covenants and familiar challenges", *Public Law*, 1999, pp. 23–34, at p. 33.
2. First Report, HC 163, 2000–01, para. 3.
3. Ibid., paras 155–156.
4. Ibid.
5. "Blunkett Defends 'swamping' remark", *The Guardian*, 25 April 2002.
6. D. Butler and D. Kavanagh, *The British General Election of 1992*, Macmillan, 1992, p. 114.
7. Ibid., p. 111.
8. *Building A Fairer Britain* Labour Party 2001 – available on the Labour Party website at http://www.labour.org.uk/.
9. *Time For Common Sense* Conservative Party 2001 – available on the Conservative Party website at http://www.conservatives.com/pdf/manifesto_uk.pdf.
10. *Freedom, Justice, Honesty* Liberal Democrat 2001 General Election Manifesto – available at www.libdems.org.uk/documents/policies/Manifestos/Fed2001.doc.
11. Cm. 4018; 17 July 1998.
12. HC Debs, Vol. 326, Col. 37.
13. Special Standing Committee, evidence, 22 March 1999.
14. "Union Leader's Blast At 'Racist Government' " *(Edinburgh) Evening News* 14 April 2000.
15. *An Effective Protection Regime for the Twenty-first Century: Speech to IPPR*, 6 February 2001 by the home secretary, Rt Hon Jack Straw MP – available on the Home Office website at http://www.homeoffice.gov.uk/speeches/speech60201.pdf.

16. "Immigrants are Seeking Asylum in Outdated Law", *Times*, 4 May 2001.
17. Chapter 7, p. 162. Available online from the UNHCR website from: http://www.unhcr.ch/pubs/sowr2000/ch07.pdf.
18. See http://europa.eu.int/comm/justice_home/news/intro/printer/news_191202_en.htm.
19. At http://europa.eu.int/scadplus/leg/en/lvb/a11000.htm.
20. Chapter 7, p. 164. Available online from the UNHCR website from: http://www.unhcr.ch/pubs/sowr2000/ch07.pdf.
21. *Refugees and Asylum Seekers*, Justice (2002), p. 170.
22. Select Committee on Foreign Affairs, Fourth Report, 1997–98, HC 515, *Entry Clearance Procedures, with Particular Reference to Islamabad and New Delhi* (including evidence taken before the Entry Clearance Sub-committee).
23. Public Accounts Committee, Seventh Report, 1999–2000, HC 130, *The Immigration and Nationality Directorates Casework Programme*.
24. Home Affairs Committee, First Report, 2000–01, HC 130, *Border Controls*.
25. Home Affairs Committee, Fourth Special Report, 2001–02, HC 375.
26. Select Committee on the European Union *Minimum Standards in Asylum Procedures, Eleventh* Report with Evidence, 27 March 2001 (Session 2000–01), HL 59 – available at http://pubs1.tso.parliament.uk/pa/ld200001/ldselect/ldeucom/59/5901.htm.
27. Ibid., p. 7.
28. *Communication from the Commission to the Council and the European Parliament on a Community Immigration Policy* (COM (2000) 757 final), European Commission, November 2000 – available at http://europa.eu.int/eur-lex/en/com/pdf/2000/com2000_0757en01.pdf.
29. Select Committee on the European Union *A Community Immigration Policy, Thirteenth Report with evidence*, 27 March 2001 (Session 2000–01) HL 64 – available at http://www.parliament.the-stationery-office.co.uk/pa/ld200001/ldselect/ldeucom/64/6401.htm.
30. Ibid., paras 123, 124.
31. Ibid., para. 131.
32. Ibid., para. 165.
33. Introduction to *The Politics of Education*, Harmondsworth: Penguin, 1971, p. 42.

# 10
# Devolution, Westminster and the EU

*Alex Wright*

Scotland now has a Parliament, Wales a National Assembly, and, although it is suspended at the time of writing, Northern Ireland a Legislative Assembly. The intention is that the governance of these territories will be transformed for the better and consequently their citizens should have more influence over the policies which affect them than was the case hitherto. But to what extent does this apply to matters concerning the European Union? To understand this we must first give a brief account of devolution itself.

## The apparatus of devolution

First, the competence of the devolved governments in the UK varies from territory to territory. At the upper end of the scale the Scottish Parliament can enact primary legislation and it could vary tax by plus or minus three per cent (albeit that 'Scottish Labour' has decided against varying tax for the moment). In the middle, the Northern Ireland Legislative Assembly can enact primary legislation but it lacks tax varying powers. At the lower end, the National Assembly for Wales cannot even enact primary legislation: it is, in strict terms, executive rather than legislative devolution.[1] This was to have far reaching consequences because for Wales in particular the result was a demand for greater powers,[2] whereas at 'Holyrood' (i.e. the Scottish Parliament) the emphasis has been on maximising the powers that had already been assigned to Scotland.

Second, there is a clear distinction between the Scottish Executive and the Scottish Parliament. Scottish ministers are accountable to a legislature. The position is somewhat similar in Northern Ireland, although the executive there is constructed differently. In Scotland the executive is drawn from the majority party, or as between 1999 and 2003, the two parties which formed the governing coalition. In Northern Ireland ministerial portfolios were allocated between a number of parties using a formula based on the D'Hondt system. Whereas in Scotland legislative devolution was the result of aspirations for further autonomy from Westminster, in Northern Ireland it was the product of a peace settlement. The National Assembly for Wales was quite distinct from the other two because it was also a 'corporate body'; technically, the members of the assembly also comprised the executive.

As a result, in Wales there has been a degree of confusion over accountability, in part because there has actually been a cabinet of sorts, consisting of a First Minister (initially entitled 'First Secretary') and his ministerial team. Unsurprisingly, some commentators referred to the Assembly's first year as a 'constitutional convention by other means'.[3] It could therefore be said that, in contrast to the Scottish Parliament, the National Assembly for Wales lacked a sense of purpose and direction during its early years. The same was so to some extent with Northern Ireland, albeit that in this instance legislative devolution has been somewhat intermittent to-date. Given that the origins, powers and procedures of each of these bodies are so diverse what are the implications for their relations with the EU? Can they, for example, have a formal relationship with the latter's institutions (e.g. vote in the Council of Ministers)?

## Relating to the EU

At the turn of the Millennium, the EU was addressing its own 'democratic deficit' and taking the view that this could be ameliorated by a closer engagement with its territories (i.e. regions and stateless nations). In its White Paper on Governance the European Commission acknowledged that for the most part a chasm remained between the EU and its territories[4] which threatened to undermine the legitimacy of the EU itself.[5] The Commission acknowledged that the regions and stateless nations offered the EU the chance to re-connect to its citizens. That might also act as a stimulant for the devolved governments in the UK and their democratic assemblies;[6] which might seek a closer relationship with the EU. But it was the member states (and/ or their constitutions) not the EU which determined the extent to which their territories could open up formal channels with the EU.[7]

As far as the UK is concerned, foreign affairs, including relations with the EU is 'reserved' to Westminster (i.e. not devolved to the three territorial governments). This had a number of consequences. It implied that as far as the devolved territories were concerned, Westminster and its 'European' committees would continue to have an important role to play in relation to European matters. It ensured that the territorial (i.e. devolved) governments would for the most part remain one step removed from decision-making in the Council of Ministers. This semi-detachment from the EU posed its own challenge to the devolved assemblies because over time increasingly the EU had acquired competence for policies which now were their responsibilities. It was therefore likely that they would wish to influence EU policies. How, if at all, could they achieve this if the UK Government was pivotal to the outcome?

## Inter-governmental mechanisms

In some respects the inter-governmental mechanisms were similar to those that pre-dated devolution. The territorial executives would be responsible for aggregating local interests when responding to an EU proposal and then transmitting their views upwards to whichever UK department was acting as the 'lead'. Where necessary territorial officials might be a part of the UK delegation at the Council of Ministers, and where so permitted their ministers might attend meetings of the Council. But the latter could do so only with the consent of the minister from the lead department and if a territorial minister did actually vote in the Council then *de facto* that individual at that moment would be a UK minister not a territorial one. But under devolution new arrangements had to be made.

Under devolution clearly the territorial administrations and the UK Government needed to work closely together on many issues, including European matters. That need produced the Memorandum of Understanding (MoU), the Joint Ministerial Committee (JMC) and the Concordats. As the MoU intimated, in principle the relationship between the two tiers of government in the UK was supposed to be relatively benign. The MoU therefore highlighted the need for communication and consultation; co-operation; the exchange of information, statistics and research; and confidentiality.[8] In part this was deemed necessary for occasions when the UK Government and devolved administrations adopted conflicting positions over a particular policy (especially if different parties were in power in territorial and the UK tiers of government). Thus, the terms of reference of the JMC included:

> To keep the arrangements for liaison between the UK Government and the devolved administrations under review; and
> To consider disputes between the administrations.[9]

The Concordats were 'intended to be binding in honour only' and 'not a legally enforceable contract'. The EU Concordat covered, 'the provision of information, the formulation of UK policy, attendance at the Council of Ministers, implementation of EU obligations; and infraction proceedings'.[10] However, these arrangements posed a problem for the devolved assemblies, not least by virtue of the confidentiality surrounding the work of the JMC.

## Opportunities, constraints and challenges

Although, potentially, European affairs mattered a great deal to the assemblies, when they were first established it was unclear exactly what their EU role would be. What did they want to achieve and what in practice were they capable of achieving given the constraints that they faced? Would they be limited to the scrutiny of EU legislative proposals or would they be engaged in advocacy on behalf of citizens as well as interest groups? Would they be responsible for overseeing the implementation of EU policy in their territories? Could they act as drivers for change on issues of strategic interest to their territories?[11] Would they encourage their respective executives to adopt a more strategic and proactive approach to the EU and its policies?

However, there were a number of caveats as well. Would the volume of EU legislative proposals overwhelm them? Would they possess sufficient resources to fulfil their role? Would they be able to exercise some control over the ministers in their own executives who were responsible for EU matters, despite the reserved status of foreign affairs? Would their views carry much weight if they were aimed primarily at their own executives, given that European matters were reserved? Should they therefore focus their attention on the committees at Westminster or should they go direct to the relevant UK minister? These were some of the challenges confronting the assemblies in 1999.

## The Devolved Assemblies and the EU: The first few years

### Scotland

Even before the Scottish Parliament reconvened it was clear that relations with the EU would not be neglected. The 1997 White Paper devoted an entire chapter to relations with 'Europe'.[12] The following year the Consultative Steering Group (a body which in part was established to 'consider the operational needs and working methods of the Scottish Parliament') recommended that there should be a 'European committee' because it was 'so fundamental to the running of the parliament'.[13] Accordingly, a committee was established under Rule 6.8 of the Parliament's Standing Orders. Its remit was:

> To consider and report on:
> - proposals for European Communities legislation
> - the implementation of European Communities legislation
> - any European Communities or European Issue.[14]

When the Committee first met to consider how best it should fulfil its remit, discussion focused on the scrutiny of EU legislative proposals[15] and how best it might influence the outcome. Members of the Scottish Parliament (MSP) on the Committee were advised that the EU despatched circa 8000 documents to the UK Government annually, of which 1200 were referred to the UK Parliament of which more than 800 were earmarked for scrutiny. Although the Scottish Parliament would be given these papers it was suggested that it would be impractical for them to scrutinise the same proportion: 200 might be a more realistic figure.[16]

Should they wish to express an opinion on an EU proposal, MSPs had a variety of channels available to them (the same applied to the other two devolved assemblies). If an EU proposal was extremely significant they could call for it to be debated in a plenary session in the Parliament. If they believed it was necessary for one of their ministers (or his or her officials) to discuss it with colleagues in the 'lead department' in London, then they could invite their executive to take the necessary steps. What they could not do, however, was convey their opinion direct to the lead department or its minister – that was the responsibility of the European Scrutiny Committee in the Commons. Moreover, since under the Scrutiny Reserve UK ministers were obliged to await the views of the Committees at Westminster before voting on a particular proposal in the Council of Ministers, it was supposed that territorial committees would transmit their opinions to the Commons Committee which could then if it so wished incorporate them in its own position on the relevant proposal. That surprised the MSPs on the Holyrood Committee when they learned of this in September 1999. This was in part because it was unclear what would happen to their opinion after it reached Westminster, since the Commons Committee was not duty bound to incorporate it in its own deliberations.

However, at the time of writing the European and External Affairs Committee (EEAC) [now the European and External Relations Committee, EERC] of the Scottish Parliament has not conveyed a single opinion to the committee at Westminster in response to a legislative proposal from the European Commission. The reason for this is that there simply has been insufficient time for the Committee to consider proposals before they come before the Council of Ministers in Brussels.[17] That has called into question the practicality of detailed sifts of EU legislation with the result that the main channel of influence for the Scottish Parliament (and presumably the other two assemblies) is not the Commons scrutiny process but its own executive.

By May 2000, it was apparent that the EEAC's working practices and work programme needed to be revised. Its members agreed that the Committee's remit should continue to focus on scrutiny, relations with the Scottish Executive and advocacy. But the Committee acknowledged that it had been too reactive vis-à-vis the Executive's European agenda. Members now wanted to be more proactive, stimulating debate on strategic issues such as enlargement of the EU and the Single Currency. It was therefore decided to change the future work programme, putting more emphasis on conducting inquiries. For the time being scrutiny would not be abandoned, far from it, but the Committee would focus more deeply on major inquiries rather than the multiplicity of proposals emanating from Brussels.

*Governance: the role for Scotland*

The EEAC's most significant inquiry generated the 'Report on the Governance of the European Union and the future of Europe: What Role for Scotland?' The report made a series of key recommendations:

- On scrutiny, unsurprisingly it called for 'better standards of information flow between EU institutions and national/sub-national parliaments and their scrutiny committees'. The Committee also suggested that Council of Ministers' working groups should be subject to greater scrutiny.
- On regionalism, MSPs called for the establishment of a 'Regional Affairs Council involving ministers from the various constitutional regions with legislative powers.'[18]
- On the Convention for the Future of Europe, the Committee suggested that if the devolved administrations in the UK were not involved directly in the Convention, then 'systems should be in place for their voice to be heard'.[19] In practice Jack Straw, the Foreign Secretary has given the devolved governments an assurance that he would convene a Joint Ministerial Committee Europe (JMCE) if any significant developments were to occur as a result of the Convention.[20]
- On the *Concordats* the MSPs recommended that they be re-written so 'at the very least the interpretation of what should be – not what might be – kept private should be reviewed'. It also called for Scottish ministers to be automatically entitled to attend the Council of Ministers when devolved matters were due to be discussed and that the Concordats 'should spell out more clearly the nature of the information that should be provided by Whitehall to the devolved administrations'.[21]

But by far the most significant proposal was that there should be a 'Scottish scrutiny reserve for governance in Scotland'. The EEAC stated:

In such a scheme, a Scottish Executive Minister could not agree a [sic] its own final position with their UK counterpart in advance of a relevant JMC or Council meeting if the European Committee (or another committee) had previously identified a wish to provide its view and had not yet done so. Such a system should not be allowed to slow down unnecessarily the work of the Executive, but provide a check on the ability for a Minister to agree a final position if a parliamentary committee still wished to comment.[22]

It was stressed subsequently that the 'reserve would no way apply to the legitimate functions of the UK Government or the UK Parliament'.

Whilst the EEAC's report on governance appeared wildly ambitious it did receive a favourable response from the Deputy First Minister, Jim Wallace who promised to 'revisit the issue once we have had some experience of the new arrangements in operation'.[23] However, a short while later, the Executive rejected the scrutiny reserve proposal. That came as little surprise but the report was as much a statement of principle as a request for reform. Since then, however, the working relationship between the Committee and Executive has grown apace. The Executive currently provides not just pre- and post-briefings to MSPs in relation to EU Council meetings but also for those of JMCE and Minecor Europe – the latter is responsible for promoting ministerial co-ordination within the UK.[24]

*The Committee's remit*

In the early part of 2002 there were two further developments. It was proposed that there should be still less scrutiny and greater emphasis on overseeing implementation. There were two reasons for this. First, the Scottish Executive faced criticism from the European Commission over its failure to implement environmental legislation. Non-compliance was a matter of public concern which needed to be addressed by the Committee. Second, if the Executive was fined by the European Court of Justice for non-compliance this would be met from tax payers' money and the Parliament had a right to be involved.

It was also suggested in January 2002 that the Committee's remit should be extended to include external affairs (i.e. foreign relations beyond the EU). This came to fruition on 5 March 2003 when the Committee was renamed the European and External Affairs Committee. Under Standing Orders, Rule 6.8.1, its remit now also includes:

The development and implementation of the Scottish Administration, links with countries and territories outside Scotland, the European Communities (and their institutions) and other international organisations.

Co-ordination of the international activities of the Scottish Administration.

It will be interesting to see how far the external relations remit imposes its own strains on the Committee's time and resources. In sum, the EEAC (now EERC) has made considerable progress in terms of securing a role for itself and avoiding becoming submerged in scrutinising a plethora of EU proposals. It has identified and investigated issues of strategic importance to Scotland and these in turn have been debated in plenary session in the Parliament. It has called for the reform of the EU's institutions and procedures, for the revision of the Concordats and for transparency in intergovernmental relations between the Scottish and UK Governments. But conceivably its greatest achievement is to have identified the need for a scrutiny reserve on its own ministers. Whether that remains simply 'blue sky thinking' remains to be seen but already MSPs have succeeded in maintaining a close watch on their executive.

## Wales

The 1997 White Paper affirmed that the Assembly would have a role to play regarding European matters[25] and when the Assembly was first established it was agreed that there should be a European Committee. Under Standing Order 15 the role of the Committee was to:

- review the interaction between the Assembly and the EU
- review the interaction between the Assembly and UK Rep and UK Government
- monitor the general impact and consequences of EU policies for Wales
- review the Assembly's methods of dealing with EU issues
- alert subject committees to EU issues of relevance
- recommend Assembly responses to EU activity within the remit of more than one subject committee
- report to the Assembly on the above from time to time.[26]

## European Committees: Wales and Scotland compared

The Welsh Committee differs from its counterpart in Scotland in two significant respects. First, it was intended that EU scrutiny should be decentralised to the other subject committees – so, the Committee on Agriculture and Rural Affairs would handle proposals under the EU's common agricultural policy, for example. For its part the European Committee would have something of a co-ordinating role vis-à-vis EU matters and it would become more closely involved where an EU policy overlapped the competence of two or more committees. The danger with this is that because it would be extremely difficult in practice for the European Committee to monitor the work of the other committees there was no absolute certainty that EU proposals were being scrutinised effectively.

The second substantive difference related to the membership of the Committee. Since the Assembly was in effect a corporate body it was regarded as perfectly proper for a minister to sit on, or 'head' a committee. Consequently First Minister Rhodri Morgan chaired the European Committee. This had its advantages because he represented Wales in the JMCE and he also could attend meetings of the Council of Ministers (where permitted by the lead department). But it was potentially disadvantageous insofar as the First Minister could less easily be held to account for the Executive's handling of European matters – which was quite distinct from the situation in Scotland. The Committee was well aware of this problem. When Committee members reviewed its future role in January 2001 a discussion paper noted:

> The structure of the Committee with an Assembly Minister as Chair makes it difficult for the Committee to be, or appear to be, an effective agent for scrutiny of the Assembly's Cabinet's handling of European Affairs.[27]

This was not unique to the EEAC: it could be said of all the other committees and was symptomatic in some people's view of just how flawed the National Assembly was. As Osmond put it:

> The Assembly was established as a corporate body, combining its legislative and executive functions rather than separating them as

is normal in parliamentary institutions. Many of the tensions that
arose in the first year arose as part of this conundrum.[28]

But is it really that simple? As Osmond has subsequently observed,[29]
whilst 'all members of the Assembly shared responsibility for decisions,
*de facto* there was a separate cabinet'. This was wholly unsatisfactory
because it created ambiguity over accountability.

Membership, though, was not the only problem. The Assembly has
considerably fewer 'members' (60) than Scotland (129) or Northern
Ireland (108). This meant that its resources were stretched because
those same individuals were supposed to sit on the Assembly's
committees, as well as providing from their ranks its officers (e.g. the
Presiding Officer) and its ministers. As a result there was the likeli-
hood that they could not meet as frequently as their opposite
numbers in the Scottish Parliament. The net effect was that the
European Committee in Cardiff has been able to cover less ground
than its equivalent in Scotland. 'The limited time available for meetings of the Committee makes it difficult for the Committee to be
apprised of all issues raised within European fora or to monitor and
scrutinise their day to day output, such as European legislation and
directives.'[30]

All-in-all the Assembly was in a much weaker situation than Holyrood. This was particularly apparent in relation to its European
Committee which was regarded as something of a failure during its
early years. As Jones observed, 'the devolution debate, in Wales and
success in securing Objective 1 status (under the EU's Structural
Funds), helped fuel public expectations about the extent to which
the Assembly would act as a driver for greater influence over
European matters. In practice, this simply did not occur during
the first twelve months of the Committee's existence'. He also noted
that as far as scrutinising draft legislation from the EU was concerned, the Committee itself in its annual report had conceded that,
in Jones' words, 'the array of legislation is so vast that it is beyond its
capacity' – which mirrored the situation in Scotland. In some
respects the Committee's failure could be attributed to factors outside
its control such as the Concordats and the relative lack of consultation
between Welsh and UK officials. But as Jones also observed, the
Committee had to be 'more proactive' and it needed to generate
more 'policy orientated reports'.[31]

## The Committee reviewed

For a time there were deep misgivings about the quality of the Committee's work. In its submission of evidence on the Committee's future role, Plaid Cymru posed the fundamental problem: 'what was the point in having such a committee?'[32] This was first raised during one of its sessions in March 2000 when all the papers which were due to be considered by the Committee were 'for information to note their contents'. In this instance the views of its members were largely irrelevant, because they would be retrospective of what had already been agreed or determined by others. Consequently when the Committee met in June of that year it was agreed that the political parties should have the opportunity to present their own proposals on what the Committee's future role should be. Plaid Cymru, in response, recommended that there should be:

- A thorough review of the Committee, its functions and perceived failings is required. This should involve asking external bodies within Wales which have an interest in European Affairs how they wish to see the Committee operating.
- The Committee should meet on a more regular basis to ensure more detailed discussion and the creation of more productive proceedings.
- The work and role of the House of Commons and the House of Lords European Legislation Committees be examined to establish the wider framework within which the National Assembly's European Affairs Committee has to operate.
- The role of European Committees within other devolved administrations be considered for relevance to Wales.
- Each subject Committee should appoint one of its members to be its European co-ordinator/rapporteur.
- The Committee has to have a proper strategy in place.
- It should also act as an overarching Committee.[33]

When the Committee met in May 2001, it adopted much of Plaid Cymru's recommendations. Its members resolved:

That...all subject committees are represented on the European Affairs Committee and...that a system of rapporteurs be established.[34]

The significance of this was that there would be greater co-ordination by the Committee as to how the Assembly was or was not responding to a particular European matter. It also ensured that the Committee itself would be better informed as to what was happening elsewhere in the Assembly. It was also agreed that the 'agendas, reports and notification of inquiries received from other UK parliamentary committees' should be monitored. This made sense as it could expose an issue that for one reason or another the Committee or the other subject committees had neglected to address.

In contrast to Scotland, where to-date the links with MEPs and delegates to the Committee of the Regions and Economic and Social Committee have been rather modest, it was agreed that individuals from these bodies (i.e. those from Wales), would be given time to provide a 'brief report' when they were present at a meeting of the Welsh Committee. The latter also requested that:

> The First Minister provide the Committee with a report as soon as possible following the release of each work programme of the European Commission noting issues of potential significance arising from the programme falling within the responsibility of each Assembly Minister.[35]

Although this was not the same as actually holding the First Minister to account it follows that he would have to identify issues that were of concern to Wales in the future, and more latently, these would then be addressed by the Committee.

Although the European Committee has not been without its setbacks, it has also made some headway despite the constitutional constraints that both it and the Assembly have had to endure. As Holyrood discovered, the potential to scrutinise EU proposals is circumscribed by the volume of legislation produced by the EU and there is some merit in decentralising this to other subject committees.[36] When it was clear that this was not always working satisfactorily the Committee then set up a system of rapporteurs to monitor the work and ensure a degree of co-ordination. Even though, because of its corporate nature, the Assembly cannot effectively hold its own executive to account, it has sought to capitalise on the fact that it is chaired by the First Minister. In some respects it has been more inclusive than its Scottish counterpart in opening up a dialogue and developing links with MEPs and civil society in Wales – for example, by establishing the European Forum for Wales.[37] As Jones rightly intimated after the Committee's first year or so – 'it had yet to find a role for itself'. There are signs that this has now begun to come to fruition. The Committee has recently summed up its role as follows: 'to provide strategic guidance on European issues and to consider in detail those matters that impact most directly on Wales'.[38]

## Northern Ireland

Understandably, given that its primary goal was to resolve the conflict in Ulster, the 'Belfast Agreement' made little mention of the EU. Strand One of the Agreement simply stated:

> Terms will be agreed between appropriate Assembly representatives and the Government of the United Kingdom to ensure effective co-ordination and input by Ministers to national policy-making, including EU issues.[39]

The EU was also referred to in the context of Strand Two which related to the North/South Ministerial Council, with the underlying implication that the Council might have an interest in cross-sectoral matters. It was also mentioned under Strand Three, which was concerned with the British-Irish Council, where again the implication was that there might be an EU issue that would be of common interest to the constituent members of the Council.[40] In practice the EU was rather overshadowed by the 'Peace Process' in Northern Ireland until the autumn of 2001. That is not to say that it was wholly neglected but the Legislative Assembly's (LA) involvement was extremely modest at first.

On 8 December 1999 the LA agreed to the formation of a European committee. This was accompanied by a proposal for a standing committee on Equality, Human Rights and Community Relations – all designed to ensure greater accountability of the Office of the First Minister and Deputy First Minister. As it happened within a week the First Minister and Deputy First Minister called for both Committees to be replaced by a 'Committee of the Centre' and this duly came to pass. External matters were initially excluded from the Committee's scrutiny role and the 'committee failed to get off the ground' to begin with because of divisions between the chair and sub-chair (who were 'Unionists') and the Sinn Fein members. The result was an impasse: during the first year of devolved government, the Committee had apparently not even issued a press release on EU matters.[41] As McGown and Murphy observed, 'To-date the Committee of the Centre has devoted little time to European Affairs, and its programme of work for the first half of 2001 lists no European topic.'[42]

After September 2001 the LA's Committees, including the Committee of the Centre (which now had a new chair) began to work together at last.[43] There was a growing awareness of the governance debate within the EU and the extent to which the two other devolved assemblies in the UK had involved themselves in European matters. In June 2001, the Committee's chair had acknowledged how significant the EU was to Northern Ireland and the following January it was announced that the Committee would conduct an inquiry into Northern Ireland's relations with the EU.[44] Its members subsequently visited Brussels. They also took a close interest in Scotland's arrangements taking evidence from officials at Scotland House in Brussels and from MSPs when a further fact-finding tour was undertaken in Edinburgh. Revealingly the Committee's chair conceded that 'the Committee has already identified a number of EU issues where Northern Ireland is not being well served'.[45]

The experience of Northern Ireland is informative when compared to the situation in Scotland and Wales. The political leadership was divided and the very future of the Northern Ireland Legislative Assembly was open to doubt. This had a number of repercussions. There was virtually no ministerial leadership vis-à-vis the EU, and Members of the LA were more interested in constitutional matters and the decommissioning of arms. Until 2002, therefore, for the most part European affairs had been dealt with by the subject committees rather than by the Committee of the Centre and the executive's attention was focused elsewhere. By 2002 this could no longer continue. It was clear that Northern Ireland lagged far behind Scotland and Wales both in terms of its capacity to monitor the executive's handling of EU matters and its potential to influence the EU's agenda. As McGowan and Murphy observed, some of the political parties were lukewarm at best towards the EU. That can have two possible consequences. It could mean that they avoid pursuing a proactive approach towards the EU. Alternatively, the fact that some of them are suspicious might encourage them to keep a close watch on it.[46] Much more important, however, is the extent to which the LA can hold its own executive to account over European matters.

At the time of writing there is reason to hope that progress will now be made on the LA's handling of European matters. In March 2002 the Committee of the Centre published a substantial report on the 'Approach of the Northern Ireland Assembly and the Devolved Government on European Union Issues.' Its recommendations were wide-ranging. The Committee called not only for greater transparency surrounding the EU-related work of the Office of the First Minister and Deputy First Minister; it also argued that 'a higher priority (should be) given to the attendance of Northern Ireland Ministers at the relevant Council of Ministers meetings'. It also suggested that a 'Standing Committee on EU affairs' should be established.[47] Although the Assembly is currently suspended, there are good grounds for supposing that when this is lifted, EU affairs will be accorded a higher priority than was the case hitherto.

## Devolution, Westminster and the EU: a conundrum?

In some respects it should not be surprising that devolution has as yet had little significant impact on the work of the European committees at Westminster. The House of Lords continues to examine substantive issues and produces detailed reports on the EU. The European Scrutiny Committee at the Commons continues to examine EU legislative proposals. There simply is not the time to wait for the devolved assemblies to transmit their view on a particular EU proposal. So, the principle of Scrutiny Reserve, as currently applies to Westminster, is of little value to the territorial committees. As we have seen this was not what was envisaged by MSPs on the Scottish Committee when they met in the autumn of 1999 and it *is* of consequence. At the time it was believed that this would be one of the primary routes through which they could influence relevant UK ministers and their departments on European matters.

Instead, to-date it would seem that the only example of their views being taken into account occurred when the European Legislation Committee at the Commons conducted an inquiry into 'democracy and accountability in the EU, the role of national parliaments'. Although the Scottish Committee's report on Scotland's role in the EU was highly relevant to this inquiry, the inquiry itself was not without its critics. For instance, Plaid Cymru, in a submission to the Welsh Committee on European Affairs, maintained that the questions raised by the Westminster inquiry were 'too narrow: they failed to take into account the role of small nations and regions in Europe and only one of the eleven questions specifically referred to these tiers of government'.[48] So, formally, the links between Westminster and the devolved assemblies have been relatively modest. Nonetheless, informally, there is a good working relationship and ideas about best practice are exchanged when officials and chairs of the European Committees (or their equivalent) meet circa three times per annum.

There have been setbacks, however. When MSPs on the Scottish Committee applied to join COSAC (the Conference of Community and European Affairs Committees of Parliaments of the European Union) their application was apparently vetoed by the French.[49] Consequently at the time of writing only Westminster is represented on COSAC, the body which articulates the interests of 'national' parliaments in the EU and there is no sign that it seeks to aggregate the views of the territorial committees prior to its meetings.

Another recent notable development is the inquiry undertaken by the House of Lords Select Committee on the Constitution. Its report *Devolution: Inter-institutional Relations in the UK* contains a substantial chapter on EU matters. The report points out that there is too much reliance on goodwill rather than formal mechanisms between the various tiers of government. More particularly it noted that both formal and informal consultation processes were bound by confidentiality which ensured that it was difficult for parliamentarians to determine how successfully the devolved administrations had fought their corner in relation to EU affairs. The Committee therefore suggested that more information should be in the public domain. For example, the UK Government should issue a press release after a meeting of the JMC and the Prime Minister should make a statement to the Commons after a plenary session of the JMC.[50] It remains to be seen whether the government will meet these recommendations.

In the meantime the underlying dilemma is that, although the EU impacts in all sorts of ways on policies which now fall within their remit, devolution has not really enabled the assemblies to exercise any substantive influence over how the UK Government conducts itself in the EU. For the moment the territorial executives remain one step removed from the Council of Ministers, and the assemblies' European Committees cannot hold UK ministers to account. Although Peter Hain the UK minister for Europe appeared before the Scottish Committee during 2001, it should be noted that technically he was not giving evidence: rather, he 'addressed' MSPs. What the European Committees could attempt – and in Scotland's case have attempted – to do is to hold their own Executives to account. But herein lie the problems.

First, those ministers' input into EU matters is potentially limited. As we have seen, they do not automatically have the right to attend meetings of the Council of Ministers. In addition, much of the work of the Council is determined by officials whose meetings (in the Council's 'Working Groups') are held in private. They remain well beyond the scrutiny of state and sub-state parliaments. Moreover, as far as the UK is concerned, although officials from the territorial administrations can and do attend meetings of the Working Groups, they are a part of a UK delegation under the leadership of a civil servant from the 'lead department' in London.

Second, as the Lords' Committee on the Constitution has observed, there is considerable secrecy surrounding intergovernmental meetings between ministers. To-date the Cabinet Office has been unwilling to divulge much if anything on JMCE but ironically it is referred to briefly on the Welsh Assembly's website under the section entitled First Minister's report in December 2001. The same is true for 'Minecor'. It will be interesting to see how much information the Scottish Committee gleans now that the Executive has agreed to pre- and post-briefings when these bodies convene.

What the Committees can do, and in the case of Scotland and Wales have succeeded in doing, is act as vehicles for reform. They can conduct inquiries into the extent to which their Executives have formulated an EU strategy. They can identify issues that are of strategic importance to their territories and invite relevant parties to submit evidence. They can establish working groups, to investigate complex matters such as EU enlargement and as a result formulate a strategy on a suitable response. In responding to the European Commission's White Paper on Governance they can call for a closer relationship with the EU and in so doing they have played a con- structive part in the debate surrounding the future governance of the EU.

What they can do less easily is scrutinise EU legislative proposals. This is primarily because too many proposals emanate from
Brussels for them to handle. Unlike Westminster there is only one
European Committee in each of the devolved assemblies, thereby
stretching their resources. That is further compounded by the
relatively short time available for them to frame a reply. Although
the Scottish Committee did attempt to sift through EU proposals
and established an informal network to identify those that were
pertinent to Scotland, for the most part this proved impractical.
The Committee still undertakes sifting but scrutiny is less of a
priority now.

So we are faced with the conundrum that for the most part the UK
Government remains pivotal to the devolved administrations' relations
with the EU, whilst the EU's policies can impact directly on their
territories. Despite the existence of new democratic assemblies at the
sub-state level there appears to be little more constraint on how UK
ministers conduct themselves in the Council of Ministers than was
the case hitherto. The committees at Westminster have had to endure
similar problems in the past and thanks in part to the Scrutiny
Reserve (as applicable to Westminster) they have had some success in
overcoming this. It is just about conceivable though that they might
take the lead in calling for increased power for state *and* sub-state
assemblies in the UK over UK ministers handling of EU affairs. Such
a thing is conceivable but unlikely.

In the meantime as far as the EU is concerned Scotland, Wales and
Northern Ireland are not much better off in terms of democratic
accountability. At the time of writing the assemblies have little, if
no, influence over how UK ministers conduct themselves in the EU.
From their perspective, the European Committee at the Commons is
unable to function as a channel of influence. Whilst the territorial
committees have been increasingly active, with Scotland as pace
setter, for understandable reasons, their scrutiny and advocacy roles
are focused on their own executives rather than on the UK Government.
But ministers and officials from the territorial executives usually have
a subordinate role with regard to intergovernmental relations between
the UK and the EU, a process which itself lacks transparency. The
Scottish Parliament has highlighted these and other deficiencies in
its landmark report on Governance. It remains to be seen whether
this can be remedied under the existing constitutional framework in

the UK, at a point in time when the EU looks set to increase its competence once more.

## Notes

1. This occurs whereby territorial departments of government possess the 'power to take decisions over a wide range of executive matters' (HMSO 1973, Cmnd 5460, Royal Commission on the Constitution 1969–73, Vol. 1 Report, 377, para. 1256).
2. See B. Jones and J. Osmond, *Inclusive Government and Party Management. The National Assembly for Wales and the Work of its Committees*, Institute of Welsh Affairs and the Welsh Governance Centre, Cardiff, 2001, pp. 164; and J. Osmond, in Search of Stability, in A. Trench (ed.) *The State of the Nations 2001. The Second Year of Devolution in the United Kingdom*, Imprint Academic, Thorverton, 2001, p. 41.
3. J. Osmond, A Constitutional Convention by Other Means, in R. Hazell (ed.), *The State and the Nations. The First Year of Devolution*, Imprint Academic, Thorverton, 2000, p. 76.
4. European Commission, *European Governance*, A White Paper, Com (2001) 428, Brussels, 2001, p. 12.
5. Ibid., p. 3.
6. Although Scotland has a parliament, collectively they are referred to here as 'assemblies' for simplicity.
7. There needs to be a stronger interaction with regional and local governments and civil society. Member States bear the principal responsibility for achieving this (European Commission, op. cit., p. 4).
8. Memorandum of Understanding.
9. Ibid.
10. Concordat on Co-ordination of European Union policy.
11. See A. Wright, 'The Europeanisation of Scotland'. A Driver for Autonomy', in M. Graves and G. Girrard (eds) *Europe United, the United Kingdom Disunited?* University of Brest, 2000; and 'Scotland and the EU: All Bark and no Bite?' in A. Wright (ed.), *Scotland: the Challenge of Devolution*, Ashgate, Aldershot, 2000.
12. Cm. 3658, *Scotland's Parliament*, HMSO, 1997, p. 3.
13. Report of Consultative Steering Group, Scottish Office, Edinburgh, 1998, p. 26.
14. Scottish Parliament, *Standing Orders*, Rule 6.8.
15. The author was present as an observer.
16. Information based on interview with an official at the Scottish Parliament. In practice the committee received 4100 EU documents during its first four years – 'all of which were deliberated upon to some degree by the committee' (Scottish Parliament, *Legacy Paper: A Review of the First Parliamentary Session of the European Committee – Advice to Successors*, 2003).
17. A. Wright, 'The European Committee of the Scottish Parliament. Representation, Advocacy, Legitimation and Agenda Setting', Second Conference for the

Network of Scottish and Nordic Political Scientists June 2001, 'The Nordic model at the cross roads? Governance, Representation and Accountability.' Gothenburg, 2001.

18. Scottish Parliament, European Committee, Ninth Report, 2001, Report on the Governance of the European Union and the Future of Europe: What Role for Scotland, Vol. 1 – Main Report, p. 65.
19. Ibid., p. 67.
20. Interview with member of Scottish Executive responsible for foreign relations.
21. Scottish Parliament, European Committee, Ninth Report, 2001, Report on the Governance of the European Union and the Future of Europe: What Role for Scotland, Vol. 1 – Main Report, p. 69.
22. Ibid.
23. Scottish Parliament, *Official Report*, 28 February 2002, c. 9793.
24. Scottish Parliament, 'Legacy Paper: A Review of the First Parliamentary Session of the European Committee – advice to successors', 2003.
25. *Voice in Wales*, White Paper, Chapter 3, 'The Assembly and its partners', www.wales.gov.uk.
26. National Assembly for Wales Committee on European Affairs, Minutes, 4 April 2001.
27. National Assembly for Wales Committee on European Affairs, 'The Future Role of the European Affairs Committee', 31 January 2001.
28. J. Osmond, in R. Hazell (ed.), *The State and the Nations: the First Year of Devolution*, The Constitution Unit, London, pp. 37–39.
29. J. Osmond, in R. Hazell (ed.), *The State of the Nations 2001*, The Constitution Unit, London, p. 19.
30. National Assembly for Wales Committee on European Affairs, 31 January 2001, 'The Future Role of the European Affairs Committee'.
31. B. Jones, 'Searching for a Role. "The Committee on European Affairs"', in B. Jones and J. Osmond (eds), 'Inclusive Government and Party Management', in *The National Assembly for Wales and the Work of its Committees*, Institute of Welsh Affairs and the Welsh Governance Centre, Cardiff, 2001, pp. 154, 156.
32. National Assembly for Wales Committee on European Affairs, 'The Future Role of the European Affairs Committee', 31 January 2001.
33. Ibid., Annex. A.
34. National Assembly for Wales Committee on European Affairs, 23 May 2001.
35. Ibid.
36. National Assembly for Wales Committee on European Affairs, 1999–2000 Report 2.6.
37. Ibid., Report 2.30.
38. National Assembly for Wales European and External Affairs Committee, EUR-01–02, 13 February 2002, p. 2.
39. Agreement reached in the multi-party negotiations (the Belfast Agreement), 10 April 1998, para. 31.
40. Ibid.

41. R. Wilford and R. Wilson, 'A Bare Knuckle Ride: Northern Ireland', in R. Hazell (ed.), *The State and the Nations. The First Year of Devolution*, Imprint Academic, Thorverton, 2000.
42. L. McGowan and M. Murphy, *Northern Ireland under Devolution: Facing the Challenge of Institutional Adaptation to EU Policy Formulation*, paper presented at the 6th UACES Research Conference, the State of the Union, Bristol, 3–5 September 2001.
43. Wilford and Wilson, op. cit., p. 95.
44. Northern Ireland Assembly, Committee of the Centre, Press Notices 161/2001 and 170/2002, 22 June 2001 and 8 January 2002.
45. Northern Ireland Assembly, Committee of the Centre, Press Notices 20/2002, 21 January 2002.
46. For an interesting analysis of the effect opposition parties can have on EU scrutiny, see T. Raunio and S. Hix, 'Backbenchers Learn to Fight Back: European integration and Parliamentary Government', *West European Politics*, 23:4, October 2000.
47. Northern Ireland Assembly, *Inquiry into the Approach of the Northern Ireland Assembly and the Devolved Government on European Union Issues*, Report 02/01R, Committee of the Centre, 2002.
48. Plaid Cymru, 'Submission to the Committee on European Affairs', National Assembly for Wales, 17 October 2001.
49. See A. Wright, 'A Federalised Polity – An Alternative to Scottish "Independence" in Europe?' in S. Henig (ed.), *Modernising Britain. Central, Devolved, Federal?* The Federal Trust, London, 2002.
50. House of Lords Select Committee on the Constitution, *Devolution: Inter-Institutional Relations in the UK*, HL 28, 2002–03.

# 11
# Finding the Way Forward

*Philip Giddings and Gavin Drewry*

## Challenge and change – for the Union

The ten years following ratification of the Treaty of Maastricht have been years of challenge and change for the European Union and its Member States. They include: enlargement to fifteen agreed and to twenty-five to come; economic and monetary union and a single currency planned and adopted for most if not all of the Member States; and new pillars of governance for justice, home affairs, foreign and defence policy, the extension of the single market, labour and social reforms. It is by any standard a substantial catalogue. And governance itself, for a Union which has doubled in size, is being tackled as Member States grapple with the question how to improve the EU's decision-making procedures after the 2004 enlargement. Failure to agree on a draft constitutional treaty at the December 2003 IGC demonstrated the magnitude of that task.

All that itself is a substantial challenge as we shall see later, but first the Union has to recover from the seismic shock of the failure to achieve a common position amongst its Member States with regard to the crisis in Iraq. After the rapid moves forward together after the terrorist attacks on the United States in September 11, 2001, the spectacle of different groups of Member States apparently working against each other in the corridors of the UN made the notion of a European Foreign Policy look literally incredible. Even if relationships are being restored – in June 2003 the Government announced UK participation under the Common European Security and Defence Policy (CESDP) process in a small multinational force for the Democratic Republic of the Congo, the first EU-led operation outside

Europe – the Iraq crisis has laid bare the size of the gap between aspiration and reality: there continue to be deep differences in perceptions of strategic interest between some Members States of the Union. Without shared strategic interest, a common foreign and security policy cannot begin to get off the ground. Words may be found to paper over the differences, but when events demand action, Member States still seem unwilling to set aside what their governments perceive to be their national strategic interests in pursuit of a conflicting common objective. Which, we ask, is the more reliable sign for the future: the successful introduction of the Euro in 2002 or the debacle of a common foreign policy in 2003?

## Challenge and change – at Westminster

At Westminster, 2003 was very different from 1994. Withdrawal from the ERM and the protracted struggle over the Maastricht Treaty dealt to John Major's Government blows from which it never recovered. The remainder of that Parliament saw the Government's authority, and its majority, ebb away as the pro- and anti-EU factions in the Conservative Parliamentary Party fought for its soul with increasing bitterness. The election of the Blair Government with an overwhelming majority and without the incubus of a strong and articulate Eurosceptic tendency able to rock the boat produced a more stable and positive line of policy. It was also a government committed to constitutional reform, at least in the sense of measures to change important aspects of British constitutional processes (House of Lords reform, devolution and human rights). Allied to that were commitments to the somewhat esoteric concepts of 'modernisation' and 'joined-up government' which had knock-on effects on the way in which Parliament in general, and the House of Commons in particular, went about its business, including its European business.

The second Blair landslide in 2001 reinforced the Prime Minister's authority. But beneath the surface of those party-political headlines deeper currents were running. The parliamentary mechanisms which mediate Westminster's relationship with the EU's institutions continued to evolve. To such hardy perennials as reform of the common agricultural policy, fishery quotas and competition rules were added evolving economic and monetary union, foreign policy (the Balkans, Afghanistan, Zimbabwe and Iraq), security and defence issues (relations with WEU and NATO), the Social Chapter, justice and home affairs, the consequences of devolution: all these brought challenges and opportunities. Nor were they in watertight boxes, as the spillover from immigration and asylum policy frequently demonstrated. The ambiguity of the British position on the single currency remained. And as Westminster politicians began to appreciate the looming significance of the constitutional endeavours and ambitions placed in the Convention for the Future of Europe and its draft constitutional treaty, some of the most basic issues concerning the nature of the United Kingdom's relationship with the EU once again broke surface. Prominent amongst those issues was, and is, the vexed question of the role of national parliaments and their scrutiny mechanisms.

## Evolving scrutiny processes

In the earlier chapters of this book we have seen how the practices and procedures of the Westminster Parliament have continued to evolve in response to business arising from the EU. The scrutiny processes of both Houses, originally conceived to deal with legislation, have been adapted to cover a wide range of other European documentation. The EU consumes mountains of paper, and the work of the European Scrutiny Committees, especially the Commons Committee, is document-based. In the 2001–02 Session the Commons Scrutiny Committee considered 1860 documents. This makes it, as Priscilla Baines points out, enclosed and inward-looking and not very attractive to Members since it rarely deals with substantive policy issues. This may help to explain the contrast between Members' expressed desire for effective scrutiny and their lack of engagement with the procedures which deliver that scrutiny.[1]

For governments the primary objective is to get the business through – to complete the scrutiny process so that the reserve can be lifted and negotiating space in Brussels maximised. It is not difficult to imagine how policy-makers in Whitehall might come to see the need to obtain clearance for documents as an irritating additional hurdle in the already difficult steeple-chase which is EU decision-making. Nor how that irritation might lead either to overlooking the need to obtain clearance or too readily accepting that negotiating priorities require it to be set aside.

There is no doubt that if Westminster scrutiny is to be a reality, constant vigilance and persistence is needed on the part of the scrutiny committees' staff and leading Members to ensure that the Government lives up to its promises to make it work. The process relies on Government respecting the reserve and providing documentation, especially explanatory memoranda, in a timely and efficient manner. It also requires Government to show a generous rather than niggardly approach to the question which documents are to be scrutinised. It was to the credit of the Commons' Modernisation Committee that it broke out of the previously restrictive approach to second and third pillar documentation and formally ensured that the European Scrutiny Committee (ESC) was able to scrutinise the whole range.

It must always be borne in mind that what happens at Westminster is at best marginal to the outcome. As Priscilla Baines has so well expressed it, no amount of tweaking of the scrutiny process will remove the reality that the United Kingdom is only one among ... fifteen member states, all seeking to protect their own positions. What has been given up in extensions of the competence of the Union in successive treaties and their consequential European Community (Amendment) Acts cannot be recalled by revising the mandates of the scrutiny committees. The Community Legislator is the Council of the European Union in co-operation with the European Parliament (EP), not the Parliament of the United Kingdom, either on its own or in association with the national parliaments of the Member States – which in any case have different roles, powers and cultures. This is a point to which we will return.

## The policy challenges of the 1990s

Our earlier chapters have shown how the evolution of the United Kingdom's membership of the EU in the 1990s was reflected at Westminster in significant areas of public policy which stretch beyond the core trade and commercial policy issues which lay at the heart of the concept of the single market in the previous decade. The Union has evolved at different speeds and in different ways in different policy sectors, as has British participation in that evolution. The protocols in respect of EMU and social policy which were negotiated at Maastricht required different Westminster responses from those applicable to the second and third pillars created by that same treaty.

## The single currency

In the case of EMU, as we have seen in Chapter 7, the 'wait and see' stance of both the Major and the Blair governments meant that peers and MPs were able, repeatedly, to provide in parliament a forum for debate on the desirability and likely consequences of UK participation. They were also able to exploit the whole range of Westminster processes to require ministers to explain and defend their position, thereby exposing the range and passion of views between and across the major political parties on this deeply controversial question and contributing significantly to the undermining of the Major Government.

## The Social Chapter

In the case of social policy the position has been more complex, both because of the availability of an alternative treaty base in some instances and the ending of the protocol after the election of the Blair Government. As Julia Lourie has shown, the protocol itself created difficulties for the scrutiny system and the subsequent use of framework agreements, excluding Ministers as well as Parliament from involvement in examination of detailed legislative provision has underlined the relative impotence of national governments and parliaments in the areas in which QMV applies. Both the Major Government with the Working Time Directive and the Blair Government with the Information and Consultation Directive found themselves unable to exert influence upon important pieces of employment legislation to which they were opposed but the governments of other Member States were not. About that the Westminster Parliament could do nothing, other than listen to Eurosceptics gleefully using it to illustrate their argument about loss of sovereignty.

## Foreign policy, security and defence

The evolution of the EU's second pillar took parliamentary scrutiny into new and more difficult territory. Foreign, security and defence policy has always been executive-led and accountability general rather than detailed. There is little by way of legislation and the document-based processes of the Westminster European Committees were not well suited to its format. Perseverance on the part of the committees has enabled them to engage with some of the major issues but, as Ware and Wright point out, there is general agreement that the processes and mechanisms are not adequate. The debacle over military intervention in Iraq revealed the fragile nature of the 'commonness' of Member States' policies which will add to the ministers' sensitivities to the risks of over-exposure of delicate inter-governmental policy positions. Although there is general awareness of the weaknesses in the scrutiny of the second pillar, there is no clear consensus on how the problem might be solved. The second chamber idea has not found favour: the ESC's preference for 'collective scrutiny' through joint meetings with the committees of other national parliaments seems to ignore the substantial differences in their roles and powers, not to mention the differences in the foreign, security and defence postures of the Member States. Accountability seems bound to remain ex post facto.

### Immigration and asylum

In contrast to experience with the second pillar, the momentum for greater integration of justice and home affairs matters seems to have been maintained. As we have seen in Chapter 9, immigration and asylum issues have revealed the extent to which the various fields of policy have inter-penetrated one another. The consequences of international developments such as terrorist attacks on the United States and the war in Afghanistan as well as the continuing tensions in the Balkans and on the fringes of former USSR have increased the incentives for common action by EU Member States. Although immigration and asylum policy has had a very high public and media profile, and aroused very strong feelings, parliamentarians have found it difficult to exert direct influence upon policy development. They can, and do, generate a good deal of background noise which cannot be ignored by responsible ministers. But the decision-making levers continue to rest in the hands of government officials and ministers operating collectively through the complex and far from transparent EU networks. Parliamentary reaction back home is as much a ploy to be used in negotiation as a constraint on the process of crafting a common policy. And when the pressure of events and public opinion becomes very high, as in the aftermath of 9/11, then the speedy and decisive action required is taken – as it always has been in the past – by ministers in conclave.

## Governance

'Deepening and widening' the EU has brought significant challenges to its governance, which have been accentuated by growing concerns about the 'democratic deficit' and the need to make the EU more 'citizen friendly'. As far as widening was concerned, the EFTA enlargement was accomplished without great difficulty. In contrast to Maastricht the consequential legislation to amend the European Communities Act presented no problems – there was general support across all parties for both enlargements. The Government kept Parliament reasonably well informed about progress in the accession negotiations. The key issues were explored by the committees in both Houses, although Andrews and Miller point out that there was not much evidence of engagement with the complex financial issues arising out of enlargement.

With the number of Member States doubling, governance was bound to be a major issue. Anxieties about negative referendum results, low turn-out in EP elections, and fraud and corruption added to the concerns about the democratic deficit. One of the major aspects of the debate about the democratic deficit was the controversy about the appropriate role for national parliaments, a question dear to the heart to many at Westminster and not just a few ministers and would-be ministers. Attempts to address these governance issues at the Amsterdam and Nice IGCs produced only the minimum adjustments to enable enlargement to go ahead but 'skimmed over the vital question of efficiency. At the heart of the problem remained the distribution of power between Member States, in particular the balance between large and small states . . . fundamental . . . in view of the large number of small states likely to accede.'[2] And indeed this issue of distribution of power was to be the rock on which the draft constitutional treaty came to grief at the brussels IGC of December 2003.

It was agreed at Nice that there would be another IGC in 2004 to address the question of treaty simplification and specifically the role of national parliaments, the status of the Charter of Fundamental Rights, and the division of competencies between European, national and regional authorities. Moreover, the Member States recognised that, if public disenchantment with the EU was to be reversed, these issues would have to be addressed in a more open and inclusive way than the processes adopted for previous IGCs. Thus, in a Declaration in Annex IV to the Treaty of Nice the governments of the Member States committed themselves to a far-reaching public debate on the future of Europe.

The debate, which was formally launched by the Swedish Presidency in March 2001 as a follow-up to the Nice Treaty, had in fact begun a year earlier when the Commission presented its White Paper on European Governance to the EP. Added impetus came from a controversial speech by the German Foreign Minister in May 2000 advocating federation as ultimate goal for European integration.[3] Building on the successful precedent established by the Convention which drafted the Charter of Fundamental Rights (CFR),[4] the Laeken European Council agreed to establish a Convention on the Future of Europe which would examine governance issues in preparation for the IGC planned for 2004.

## The Convention on the Future of Europe

Moving beyond the time frame of the earlier chapters, we now conclude by looking at some of the prospective European issues that face Parliament in the future. We begin with debates about the future governance of the EU – debates that look set to form the backcloth to much Westminster debate and scrutiny of European business in the years to come, and which has already prompted an interesting addition to the committee structure of the House of Commons.

Contrary to some interpretations, the Convention was not set up to draft a Constitution for Europe but rather to prepare the ground for the governments of the Member States to tackle the issues of governance and democratic deficit in at their next IGC. The Laeken Declaration in fact set a total of 54 questions for the Convention to answer, grouped under four headings:

1. a better division and definition of competencies in the EU;
2. simplification of the treaties;
3. more democracy, transparency and efficiency in the EU;
4. examining the case for a Constitution for Europe.

To achieve this the four major stakeholders – the Commission, the European Parliament, the governments and parliaments of the Member States – were brought together in the Convention which held its inaugural meeting in Brussels on 28 February 2002. The EP had a delegation of 16 MEPs; the Commission was represented by two Commissioners; each Member State had one government and two parliamentary representatives. The thirteen (i.e. including Turkey) candidate states had the same representation as Member States.[5] Although this meant that members of national parliaments were in the majority (58 out of 105), they did not operate as a cohesive group in the way that, for example, the EP group did.[6] The whole enterprise was directed by the former President of France, Valéry Giscard d'Estaing, assisted by a former Prime Minister of Belgium (Jean-Luc Dehaene) and a former Prime Minister of Italy (Giuliano Amato) who worked with the Convention's Praesidium to guide the Convention's work. That work was done first through a series of ten 'working groups'[7] whose reports were to be considered in plenary sessions with the intention of producing a final report for the European Council in June 2003. Although there was some debate about whether that timescale would prove feasible, in the event the Convention agreed its report on 13 June 2003.

The Laeken Council Declaration did not mandate the Convention to produce a Constitution. Rather it asked for 'a final document which may comprise either different options, including the degree of support which they received, or recommendations if consensus is achieved'.[8] Nevertheless, a strong body of opinion within the Convention itself, including especially its President, M. Giscard, wanted it to produce a single document, a draft Constitutional Treaty. That alarmed some national parliamentarians, and others, including some Member State governments. British Ministers made clear on a number of occasions that the Convention's recommendations would not be binding and that the real decisions would be taken by Member governments at the IGC. Indeed it was not inevitable that its conclusions would go to the IGC: thus Baroness Symons of Vernham Dean assured the House of Lords soon after the Convention got under way that 'the status of the Convention conclusions is that they will be submitted to parliaments for discussion before governments then move forward – on the basis of having heard those parliamentary discussions – to consider what should go to the IGC'.[9]

Notwithstanding such assurances, Members of both Houses of the British Parliament were anxious to keep a close eye on what was happening at the Convention and out of that desire there developed a unique parliamentary instrument – the Standing Committee on the Convention. But first it had to be agreed who the British members of the Convention would be. A Foreign Office Minister

Peter Hain was appointed the Government's representative – and he continued in this role when he was promoted to the Cabinet as Secretary of State for Wales. At the previous Convention on the CFR, the four parliamentary representatives had been one from each House, and with a cross-party membership. For the CFE the Government decided that both the full members should come from the Commons, one Labour and one Conservative, and the two alternates should come from the Lords (one Labour and one Liberal Democrat).

The Government's approach caused a good deal of resentment in the Lords, particularly amongst the Cross-Benchers. The Euro-sceptics were also quick to point out that both peers were pro-European.[10] The matter was also raised at Question Time in the Commons[11] and the Foreign Affairs Committee, after an exchange of correspondence between its Chairman and the Foreign Secretary and the Prime Minister, issued a Special Report in which it drew attention to the 'key constitutional principle involved. National Parliaments are to be represented separately from Governments. Those representing Parliament should be, and seen to be, true representatives of Parliament and not the choice of Government. If they are to enjoy the confidence of Parliament, they must be selected only after full consultation with relevant parliamentary bodies'.[12] Notwithstanding these criticisms, the Government nominations – Gisella Stuart and David Heathcoat-Amory as full members and Lords Tomlinson and McLennan of Rogart as alternates – were accepted without a division in both Houses on 28 January 2002.[13]

## The Standing Committee on the Convention

Perhaps because of the controversy about the appointment of the parliamentary representatives, the Government proved accommodating and innovative with the question of how Parliament would be kept in touch with the ongoing work of the Convention. Some delicacy was required given the obvious claims of the two Houses' European Select Committees and the Commons' Foreign Affairs Committee. Using the model of the ESCs, the Government proposed that the parliamentary representatives should report to a Standing Committee composed of the combined membership (28) of the Commons European Scrutiny and Foreign Affairs Committees.

Non-members of the Committee, including Peers, would be allowed to attend, ask questions and contribute to the debate. Proceedings would begin with statements from the representatives and the alternates, followed by questions, for a maximum of one and a half hours, after which there would be a further one hour's debate on the motion, moved from the chair, that the Committee has considered the report. These arrangements were embodied in a Standing Order approved by the Commons on 12 June 2002, and renewed for the 2002–03 session on 4 December 2002.[14]

This innovation proved a considerable success,[15] with full participation from and dialogue between the representatives, alternates, Committee members and 'visiting' MPs and peers. Between July 2002 and April 2003 the Committee met four times. Attendance by Members averaged 58 per cent; 16 other MPs and 37 peers have also attended. The proceedings of the Committee – though not the reports of the representatives – were made available in Hansard and on the Internet.

In addition to reporting to the Standing Committee, the parliamentary representatives, and Mr Hain on behalf of the Government, gave evidence to the Lords' EUC[16] and the Commons' ESC.[17] There were two debates on the work of the Convention in the Commons[18] and one in the House of Lords.[19] The Lords' EUC produced a series of informative reports on the Convention and particularly on the draft Constitutional Treaty and its Protocols which the Convention published in February 2003.[20] The ESC produced a report on the Convention in December 2001[21] and a second, major report on *Democracy and Accountability in the EU and the Role of National Parliaments*[22] which was written with an eye to the Convention's work and formally submitted to it. The ESC also issued a Press Notice in October 2002 which was highly critical of the report of the Convention's Working Group on National Parliaments[23] and took evidence from the Convention's work on three occasions.[24] The ESC published a report on The Convention on the Future of Europe and the Role of National Parliaments[25] in June 2003. With the addition of Questions this adds up to a formidable amount of parliamentary activity, even though much of it went unremarked in the media, perhaps because of the latter's pre-occupation with the Iraq crisis.

The impact of all this activity is difficult to assess when the whole issue of a Constitution for Europe remains undecided following the failure to reach agreement at the December 2003 IGC in Brussels.

It can certainly be said that both government and parliamentary representatives from the United Kingdom were kept well aware of the sensitivities of the constitutional issues at Westminster – and of serious anxieties about the process – anxieties which some of the representatives themselves shared. Both Peter Hain and David Heath-coat-Amory put down many pages of amendments to the Draft Articles[26] and Gisella Stuart fought hard to strengthen the line on the role of national parliaments and the monitoring of subsidiarity. Nevertheless, the trend of Convention thinking, as interpreted by its President and reflected in the Draft Articles, was more heavily influenced by the EP's representation and those in favour of reducing the obstacles (such as the three pillar structure and requirement for unanimity) as they saw them to more efficient decision-making. Moreover, the different understandings of the status and role of 'constitutions' and indeed the law itself between the Continental European and Common Law traditions seem not to be fully appreciated.

Parliaments can make a fuss and to that extent raise the level of background noise which may influence the final decision-makers. In this instance the decision whether to adopt the Convention's proposals was, and still is, for Member States' Governments at the IGC. And there Prime Ministers like Mr Blair will face the familiar choice between accepting particular provisions which he does not like and using the veto to scupper the whole deal, as in the event happened over QMV voting weights at the December 2003. Although part of the purpose of the Convention was to relieve the IGC of the need to get into the particularities – and thus to discourage heads of government from discussing the detail much depends upon what is fundamental principle and what is detail. Amongst the large questions upon which British ministers and parliamentarians have strong views are:

- Is the Union to be a federal state with a separate legal personality or a Union of States?
- Should Charter Rights be made justiciable or not?
- Do the Member States confer competences on the Union or the Union on the Member States?
- Should national parliaments be given a role in making proportionality- and subsidiarity-effective constraints on Union activity?
- Should that role amount to a veto?

- Can inter-governmentalism be combined with a stronger role for the Union in foreign policy, security and defence matters?
- Should future amendments to the Constitutional Treaty require unanimity?
- Under what circumstances, if at all, should Member States be able to withdraw from the Union?

Although a draft treaty was not finally agreed at the December 2003 IGC 'consensus was close' on key changes to the Convention draft which were important to the UK Government and Parliament. In his report to Parliament on the IGC outcome,[27] Prime Minister Blair specifically instanced four items:

1. tax, EU finance, social security and criminal law will remain the province of the nation-state, and so subject to decision-making by unanimity;
2. any further treaty change will be subject to appoval by national parliaments;
3. a clear statement that the EU has only the powers that the nations give it. The Union acts only when objectives cannot be achieved by individual countries acting alone;
4. new powers for national parliaments to be involved in EU legislation.

However, in such negotiations nothing is actually agreed until everything is agreed. Whether any of these items will change as part of a package to achieve agreement on voting rights remains to be seen. For the time being the EU continues under its existing treaty (Nice) framework, through which a new financing network for the period from 2007 will have to be agreed. British parliamentarians, and no doubt also those from other Member States, will be watching developments on these issues very closely.

The view of the British Government is that whatever form of treaty that emerges from a future IGC will require ratification in the normal way – which in the case of the United Kingdom means by due process in Parliament. The Government has strongly resisted pressure for a referendum. Given the magnitude of the issues listed above, if the IGC produces a treaty similar in content to the draft articles which emerged from the Convention, then it will set Westminster some very stiff challenges indeed.

For political scientists and lawyers the customs, rules and procedures which provide the context for governance are often of all-consuming interest. For most citizens, however, and probably the majority of their elected representatives, the currency in which they are paid and with which they buy and sell is of much greater significance. And for Westminster that question too raises some challenging issues. In June 2003 Gordon Brown reported to Parliament the outcome of the Treasury's assessment of his five economic tests – 'yes, but not yet'. Although the Government had not been able to decide upon the date of a possible referendum on entry, the Chancellor did announce that a draft referendum Bill would be published in the autumn, along with further paving legislation for additional departmental allocations for preparations. He also announced that, inside EMU, the Government would move to a new 'open letter' system on fiscal policy. He proposed 'a regular fiscal stability report published on a pre-announced table to Parliament ... [with] an assessment in the report of the gap between actual and trend output in the economy; and when output materially diverges from its trend, an open letter sent by the Treasury to Parliament setting out the Government's response'. On the same day as his statement the Government published the 'full and complete' version of the British national changeover plan. It is therefore evident that, even though a referendum may be some time away, in the Westminster Parliament there is much debate and controversy about the United Kingdom and the Euro still to come.

The immediate future, then, is one in which major controversies will be taking place about Britain's place in the EU, about the way in which it is structured by treaty and/or constitution, and about how it impacts our day-to-day economic life. Parliament provides a forum in which that controversy can be played out. Its structures and procedures, as we have seen, gives ample opportunity for debating policy, scrutinising decisions, exploring the implications of proposals and holding governments to account. But it is governments, not parliaments, who take the key decisions in the EU. Parliamentary influence upon government largely depends on the extent to which parliamentarians' concerns engage with and reflect the concerns of the public in general, and voters in particular. That is the leverage which representative democracy gives to parliamentary assemblies.

The question is, as Austin Mitchell's comparison with the Sealed Knot society (see the epigraph in Chapter 7) sharply shows, whether anyone is listening: Are the public are taking any notice? Are parliamentarians making the connections between public and government which in a liberal democracy should ensure that they march in step? As the Westminster Parliament wrestles with the issues raised by the proposed Constitution for Europe and the anxieties about the EU's democratic deficit, they will surely need to spare some time to reflect on the quality of their own engagement with the public they represent, the quality upon which their raison d'etre as well as their power depends.

## Notes

1. In the 2001–02 Session the three Commons Standing Committee recorded attendances of 59, 59 and 75 per cent.
2. Thirtieth Report of the Select Committee on the European Union, *The Convention on the Future of Europe*, HL 163, July 2002, para. 16.
3. 'From Confederacy to Federation': Thoughts on the Finality of 'European Integration', Joschka Fischer, 12 May 2001.
4. See Eighth Report of the EUC, *EU Charter of Fundamental Rights*, HL 57, 1999–2000, which praised the composition and transparency of the Convention.
5. In addition to the 105 full members; each member has an alternate. There are also 13 observers: 3 from the Economic and Social Committee; 3 representatives of the European social partners; 6 from the Committee of the Regions, and one from the European Ombudsman. See HL 163, 2001–02 for a clear and succinct account of the Convention's organisation and method of working.
6. See evidence from Gisella Stuart to the Standing Committee on the Convention. 12 February 2003, c. 005.
7. The Groups were: Subsidiarity; Charter/ECHR; Legal Personality; National Parliaments; Complementary Compentencies; Economic Governance; Internal Security and Justice; Simplification of Legislative Procedures; External Relations and Representation of the EU Abroad; and Defence and Security Policy.
8. Laeken European Council, *Presidency Conclusions*, 15 December 2000.
9. HL Deb, 27 May 2002, c. 1048.
10. HL Deb, 28 January 2002, cc. 12–25
11. HC Deb, 17 December 2001, cc. 19–37, and 8 January 2002, cc. 407–410.
12. First Special Report of the Foreign Affairs Committee, *Appointment of Parliamentary Representatives to the Convention on the Future of Europe*, HC 509, 2001–02, para. 3.
13. HC Deb, 28 January 2002, c. 125 (no debate); HL Deb, 28 January 2002, c. 26 (after fifty minutes' debate).
14. The full text of the Standing Order is available on the Parliament website at www.publications.parliament.uk/pa/cm200203/cmstords/17523.htm.

15. 'One of the successes of the whole process', Jimmy Hood, MP, Chairman of the ESC, Standing Committee on the Convention, 12 February 2003, c. 025.
16. Select Committee on European Union, *Minutes of Evidence*, 8 October 2002.
17. European Scrutiny Committee, *Minutes of Evidence*, 16 July 2002, 'The Seville Council and the Convention on the Future of Europe', HC 1112-I, 2001–02, QQ 17–28; *Minutes of Evidence*, 20 November 2002, 'European Council Enlargement and the Convention on the Future of Europe', HC 103-I, 2002–03; *Uncorrected Evidence*, 31 March 2003, 'Report of the Convention Working Group X on "Freedom, Security and Justice"', HC 554-ii, 2002–03.
18. HC Deb, 2 December 2002, cc. 673–722; HC Deb, 20 March 2003, cc. 303–348WH.
19. HL Deb, 7 January 2003, cc. 897–986.
20. Thirtieth Report, *The Convention on the Future of Europe*, HL 163, 2001–02, July 2002; Sixth Report, *The Future Status of the EU Charter of Fundamental Rights*, HL 48, 2002–03, 3 February 03; Ninth Report, *The Future of Europe: Constitutional Treaty – Draft Articles 1–16*, HL 61, 2002–03, 25 February 2003; Eleventh Report, *The Future of Europe: National Parliaments and Subisidiarity: the Proposed Protocols*, HL 70, 2002–03, 11 March 2003; Twelfth Report, *The Future of Europe: Constitutional Treaty – Draft Articles 24–33*, HL 71, 2002–03, 11 March 2003.
21. Fifth Report, *Convention to Prepare for the 2004 Inter-Governmental Conference*, HC 152-v, 2001–02, November 2001.
22. Thirty-third Report of the European Scrutiny Committee, HC 152, June 2002.
23. Press Notice 24, Session 2001–02, 16 October 2002.
24. 20 November 2002, HC 103-I; 19 March 2003, HC 554-I; 25 March 2003, HC 554-ii.
25. Twenty-fourth Report of the European Scrutiny Committee, HC 63-xxiv, 16 June 2003.
26. They occupy 28 pages in Appendix II of the House of Commons Library Research Paper 03/23.
27. HC Deb, 15 December 2003, c. 1320.

# Appendix A: Chronology of/ Key Events

## 1991

Dec. 1991    Maastricht European Council Treaty on European Union agreed at Maastricht, with British opt-outs on EMU and Social Chapter

## 1992

April 1992    British General Election confirms John Major as Prime Minister
June 1992    Danish referendum's 'No' vote on Maastricht Treaty
Sept. 1992    United Kingdom forced out of ERM
Dec. 1992    Completion of 'internal market'

## 1993

July 1993    Passage of EC (Amendment) Act implementing TEU
Government defeated in Commons on vote on Social Chapter, forced to seek Vote of Confidence
Nov. 1993    TEU comes into force

## 1994

Jan. 1994    Stage 2 of EMU begins
Mar. 1994    Accession Treaty agreed with Austria, Finland, Norway and Sweden
June 1994    Elections to European Parliament
Nov. 1994    Government backbench rebellion on EU Finance Bill
Nov. 1994    EU (Accessions) Act receives Royal Assent

## 1995

Jan. 1995    Austria, Sweden and Finland join the EU

## 1996

Mar. 1996    UK White Paper *A Partnership of Nations*
BSE crisis breaks: Commission bans UK beef exports
Turin IGC

| | |
|---|---|
| May 1996 | John Major announces 'non-cooperation' within EU over beef export ban |
| June 1996 | Florence Council: Britain forced to accept 'no timetable' for lifting of beef ban |
| Nov. 1996 | ECJ rules against United Kingdom on Working Time Directive |
| Dec. 1996 | Government defeated in Commons on EU Common Fisheries Policy |
| Dec. 1996 | Dublin Council agrees 'Stability and Growth' Pact |

## 1997

| | |
|---|---|
| May 1997 | Tony Blair's 'New Labour' wins landslide victory in British General Election |
| June 1997 | Treaty of Amsterdam agreed: United Kingdom accepts Social Chapter and Article 13 anti-discrimination provisions |
| Oct. 1997 | Chancellor Gordon Brown announces 'five economic tests' for United Kingdom joining the single currency system |

## 1998

| | |
|---|---|
| Jan. 1998 | European Central Bank established |
| Mar. 1998 | Negotiations on EU enlargement commence with 'first wave' states (Czech Republic, Estonia, Hungary, Poland, Slovenian and Cyprus) |
| June 1998 | European Communities (Amendment) Act implementing the Treaty of Amsterdam receives Royal Assent |
| Oct. 1998 | Prime Minister Blair suggests gradual merger of EU and WEU |
| Dec. 1998 | United Kingdom agrees joint European defence initiative with France |
| Dec. 1998 | Terms of Reference of Commons Scrutiny Committee extended to include Second and Third Pillars |

## 1999

| | |
|---|---|
| Jan. 1999 | Stage 3 of EMU begins; change-over to Euro commences |
| Feb. 1999 | Government announces 'National Changeover Plan' in preparation for possible entry into single currency system |
| Mar. 1999 | Santer Commission resigns following report on fraud and corruption |
| May 1999 | Treaty of Amsterdam comes into force |
| June 1999 | Elections to European Parliament |
| June 1999 | EU adopts Common Strategy on Russia |
| Dec. 1999 | Helsinki European Council agrees Common European Security and Defence Policy |

## 2000

| | |
|---|---|
| Feb. 2000 | Negotiations on EU enlargement open with 'second wave' states (Bulgaria, Latvia, Lithuania, Romania, Slovakia and Malta) |
| Feb. 2000 | UK Government publishes White Paper on *Reform for Enlargement* outlining its approach to the forthcoming IGC |
| June 2000 | EU adopts Common Strategy on the Mediterranean |
| June 2000 | Article 13 Race Directive adopted |
| Sept. 2000 | Danish referendum votes 'No' to the Euro |
| Oct. 2000 | Prime Minister Blair's Warsaw Speech on 'a Europe of the Nations' |
| Nov. 2000 | Article 13 Employment Directive adopted |
| Nov. 2000 | WEU agrees transfer of most of its tasks and resources to the EU |
| Nov. 2000 | CESDP Capabilities Commitment Conference in Brussels |
| Dec. 2000 | IGC adopts *Charter of Fundamental Rights* |
| Dec. 2000 | Treaty of Nice agreed |

## 2001

| | |
|---|---|
| Mar. 2001 | Debate on 'Future of the European Union' formally opened by Swedish Prime Minister as Chairman of the Council of Ministers |
| June 2001 | British General Elections confirms Blair Government in office |
| June 2001 | Ireland votes 'No' in referendum on Treaty of Nice |
| July 2001 | Commission White Paper on European Governance |
| Sept. 2001 | Terrorist attacks on New York and Washington |
| Oct. 2001 | United States and United Kingdom launch invasion of Afghanistan |
| Nov. 2001 | CESDP Capabilities Enhancement Conference in Brussels |
| Dec. 2001 | Laeken Council agrees to hold European Constitutional Convention |

## 2002

| | |
|---|---|
| Jan. 2002 | Euro launched |
| Feb. 2002 | European Communities (Amendment) Act 2002, implementing Treaty of Nice, receives Royal Assent |
| Feb. 2002 | Inaugural Meeting of the Convention on the Future of Europe held in Brussels |
| Oct. 2002 | Ireland votes 'Yes' in second referendum on Treaty of Nice |
| Oct. 2002 | Draft EU Constitution presented to Convention on the Future of Europe |
| Nov. 2002 | Prime Minister Blair's Cardiff Speech on 'A Clear Course for Europe' |
| Dec. 2002 | European Council at Copenhagen formally invites ten states [Cyprus, Czech Republic, Estonia, Hungary, Latvia, Lithuania, Malta, Poland, Slovakia, Slovenia] to join the EU in January 2005 |

# 2003

| | |
|---|---|
| Feb. 2003 | Treaty of Nice comes into force |
| June 2003 | Gordon Brown announces Government decision to postpone referendum on the Euro |
| June 2003 | Final session of Convention on the Future of Europe |
| Dec. 2003 | Brussels IGC fails to reach agreement on European Constitution |

# Appendix B: Web links

**Note:** Web links are liable to change or disappear; all these were checked in January 2004.

## UK Parliament

www.parliament.uk

EC Law and Treaties links      http://www.parliament.uk/useful/ul_eu.cfm/

## House of Commons

European Scrutiny Committee      http://www.parliament.uk/parliamentary_ committees/european_scrutiny.cfm

European Standing Committees (and Standing Committee on the Convention on the Future of Europe)      http://www.parliament.the-stationery-office.co. uk/pa/cm/othstn.htm

Foreign Affairs Committee      http://www.parliament.uk/parliamentary_committees/ foreign_affairs_committee.cfm

Debates (Hansard)      http://www.parliament.uk/hansard/hansard.cfm

Early Day Motions      http://edm.ais.co.uk/

Home Affairs Committee      http://www.parliament.uk/parliamentary_ committees/ home_affairs_committee.cfm

Public Accounts Committee      http://www.parliament.uk/parliamentary_committees/ committee_of_public_accounts.cfm

Research Papers      http://www.parliament.uk/parliamentary_publications_and_ archives/research_papers.cfm

Trade and Industry Committee      http://www.parliament.uk/parliamentary_ committees/trade_and_industry.cfm

Treasury Committee      http://www.parliament.uk/parliamentary_committees/ treasury_committee.cfm

## House of Lords

European Union Committee    http://www.parliament.uk/parliamentary_committees/lords_eu_select_committee.cfm

Debates (Hansard)    http://www.parliament.uk/hansard/hansard2.cfm/

## UK Government Departments

Department of Trade & Industry    http://www.dti.gov.uk/

Foreign and Commonwealth Office    http://www.fco.gov.uk

Home Office    http://www.homeoffice.gov.uk/

HM Treasury    http://www.hm-treasury.gov.uk/

## Her Majesty's Stationery Office (for Acts of Parliament since 1988 and Statutory Instruments since 1987)

www.hmso.gov.uk

European Parliament (Representation) Act 2003    http://www.legislation.hmso.gov.uk/acts/acts2003/20030007.htm

European Parliamentary Elections Act 2002    http://www.legislation.hmso.gov.uk/acts/acts2002/20020024.htm

European Communities (Amendment) Act 2002    http://www.legislation.hmso.gov.uk/acts/acts2002/20020003.htm

European Communities (Finance) Act 2001    http://www.legislation.hmso.gov.uk/acts/acts2001/20010022.htm

European Parliamentary Elections Act 1999    http://www.legislation.hmso.gov.uk/acts/acts1999/19990001.htm

European Communities (Amendment) Act 1998    http://www.legislation.hmso.gov.uk/acts/acts1998/19980021.htm

European Communities (Finance) Act 1995    http://www.legislation.hmso.gov.uk/acts/acts1995/Ukpga_19950001_en_1.htm

European Union (Accessions) Act 1994    http://www.legislation.hmso.gov.uk/acts/acts1994/Ukpga_19940038_en_1.htm

European Parliamentary Elections Act 1993    http://www.legislation.hmso.gov.uk/acts/acts1993/Ukpga_19930041_en_1.htm

European Communities (Amendment) Act 1993    http://www.legislation.hmso.gov.uk/acts/acts1993/Ukpga_19930032_en_1.htm

European Communities (Finance) Act 1988    http://www.legislation.hmso. gov.uk/acts/acts1988/Ukpga_19880046_en_1.htm

## Foreign and Commonwealth Office (has section on Britain and the EU)

http://www.fco.gov.uk

IGC – Reform for Enlargement: The British Approach to the European Union Intergovernmental Conference 2000, February 2000, Cm. 4595    http://www. fco.gov.uk/files/kfile/igc.pdf

## Scottish Parliament

http://www.scottish.parliament.uk

European and External Relations Committee (formerly European Committee) http://www.scottish.parliament.uk/S1/official_report/cttee/europe.htm

Research publications on Europe 1999–2003    http://www.scottish. parliament.uk/S1/whats_happening/research/pub-europ.html

## National Assembly for Wales

http://www.wales.gov.uk/index.htm

Europe and External Affairs page    http://www.wales.gov.uk/subieurope/ index.htm

## Northern Ireland Assembly

http://www.ni-assembly.gov.uk/

Committee of the Centre    http://www.ni-assembly.gov.uk/centre/centre.htm

## European Union institutions

Europa (General Website portal for the EU)    http://europa.eu.int/ index_en.htm

European Commission    http://europa.eu.int/comm/index_en.htm

European Council    http://ue.eu.int/en/summ.htm

European Court of Justice    http://curia.eu.int/en/index.htm

European Parliament    http://www.europarl.eu.int/home/default_en.htm

Convention on the Future of Europe    http://europa.eu.int/futurum/index_en.htm

Treaties    http://europa.eu.int/eur-lex/en/search/search_treaties.html

Official Publications of the EU    http://www.euros.ch/

COSAC: Conference of Community and European Affairs Committees (of National Parliaments)    http://www.cosac.org/eng/next/index.html

## Other resources

Commission for Racial Equality    http://www.cre.gov.uk/

British-Irish Interparliamentary Body    http://www.cipbae.org/biipb/

BUBL Information service has a set of links on the European Union    http://bubl.ac.uk

Tiscali Europe    http://europe.tiscali.co.uk/

United Nations High Commission for Refugees    http://www.unhcr.ch/cgi-bin/texis/vtx/home

# Select Bibliography: Books, Chapters and Articles Cited

This list does not include newspaper reports and articles.

Arter, D. *The Politics of European Integration in the Twentieth Century*, London: Dartmouth, 1993.

Balazs, P. 'Strategies for Eastern enlargement of the EU: an integration theory approach', in P.-H. Laurent and M. Maresceau (eds), *Deepening and Widening*, The State of the European Union (Vol. 4), Oxford: Oxford University Press, 1998.

Blackburn, R. and Kennon, A. *Griffith and Ryle on Parliament*, 2nd edn, London: Sweet and Maxwell, 2003.

Bogdanor, V. 'Britain and the European Community', in J. Jowell and D. Oliver (eds), *The Changing Constitution*, 3rd edn, Oxford, Clarendon Press, 1994.

Bressand, A. 'The 1992 breakthrough and the global economic agenda', in J. Story (ed.), *The New Europe: Politics, Government and the Economy Since 1945*, Oxford: Blackwell, 1993, pp. 314ff.

Butler, D. and Kavanagh, D. *The British General Election of 1992*, Basingstoke: Macmillan, 1992.

—— *The British General Election of 2001*, Basingstoke: Palgrave, 2002.

Carstairs, C. and Ware, R. (eds) *Parliament and International Relations*, Milton Keynes: Open University Press, 1991.

Chryssochoou, D. *Theorizing European Integration*, London: Sage, 2001.

Clark, A. *Diaries*, London: Weidenfeld and Nicolson, 1993.

Cooper, R. *The Post-Modern State and the World Order*, 2nd edn, London: Demos and The Foreign Policy Centre, 2000.

Craig, P. 'Report on the United Kingdom', in A. M. Slaughter, A. S. Sweet and J. Weiler (eds), *The European Court and National Courts – Doctrine and Jurisprudence*, Oxford: Hart Publishing, 1998.

Cram, L., Dinan, D. and Nugent, N. (eds) *Developments in the European Union*, Basingstoke: Palgrave, 1999.

Daintith, T. 'Regulation', in *The International Encyclopaedia of Comparative Law*, Vol. xvii, 'Law, State and Economy', Tübingen, Mohr, 1991.

Department of Trade and Industry, *Review of the Implementation and Enforcement of EC Law in the UK*, London, 1993.

De Schoutheete, P. 'The Intergovernmental Conference', *Common Market Law Review*, 37(4), 2000, footnote to guest editorial, p. 845.

De Witte, B. 'Direct effect, supremacy and the nature of the legal order', in Craig and De Burca (eds), *The Evolution of EU Law*, Oxford: Oxford University Press, 1999.

Dicey, A. V. *An Introduction to the Study of the Law of the Constitution*, 10th edn, London and Basingstoke: Macmillan, 1959.

Dinan, D. *Ever Closer Union? An Introduction to European Integration*, 2nd edn, Basingstoke: Macmillan, 1999.

Edwards, G. 'Britain and Europe', in J. Story (ed.), *The New Europe: Politics, Government and the Economy Since 1945*, Oxford: Blackwell, 1993, pp. 187ff.

Falkner, G. and Nentwich, M. 'The Amsterdam Treaty: the Blueprint for the future institutional balance?' in K. Neunreither and A. Wiener (eds), *European Integration After Amsterdam – Institutional Dynamics and Prospects for Democracy*, Oxford: Oxford University Press, 2000.

Franklin, M. and Norton, P. (eds) *Parliamentary Questions*, Oxford: Clarendon Press, 1993.

George, S. *An Awkward Partner: Britain in the European Community*, Oxford: Oxford University Press, 1990.

Giddings, P. and Drewry, G. (eds) *Westminster and Europe: The Impact of the European Union on the Westminster Parliament*, Basingstoke: Macmillan, 1996.

Greenwood, S. *Britain and European Integration since the Second World War*, Manchester: Manchester University Press, 1996.

Griffith, J. A. G. and Ryle, M. *Parliament*, London: Sweet and Maxwell, 1989.

Gros, D. and Thygesen, N. *European Monetary Integration*, Harlow: Longman, 1998.

Harvey, C. J. 'Immigration and asylum law: new covenants and familiar challenges', *Public Law*, 1999, pp. 23ff.

Hirschman, A. *Exit, Voice and Loyalty – Responses to Decline in Firms, Organisations and States*, Cambridge MA: Harvard University Press, 1970.

Jones, B. 'Searching for a role. The committee on European Affairs, in inclusive government and party management', in B. Jones and J. Osmond (eds), *The National Assembly for Wales and the Work of its Committees*, Cardiff: Institute of Welsh Affairs and the Welsh Governance Centre, 2001.

Jones, B. and Osmond, J. *Inclusive Government and Party Management. The National Assembly for Wales and the Work of its Committees*, Cardiff: Institute of Welsh Affairs and the Welsh Governance Centre, 2001.

Kennedy, D. *Post-Agreement Northern Ireland and the European Union*, An interim report by European liaison on Northern Ireland's relations with the European Union after devolution, Belfast: Institute of European Studies, Queen's University, 1998.

Kerremans, B. 'The political and institutional consequences of widening: capacity and control in an enlarged Council', in P.-H. Laurent and M. Maresceau (eds), *Deepening and Widening*, The State of the European Union (Vol. 4), Oxford: Oxford University Press, 1998.

Kogan, M. *Introduction to The Politics of Education*, Harmondsworth: Penguin, 1971.

Lamont, N. *In Office*, London: LittleBrown, 1999.

Layton-Henry, Z. *The Politics of Immigration* (Making Contemporary Britain series: Institute of Contemporary British History), Oxford: Blackwell, 1992.

McCormick, J. *Understanding the European Union*, 2nd edn, Basingstoke: Palgrave, 2002.

Major, J. *The Autobiography*, London: Harper Collins, 1999.

—— *Making the Law: The Report of the Hansard Commission on the Legislative Process*, London: The Hansard Society, 1993.

Miers, D. and Page, A. *Legislation*, 2nd edn, London: Sweet and Maxwell, 1990.

Mitchell, J. D. B. 'British law and British membership', 6 *Europarecht*, 1971, pp. 106ff.

—— 'The Sovereignty of Parliament and Community Law: The stumbling block that isn't there', 55 *International Affairs*, 1979, pp. 33–46.

Mitchell, J., Kuipers, S. and Gall, B. 'Constitutional aspects of the Treaty and legislation relating to British membership', 9 *Common Market Law Review*, 1972, pp. 140ff.

Mitchell, J. 'Scotland: maturing devolution', in A. Trench (ed.) *The State of the Nations 2001. The Second Year of Devolution in the United Kingdom*, Thorverton: Imprint Academic, 2001.

Nicholl, W. and Salmon, T. *Understanding the New European Community*, Harlow: Longman, 2000.

Osmond, J. *The State and Nations. The First Year of Devolution* (ed. Robert Hazell), London: The Constitution Unit, 2000.

—— 'A constitutional convention by other means', in R. Hazell (ed.), *The State and the Nations. The First Year of Devolution*, Thorverton: Imprint Academic, 2000.

—— 'In search of stability', in A. Trench (ed.), *The State of the Nations 2001. The Second Year of Devolution in the United Kingdom*, Thorverton: Imprint Academic, 2001.

Owen, D. *Time to Declare*, London: Michael Joseph, 1991.

Page, E. 'The impact of European legislation on British public policy making: a research note', 76 *Public Administration*, 1998, pp. 803–809.

Rawlings, R. 'Legal politics: The United Kingdom and ratification of the Treaty on European Union', *Public Law*, 1994, pp. 254ff., 368ff.

Regelsberger, E. 'European political cooperation', in J. Story (ed.), *The New Europe: Politics, Government and the Economy Since 1945*, Oxford: Blackwell, 1993, pp. 270ff.

Seldon, A. *Major: A Political Life*, London: Weidenfeld and Nicolson, 1997.

Snyder, F. *New Directions in European Community Law*, London: Weidenfeld and Nicolson, 1990.

Soetendorp, B. *Foreign Policy in the European Union*, London: Routledge, 1999.

Stubb, A. 'Negotiating flexible integration under the Amsterdam Treaty', in K. Neunreither and A. Wiener (eds), *European Integration After Amsterdam – Institutional Dynamics and Prospects for Democracy*, Oxford: Oxford University Press, 2000.

Thatcher, M. *The Downing Street Years*, Harper Collins, 1993.

Ware, R. 'Legislation and ratification: the passage of the European Communities (Amendment) Act 1993', in P. Giddings and G. Drewry (eds), *Westminster and Europe: The Impact of the European Union on the Westminster Parliament*, London: Macmillan, 1996, pp. 261ff.

Watson, A. 'A two-speed Europe', in P.-H. Laurent and M. Maresceau (eds), *Deepening and Widening*, The State of the European Union (Vol. 4), Oxford: Oxford University Press, 1998.

Weiler, J. H. H. *The Constitution of Europe*, Cambridge: Cambridge University Press, 1999.

Wilford, R. and Wilson, R. ' "A bare knuckle ride": Northern Ireland', in R. Hazell (ed.), *The State and the Nations. The First Year of Devolution*, Thorverton: Imprint Academic, 2000.

Wilson, R. and Wilford, R. 'Northern Ireland: endgame', in A. Trench (ed.), *The State of the Nations 2001. The Second Year of Devolution in the United Kingdom*, Thorverton: Imprint Academic, 2001.

Wright, A. 'The europeanisation of Scotland'. A driver for autonomy', in M. Graves and G. Girrard (eds) *Europe United, the United Kingdom Disunited?* University of Brest, 2000.

Young, J. *Britain and European Unity 1945–1999*, Basingstoke: Palgrave, 2001.

# Index